Government as Practice

The Parliamentary Left in India is in deep trouble. Its legislative presence has shrunk both nationally and in the regions. The situation demands an open debate on possible options for building an alternative politics in a vastly unregulated rural and urban economy confronting corrupt government and corporate agencies.

This book studies a government run by a democratic-socialist coalition in postcolonial India. In the first ten years of being in power, the Left Front in West Bengal imaginatively produced a politico-administrative framework that created a substantial popular appeal keeping it in power for a record three decades and half. In those early years significant distributive policies for agrarian reforms were implemented and an elaborate structure of local representation introduced. The regime worked through an intricate web of disciplined activists – the 'party' – that mediated an 'elevated' domain of policies with an 'embedded' field of everyday practices involving various social classes. This offered a governmental conduct tuned to strategic alliances incorporating the rhetorical spirit of class struggle within the institutional protocols of a liberal constitutional system.

Based on empirical research and a critique of existing academic interpretations, the book captures such conduct within an inventive concept of 'government as practice'. It shows how these practices gradually got entrapped in the politics of electoral renewal and ritualistic management of social peace, failing to keep pace with the growing aspirations of the poor for well-being and social justice in a rapidly changing economy. Enchanted by the developmental promises of neoliberal capital, the governmental Left now failed to blend popular politics with economic imperatives which alienated its basis classes and imploded the regime.

Arguing that a radical nostalgia geared to dogmatic clichés cannot help a democratic-socialist alternative in the present impasse, the book shows how decoding certain key signals of the Left Front can critically help re-imagine a new 'government as practice'. Focused mainly on the predicaments of the Left in India, the book will have relevance for understanding a range of inclusive political options in wider fields of postcolonial democracy.

Dwaipayan Bhattacharyya is Professor at the Centre for Political Studies, Jawaharlal Nehru University, New Delhi. He was earlier at the Centre for Studies in Social Sciences, Calcutta. He has worked and published for many years in the areas of agrarian change, decentralization and democratic-socialist politics in India. A doctorate from the University of Cambridge, he has held visiting positions in several universities in India and abroad.

SOUTH ASIA IN THE SOCIAL SCIENCES

South Asia has become a laboratory for devising new institutions and practices of modern social life. Forms of capitalist enterprise, providing welfare and social services, the public role of religion, the management of ethnic conflict, popular culture and mass democracy in the countries of the region have shown a marked divergence from known patterns in other parts of the world. South Asia is now being studied for its relevance to the general theoretical understanding of modernity itself.

South Asia in the Social Sciences will feature books that offer innovative research on contemporary South Asia. It will focus on the place of the region in the various global disciplines of the social sciences and highlight research that uses unconventional sources of information and novel research methods. While recognizing that most current research is focused on the larger countries, the series will attempt to showcase research on the smaller countries of the region.

General Editor
Partha Chatterjee
Columbia University

Editorial Board
Pranab Bardhan
University of California at Berkeley

Stuart Corbridge
London School of Economics

Christophe Jaffrelot
Centre d'études et de recherches internationales, Paris

Government as Practice
Democratic Left in a Transforming India

Dwaipayan Bhattacharyya

CAMBRIDGE
UNIVERSITY PRESS

CAMBRIDGE
UNIVERSITY PRESS

4843/24, 2nd Floor, Ansari Road, Daryaganj, Delhi - 110002, India

Cambridge University Press is part of the University of Cambridge.

It furthers the University's mission by disseminating knowledge in the pursuit of
education, learning and research at the highest international levels of excellence.

www.cambridge.org
Information on this title: www.cambridge.org/9781107102262

First published 2016

Printed in India by Thomson Press India Ltd., New Delhi 110001

A catalogue record for this publication is available from the British Library

Library of Congress Cataloging-in-Publication Data

Bhattacharyya, Dwaipayan.
Government as practice : democratic left in a transforming India / Dwaipayan Bhattacharyya.
pages cm
Includes bibliographical references and index.
Summary: "Discusses the strategies of governance deployed by the mainstream Left in India"--
Provided by publisher.
ISBN 978-1-107-10226-2 (hardback)
1. Right and left (Political science)--India--West Bengal. 2. Democracy--India--West Bengal. 3.
West Bengal (India)--
Politics and government. I. Title.
JC574.2.I4B53 2015
320.954`14--dc23
2015016416

ISBN 978-1-107-10226-2 Hardback

*For Ma, who would
have been so relieved,
and Baba, who is.*

CONTENTS

PREFACE

This book waited for a closure for way too long. It is a peculiar problem of writing on the present. With each passing moment one experiences a shift in perspective calling into question some assumptions which until yesterday seemed firm. New circumstances demand a somewhat reworked frame of analysis, inviting a ripple of changes in the ordering of ongoing events and arguments. In 2011, the historical rout of the democratic left government in West Bengal brought a three and half decades of unbroken saga to its close. This gave the book, work for which started in 2009, a point of arrival.

The present impasse of the democratic left was felt simultaneously on several fronts: electoral, organizational, and more importantly, ideational. Here we will trace the lineages of the crisis more particularly through the government of the Left Front, a coalition that the left managed to maintain for a record 34 years in West Bengal. The government, in the first decade of its existence, took some important legislative steps to provide social and economic security for the disadvantaged groups and to promote local democracy for curbing the influence of the bureaucracy.

In the early years the left evolved an art of conducting its government, which the book calls 'government as practice'. It strategically combined top-down policies with the lived experience of different population groups. The art was perfected through popular movements and alliance-politics in the 1950s and the 1960s, which offered the backdrop for subsequent governmental projects of agrarian reforms and administrative decentralization in the late 1970s. This required a disciplined party and a complex structure of mass organizations for blending social democracy's ideological commitments with the everyday compulsions of postcolonial democracy. They helped the left consolidate its position among the rural and urban poor for an unprecedented duration.

However, the 'success' of the left in enlisting popular support also proved a bane, as its electoral triumphalism reproduced a stasis of predictability and famished its veins for infusing fresh ideas, so necessary to grapple with the contingencies of the 'new' economy in a rapidly transforming India. The gap proved costly, as the left failed to come up with an appropriate alternative to capital-led acquisition of farmlands, and faced a debilitating defeat with the alienation of its own constituency. Employing a mix of conceptual analysis and empirical interrogation, the book closely follows West Bengal's democratic left experiment from its record electoral run to its present political stalemate.

The book could not have been written if I did not have the opportunity of conversing over many years with Partha Chatterjee at the Centre for Studies in Social Sciences, Calcutta. His understanding of the region and its people in both their historical depth and contemporary complexities is unmatched. For me he brought home the point that the principal challenge for social science research is explaining a changing reality through conceptual tools that are widely connected yet sharply tuned to particular social, cultural and linguistic practices. With all my inadequacies, I owe a good deal of my intellectual curiosity to his generous time, his sharing of ideas and thoughts in the course of our numerous interactions.

The environment at the Centre has been central to my work. As an institution it always encouraged exchange across disciplinary boundaries within a convivial milieu through its regular seminars and M.Phil courses. Without a 'base' here, and the empathy of its current Director, Tapati Guha-Thakurta, I would not have had the chances of carrying out my fieldwork or getting a break during the last couple of months of intense writing. In working out my initial ideas, Anjan Ghosh was my most intimate sounding board. I have not known any other academic so intellectually motivated yet self-evasive, thoroughly informed yet openly sharing, firmly positioned yet tolerant of other viewpoints. He will ever be missed.

Some lines of thoughts here evolved in the course of prolonged exchanges at the Centre over the years with Anirban Das, Indrajit Mallick, Indranil Dasgupta, Janaki Nair, Jayati Gupta, Jyotsna Jalan, Keya Dasgupta, Kiran Keshavamurthy, Lakshmi Subramanian, Prachi Deshpande, Priya Sangameswaran, Prabir Basu, Rajarshi Ghose, Rimli Bhattacharya, Saibal Kar, Sohini Guha, Sugata Marjit, Sudipto Chatterjee and Trina Nileena Banerjee. The continuous provocation and questioning by Bodhisattva Kar, Manas Ray, Moinak Biswas, Pradip Bose, Pradip K. Datta, Rajarshi Dasgupta, Ritojyoti Bandyopadhyay and Sibaji Bandyopadhyay sharpened my understanding of the multivalence of politics. In addition, my time at the Centre would not have been so rewarding if I could not share the corridor, and the daily lunch conversations, with Manabi Majumdar and Rosinka Chaudhuri. In Pranab Kumar Das, I found someone to share many doubts and anxieties. He also helped me liberally for the statistical interpretations included in Appendix II. I received regular help from the Centre's Registrar, Debarshi Sen, and my colleagues at the library and the archives that included Abhijit Bhattacharya, Aseem Kumar Patra, Jayati Nayak, Kamalika Mukherjee, Kaliprasad Bose, Ranjana Dasgupta, Sanchita Bhattacharyya, Saumitra Chatterjee, Sheshadri Ghosal, Tapas Pal and the librarian Siddhartha Shankar Ray.

A few queries are carried here from a PhD thesis which I never published. Geoffrey Hawthorn, my supervisor at that time, played a critical part in its production. For me he remains a model supervisor, generous and considerate, allowing students a great deal of freedom to push arguments based, nonetheless, on demonstrable evidence. Much of my understanding of the post-Soviet leftwing politics evolved through discussions with a concerned group of students in Cambridge at that time including Andreas Janousch, Aveek Sen, Fiona Lortan, Jayanta Sengupta, Joya Chatterjee, Nandini Gooptu, Prakash Upadhyaya, Samita Sen, Selma Santos, Subha Mukherji, Subho Basu and Vinayak Srivastava.

I also had the good fortune of growing up in a broadly leftwing familial milieu, where some who surrounded me had a deep attachment to politics, either as activists or academics. Of my paternal uncles, Sankarnarayan was a disciple of M. N. Roy in his Radical Humanist phase, Natanarayan and Naranarayan were both incarcerated for their communist activities in the late-1940s, Sundarnarayan worked as a courier when the party was underground. In the extended family circle on my mother's side, political discussions and differences were rife among a large set of uncles and aunts who were either teachers or politically committed journalists. They included, among others, Alaka and Debiprasad Chattopadhyay, Asok Majumdar, Binay Bhushan Chaudhuri, Harbans Mukhia, Kumaresh Chakraborty and Sailen K. Pande. My interest in social and political affairs owes much to what I picked up in the course of recurrent conversations with all of them.

I have received cooperation from a number of individuals and institutions. My teachers from the days in Calcutta University, especially Amitabha Chandra, Buddhadeb Bhattacharya, Samir Das and Sobhanlal Dattagupta played a crucial role in shaping my life in the academia. Some material used in chapter 4 of this volume stem from a research project on rural West Bengal headed by Dilip Mookherjee of Boston University and Pranab Bardhan of University of California, Berkeley. I am grateful for their insights and comments. I also benefitted from my academic interaction with Binitha Thampi and D. Narayana of the Centre for Development Studies, Thiruvananthapuram, and Glyn Williams of University of Sheffield during our comparative study of Kerala and West Bengal. Kolkata regularly hosts a lively exchange between international scholars across disciplines thanks to the initiatives of the likes of Anasua Basu Ray Chaudhury, Paula Banerjee, Sabyasachi Basu Ray Chaudhury, Subhas Chakraborty and Suhit Sen of the Mahanirban Calcutta Research Group. Ranabir Samaddar of the same organization stands out as one of the city's most affectionate and agile intellectuals. Members of the Pratichi Trust had been especially helpful with their enormous field-data in the areas of human development. This book would have been much poorer without the generosity of Kumar Rana, the Project Director of Pratichi, who combines his inimitable energy with intimate knowledge of the ground level reality. The Lokniti group of the Centre for the Study of Developing Societies in Delhi, especially Banasmita Borah, K. C. Suri, Sanjay Kumar, Suprio Basu, Sandeep Shastri, Suhas Palshikar and Yogendra Yadav had always been generous in sharing election-related data.

A leaner and rudimentary version of the chapter on the school teachers in democratic left politics first evolved in the 1990s as a collaborative research work with some colleagues at the Centre for Political Studies in Jawaharlal Nehru University. One cannot but recall Aswini Ray, Balveer Arora, Bishnu N. Mohapatra, C. P. Bhambhri, Gurpreet Mahajan, Kuldeep Mathur and Zoya Hasan for their good wishes. Over the last couple of years Niraja Gopal Jayal, Pralay Kanungo and Sudha Pai constantly nudged me to complete this book. Shubhra and Kunal Chakrabarti, Sheila and Ramprasad Sengupta and Sanku Bose warmly opened their doors for me during my stay on campus.

My special debts are to a large pool of friends. Some – like Bhaskar Roy, Prafulla Dasgupta, Shantanu Ghosh (who shockingly passed away two years ago), Srikumar Mukhopadhyay and Ujjal Chakrabarty – were neighbourhood friends whose solidarity has withstood the test of time. My bonding with Indrapramit Roy stayed firm since I started school and merged into an enlarged circle of close mates that includes Aditi Chatterjee, Anindya Dutta, Somnath Mazumder and Subha De. Our days and nights in Shantiniketan, Kharagpur, and on the terrace of the Sambhunath Pandit Street house taught me a lot about 'life' in general and made me what I am today. Debashis Sen continues to ward off my complacence with his argumentative counterpoints on anything and everything from many seas away. Manidipa Sen still showers unconditional affection that only a childhood friend can. I consider myself fortunate to find a solid band of buddies in Anamitra Chaudhuri, Aparajita Dasgupta, Arun Ganguly, Chaitali Basu, Damandeep Singh, Debjani Sengupta, Franson Manjali, Jayanta Roy, Lili Mazumder, Malini Basu, Rita Ghosh, Sharmila Purakayastha, and Sukriti Lahori. Thank you all for your love and care. Over the years, Aloke Mukhopadhyay, Anita Agnihotri, Debjani Deb Sengupta, Satyabrata Chakrabarty, Shyamaprasad Basu, Soma Dattagupta and Sweta Ghosh have become sources of infinite warmth and fondness. In more recent years, Maidul Islam, Prasenjit Bose, Rajesh Bhattacharya, Subhas Singha Roy, Swagato Sarkar and Zaad Mahmood revived the pleasure of politically charged addas in office or at roadside cafes. My students Koyel Lahiri and Praskanva Sinharay continue to overwhelm me with their many thoughtful gestures and humane qualities. Rajashree Choudhury and Runa Chakrabarty gave me a home away from home during a stint at Claremont Graduate University. And most recently, in Göttingen, Lalit Vachani, Michaela Dimmers, Sebastian Schwecke and Srirupa Roy were unflinching in their kindness and camaraderie.

The book uses some material from fieldwork in rural West Bengal that began way back in the 1990s. But for an active support of different political parties, especially of their peasant unions, the fieldwork could simply not have been possible. My biggest debt is to Benoy Krishna Choudhury, the Left Front minister in charge of land and land reforms, who was also a peasant leader of redoubtable integrity. He helped me get in touch with other left leaders such as Tarun Roy and Surjya Kanta Mishra in Medinipur, Nakul Mahato in Purulia, Jiten Mitra in Birbhum among others. Jiten Mitra gave me access to his massive collection of rare Krishak Sabha documents, a close reading of which was vital for some of the arguments made here. I also received generous cooperation from several ordinary activists and prominent personalities of different political parties, many of whom wanted to remain anonymous. Among those whose short and long contacts can be mentioned are Ashok Ghosh, Biman Bose, Debashis Chakraborty, Gautam Deb, Gunadhar Maity, Hrishikesh Maity, Mukul Roy, Nirbed Roy and Nirupam Sen. Special thanks to Chittabhushan and Malati Dasgupta, the builders of a distinctive Gandhian ashram in Majhihira village, and Prabha, Pratap and Prasad Dasgupta, for hosting me during my work in Purulia. In the course of my recent fieldwork, I received excellent support from research associates including Abhijit Jana, Anirban Seth, Debalina Jana, Dolonchampa Chakraborty, Kanchan Mandal, Mukhlesur Rahaman Gain, Partha Sarathi Banerjee, Suparna De, Sutapa Ghosh and Tania Goldar.

I would like to thank Qudsiya Ahmed and Suvadip Bhattacharjee of

Cambridge University Press for the professionalism and care they have shown with their prompt, friendly and meticulous responses to all my queries.

Finally, I found in Bijoy Prosad Mojumder, my father-in-law, a rare combination of calmness and courage in the face of life's heaviest odds. My father, Dibyanarayan, remains a close friend, and still absorbs my tantrums with a wide smile. I have always admired his ability to find joy in the simplest of things, and his easy ways of dealing with life's many ups and downs. My mother, Mukti, taught me that an act of dissent need not be noisy. Her patience and hard work gave us a stable home while she rushed between household chores and responsibilities at work. As I sign off I fondly remember my grandmother, Charubala, whose love for me was strictly unconditional. And last, not least, I cannot but express my deep gratitude for Debjani, my comrade-in-arms and the most irreverent interlocutor, who has stood by me through happy and not-so-happy times.

ABBREVIATIONS

ABPTA	All Bengal Primary Teachers' Association
AICCCR	All India Coordination Committee of the Communist Revolutionaries
AIKS	All India Kisan Sabha
APL	Above Poverty Line
ASSOCHAM	Associated Chamber of Commerce and Industry of India
BDO	Block Development Officer
BJP	Bharatiya Janata Party
BLRO	Block Land Revenue Officer
BPL	Below Poverty Line
BUPC	Bhumi Uchchhed Pratirodh Committee
CITU	Centre of Indian Trade Unions
CMIE	Centre for Monitoring Indian Economy
CCIF	Cominform Communist Information Forum
CPI	Communist Party of India

CPI(M)	Communist Party of India (Marxist)
CPI(ML)	Communist Party of India (Marxist-Leninist)
CPSU	Communist Party of Soviet Union
CrPC	Code of Criminal Procedure
DFID	Department for International Development
EAP	Externally Aided Project
FDI	Foreign Direct Investment
GOI	Government of India
GoWB	Government of West Bengal
GP	Gram Panchayat
IBM	International Business Machines
ICDS	Integrated Child Development Services
IMF	International Monetary Fund
KJRC	Krishi Jomi Raksha Committee
KUBJRC	Krishak Uchchhed Birodhhi O Janaswartha Raksha Committee
LS	Lok Sabha
LSS	Lok Sebak Sangha
MLALAD	MLA Local Area Development
MNC	Multi-national Corporations
MoU	Memorandum of Understanding
MPLAD	MP Local Area Development

ABBREVIATIONS

NDA	National Democratic Alliance
NES	National Election Survey
NKID	New Kolkata Industrial Development
OBC	Other Backward Castes
PDF	Progressive Democratic Front
PDS	Public Distribution System
PIFRC	Price Increase and Famine Resistance Committee
PSP	Praja Socialist Party
PULF	People's United Left Front
RAF	Rapid Action Force
RCPI	Revolutionary Communist Party of India
RCRC	Refugee Central Rehabilitation Council
RSP	Revolutionary Socialist Party
SC	Scheduled Castes
SEZ	Special Economic Zone
SRD	Strengthening Rural Decentralization
SSA	Sarva Shiksha Abhiyan
SSK	Shishu Shiksha Kendra
ST	Scheduled Tribes
SUCI	Socialist Unity Centre of India
SUCI(C)	Socialist Unity Centre of India (Communist)
TFERC	Tram Fare Enhancement Resistance Committee
TMC	Trinamool Congress

UCRC	United Central Rehabilitation Council
ULF	United Left Front
UNCHR	United Nations Commission on Human Rights
UPA	United Progressive Alliance
VDC	Village Development Council
VEC	Village Education Committee
VS	Vidhan Sabha
WBIDC	West Bengal Industrial Development Corporation
WBLA	West Bengal Legislative Assembly

1

INCEPTION: GOVERNMENT AS PRACTICE

Parliamentary left parties in India never had it so bad before. In the national election of 2014, they won barely 12 seats, down from 60 odd seats they got 10 years ago, when their support proved crucial to form the Congress-led United Progressive Alliance government in New Delhi. By contrast, the left is now voted out of relevance in national politics. It is virtually wiped out in its bastion – West Bengal – where the tally came down sharply from 35 to merely 2 seats. Over the first decade of the twenty-first century, some 20 years or so after the collapse of the Soviet Union, the mainstream left slid from its historic high to an all-time low in the country's electoral battlefield. This dramatic debacle also coincides with an unprecedented rise of rightwing forces clustering around a party of religious and market fundamentalism. The question is: can India's democratic left ever hope to retrieve, and how?

An attempt to answer this cannot but move through West Bengal – an eastern Indian state with a population of 90 million – where an alliance of communist and socialist parties, the Left Front, ran a government for 34 years, from 1977 to 2011. It had been an exceptional feat for a government to win elections without a break for so long in the slippery domain that is Indian politics. Few such cases of continuity perhaps exist in the democratic world. Barring the troubling last half decade, the alliance maintained its superiority in every local, regional or national election by garnering almost half of popular votes and an overwhelming number of constituencies. Just when the regime seemed 'invincible' after a resounding triumph in 2006 election, its popular support started to wane. In 2011, the Left Front government met with its first definitive defeat. The left's rare continuity and dramatic collapse – this book argues – can be traced to the dynamics of its administrative and strategic priorities as a governmental force in West Bengal. In this chapter we travel through some major turns in its long journey over some seven decades and ask how the democratic left can think afresh beyond its restricted social, ideological and regional appeal, and hope to contribute meaningfully to the evolving ideational and public policy debates in a rapidly transforming India.

The making

The Left Front was dominated by communists who were not 'natural born citizens' of liberal democracy. Their approach to democratic government took shape since the 1940s when they were nowhere near holding administrative power in any state. On the eve of independence, in June 1947, the Communist Party of India (CPI) made a conciliatory note by deciding to 'fully cooperate' with the Congress in the 'proud task of building the Indian Republic on democratic foundations'. The party was in favour of allowing some breathing space to the new government so that it got a chance to deliver 'its promises through legal channels'. Such affability, however, was not uniformly spread within the ranks of the left. Those engaged in a bitter fight with the Nizam's dynastic rule and illegal feudal exactions in Telangana since 1946 treated the new government with utter contempt, as a purveyor of 'colonial' policies under the influence of the big bourgeoisie. They proposed a Maoist agrarian revolution to establish people's democracy. Another group, centering on Bombay, made a passionate plea in December 1947 for an armed democratic and socialist revolution in a Russian-type seizure of power.

For many left activists, a 'proletarian revolution' was imminent in the first three years of independence. The repression by the Indian state kept pace with these aspirations, causing a sharp drop in the membership of the party, which had little resilience to withstand such pressure. In several states, including West Bengal, Bombay and Madras, the party was declared illegal. The Telangana peasant struggle was brutally put down without the communists realizing even part of their demands. In 1950, the proletarian revolutionary line was rejected by none less than the Communist Information Forum (Cominform), which insisted on the Chinese path for the people in many colonial and dependent countries. The revolutionaries in the CPI were in a quandary.

Between early and mid-1950s, a number of events prompted the communists to revise their characterization of the Nehru regime. The Soviet leaders Khrushchev and Bulganin visited India, the US offered military support to India's rival Pakistan and Nehru signed *Panchsheel* with Chau-En-Lai. By 1956 CPI displayed some eagerness to ally with the 'progressive elements' in the Congress, while rejecting an extreme proposal for forging a united front. The twentieth congress of the Communist Party of Soviet Union (CPSU) proposed 'peaceful path to socialism', facilitating a CPI resolution in its fifth congress (Amritsar, 1958) that favoured containment of class struggle within the limits of the Indian Constitution. This, once again, created deep internal schism that was apparent in the sixth congress (Vijaywada, 1961) of the CPI before splitting the party on the eve of its seventh congress in 1964 (for a detailed analysis see Kaviraj, 1979).

At least four disagreements made the backdrop for the CPI split. First, there were differences on whether to accept the Soviet proposal for a 'peaceful transition to socialism'. Second, the party was divided on whom to support in the Sino-Soviet dispute or whether to maintain neutrality. Third, the Indo-China border conflict in 1962 polarized the party down the middle. In addition, no unanimity was reached on how to characterize the Indian bourgeoisie or the Congress under Nehru. The CPI strived to reconcile two main factions, a 'conservative' right and a 'radical' left.

The right followed the Soviet line on transition, merged with the nationalist position on war, backed the 'progressive' bourgeois leadership of the Congress and embraced parliamentary over extra-parliamentary activism rather uncritically. The left, by contrast, decided to maintain its autonomy with respect to Sino-Soviet rivalry, insisted that the industrial proletariat and the peasantry, not the national bourgeoisie, were the leading 'revolutionary' forces and kept open the option of extra-parliamentary struggles while participating in institutional democracy.[1] The right had a larger, if thinner, spread across the country, the left, which also absorbed the centrists, had strong organizations in three major states – Kerala, Andhra Pradesh and West Bengal. The right stayed in the CPI, while the left broke out and formed the Communist Party of India (Marxist) [CPI(M)]. Eventually the CPI(M) became the fulcrum of two coalition governments in West Bengal between 1967 and 1969, and thereafter of the Left Front government since 1977.

In the state elections in 1967, the Congress lost its uninterrupted rule over several states, including West Bengal. The preceding years were particularly turbulent with stirring effects on West Bengal. The Third Five Year Plan had faltered, industry suffered from depression and many states – West Bengal included – faced an acute food shortage.[2] The situation worsened in 1966, as the Third Plan was concluding, a severe draught wiped out the winter crop. With rupee devalued, import cost rising and high inflation, the real income of the middle class dipped. Popular discontent in West Bengal reached the brink of a political catastrophe. In midst of all this, the Congress in the state got divided; the breakaway Bangla Congress was inclined to join the communists to fight its parent party.[3] The communists and other non-Congress forces wasted little time to seize the opportunity.

Initially, the CPI(M) was hesitant to strike alliances. Unlike the CPI it refused to join Bangla Congress, a party representing the landlords and the rural rich, against the Congress. Of the three principal contestants in the 1967 state election fighting for 280 'seats' (single member constituencies), the CPI/Bangla Congress-led People's United Left Front (PULF) got 77, the CPI(M)-led United Left Front (ULF) got 74 and the Congress got 127.[4] Both CPI(M) and Bangla Congress fared well, winning 43 and 34 seats respectively. West Bengal's first non-Congress ministry seemed at a striking distance should PULF and ULF join hands.

Although it was not an easy choice for the CPI(M), a party anxious to preserve its radical image, the two merged into a United Front in March 1967. Bangla Congress leader Ajoy Mukherjee was elected the Chief Minister and CPI(M) politburo member Jyoti Basu his deputy.

The CPI(M), a party avowedly run on a set of firm political programmes, needed to explain why it came round to ally with non-left Bangla Congress. Claiming that the acute food shortage and near-famine condition had generated an extraordinary situation in the state calling for an exceptional response, it promised to sternly deal with the farmers' lobby to stop hoarding, which contributed to rapid escalation of food prices, and supported 'direct action' against the big farmers with the help of bureaucracy and peasant unions. Clearly, the CPI(M) did not see the problem of 'governing' as merely one of administering resources from the top. The party's emphasis was also on class action from below. With possible violence looming large, its partners in the United Front coalition got jittery, prompting its Food and Agriculture Minister Prafulla Chandra Ghosh, an astute Gandhian, to pit himself bluntly against the CPI(M). When Ghosh failed to meet the government's own target of procuring grains meant for selling at a controlled price from government-run shops, the tension between the CPI(M) and the non-left parties peaked.

The relentless tension wrecked the United Front from within. In early November 1967, Ghosh resigned and backed by 16 legislators formed a rival alliance – the Progressive Democratic Front (PDF) – receiving support from the Congress for staking claim to form a government without the left. Governor Dharma Vira, working in tandem with the Congress, was in no mood to wait, he asked Chief Minister Mukherjee to prove his majority within days, disregarding the latter's plea for the time he was entitled to. When Mukherjee failed the test, he was promptly dismissed. The CPI(M) claimed that the Centre unleashed its 'viciously undemocratic and conspiratorial machinations' because the party refused to give up its class commitments despite meeting all normal governmental obligations. The hurriedly forged PDF regime, fragile as it was, collapsed within days prompting the Centre to invoke President's rule in end-February 1968.[5]

A year later, on 9 February 1969, the state voted in a mid-term poll. Steeled by the recent experiences, the left parties closed ranks and formed a single coalition, the United Left Front. The CPI(M) was 'generous', allowing Bangla Congress to retain even those seats that belonged to the defectors from the party following the last election. The outcome was a rude shock for the Congress, which shrunk to only 55 seats against CPI(M)'s 83. The advantage of a pre-poll alliance in a multi-cornered fight was evident as the coalition won far more seats – 214 out of 280 – than its vote share, which was only marginally higher than the rest. Despite being the largest party, the CPI(M) offered the top job to Ajoy Mukherjee. In exchange, it kept some key portfolios like Home and General Administration, Land and Land Revenue, and Refugee Rehabilitation and Labour. The party saw its rising popularity as stemming from its capacity and readiness to combine some defining legislative steps with strident extra-legal initiatives at the field level.[6]

With the onset of the harvesting season in end-1969, as expected, clashes in the countryside and schism in the United Front saw a rapid escalation. CPI(M) insisted on using the government as an 'instrument of class struggle', Bangla Congress was determined to end the ongoing 'conflict and anarchy'. Chief Minister Mukherjee sat on a 72-hour fast holding his own government to account for fostering 'hatred and violence'. Though elements in the government sympathized with Mukherjee, none was eager to go overboard and accept the onus of breaking the coalition. The Centre was also chary of imposing presidential rule again; a decimated Congress stood as a testimony of the unpopularity of such measures. Eventually, the situation came to such a pass that Mukherjee resigned and President's rule was indeed imposed in April 1970.

While the allies blamed CPI(M)'s 'militancy' for the fall of government, leftwing factions within the party felt just the opposite. By opting to participate in a parliamentary government, they thought, the party was getting entrapped in its protocols at the cost of its radicalism. Their differences with the party's governmental actions reached a flashpoint in March 1967 over a peasant rebellion against local landlords in three villages of Siliguri subdivision – Naxalbari, Kharibari and Phansidewa.

In determining how it should respond to the rising peasants the party swung between two poles. While support for the upsurge was surely to destabilize the United Front government, suppressing the peasants looked like abandoning the project for rebellion. After some heated exchanges, the party decided to send police to put down the peasants. The action was strongly opposed by the leftists who eventually, in April–May 1969, broke with the CPI(M) and formed its own outfit – the Communist Party of India (Marxist-Leninist) [CPI(ML)].[7]

A prime theatre for this second major split in Indian communist movement was the Krishak Sabha, the CPI(M)'s peasant union (more on this in chapter 2). As late as in 1966, the Krishak Sabha anticipated that peasant movement in the country was approaching a 'revolutionary turning point' (WBPKS, 1966a and, 1966b). The line was maintained even in the early United Front days when Harekrishna Konar, the peasant leader and land minister, welcomed extra-constitutional steps to procure 'substantial benefits', considering it unhelpful to depend entirely on the government. In support, the United Front in its *Programme* pledged to keep police away from 'democratic movements'[8] and insisted that there was no contradiction between class mobilization and governmental stability.[9] The position changed dramatically after Y. B. Chavan, the Union Home Minister, issued an ultimatum on 13 June 1967 threatening central intervention if the state government failed to put down the rebellion in Naxalbari (Ghosh, 1981, 73; Banerjee, 1980, 114).

Faced with the stark choice, the CPI(M) politburo decided to purge the 'adventurist' trend in the party which now had allegedly pushed the movement so far as to put the government in danger.[10] The so-called adventurists stood by the rebellious peasants in Naxalbari (and Srikakulam in Andhra Pradesh), drew inspiration from Mao Ze Dong's leadership and received support from the Communist Party of China, which called the uprising 'the front paw of the Indian revolution'. They eventually formed the All India Coordination Committee of the Communist Revolutionaries (AICCCR) as they broke out of the CPI(M) to form the CPI(M-L) (see Dasgupta, 1974; Banerjee, 1984; Sen, 1980; Banerjee, 1980; Ray, 2002; Ghosh, 1981). Cleansed of the 'radicals', the CPI(M) clarified its position on a host of issues. It defended coalitions with non-left parties, which the radicals saw as 'class enemies', and reiterated that it would follow neither the Chinese nor the Soviets in international communist movement. In a draft resolution the central committee of the party expressed its determination to 'guard itself against any such outside interference and jealously defend its independence and independent political line'.[11] Alliance with so-called bourgeois parties was found necessary for a 'united action against a common enemy, at a particular stage of development, together with several other classes and parties with whom the proletariat has contradictions, including antagonistic contradictions at times'.[12] Critically, the CPI(M) was now prepared to join hands with smaller 'class enemies' to fight its bigger 'class enemy', the Congress.

To digress a little, the first lessons of coalitional politics were learnt by the left in the form of multi-class popular movements of the 1950s and 1960s, well before the United Front. Three mobilizations in particular – against a raise in tram-fares in Calcutta (1953), and two phases (1957–59 and 1966) of protest against acute food shortage, put West Bengal on the boil (Franda, 1971b). The communists no doubt gained the maximum mileage from these stirrings, but not until they gave up shreds of unilateralism, which had kept them apart from non-communist left and left-of-centre parties. As Prafulla Chakrabarti shows, the communists played a leading role in the United Central Rehabilitation Council (UCRC), an alliance that articulated the demands of a large and heterogeneous refugee population in and around Calcutta after the Partition of 1947. What the CPI leaders in UCRC could not achieve for years – galvanizing a simmering discontent into a flashpoint of popular unrest against the government – became possible in 1953 when another alliance – the Tram Fare Enhancement Resistance Committee (TFERC) – was rapidly formed against the raise of the tram fare by just a pice, i.e., one-sixty fourth of a rupee. However ridiculously low the amount may appear, the raise was widely seen as the last straw that an insensitive government placed on a severely distraught population in punishing post-Partition conditions. 'The UCRC had fashioned a model for the joint functioning of the parties of the Left' and the TFERC was 'created in its image ... for conducting the joint struggle of the parties of the Opposition against the Establishment' (Chakrabarti, 1990, 330–31). In the course of the agitation, the UCRC aligned with its rival organization, the Refugee Central Rehabilitation Council (RCRC) that was attached to the Krishak Mazdoor Praja Party. This catapulted a city-based movement against a small change in tram fare (a 'politics of small change' – about which more later) in July 1953 to larger segments of the refugee population (lower middle class students and mostly unemployed youth), workers in the industry and toiling peasants in the countryside. 'The TFERC may be regarded as the present-day Left Front in embryo', writes Chakrabarti, '... the leadership now claimed to represent the radical opinion of the whole of West Bengal' (Chakrabarti, 1990, 337).

Another factor that united almost all segments of West Bengal's population in the 1950s and 1960s was food. Between 1951 and 1961, West Bengal's population rose by 32.2 per cent (India 21.6 per cent) with more that 6 million refugees crossing the border. This happened at a time when arable land devoted to foodgrain cultivation depleted to make for the drop in supply of raw jute from East Pakistan for the mills lining up the river Hooghly. The problem was compounded by illegal stocking of paddy by the hoarders, who sought to take advantage of the crisis through black market operations. The B. C. Roy government first attempted to regulate transactions by statutory procurement and penal measures of levy on evaders which, when proved counterproductive, had to be discontinued in September 1959 by opening the market and making up the shortage with supplementary supplies from the central government. The crisis, however, returned in an acute form in 1966, and P. C. Sen, the Gandhian Food Minister, revoked the control regime only to realize eventually that the desired results were difficult, if not impossible, with most violators of government control – the large and intermediate landowners, millers, transporters and shopkeepers – made up the machinery of his own Congress party. Such policy flip-flop and indeterminate action gave the opposition left a large room to manoeuvre. Since 1952, agitation and demonstration against the government's 'inaction' became almost a routine affair. The CPI along with other left parties gelled into the Price Increase and Famine Resistance Committee (PIFRC) holding numerous rallies in the 1950s that peaked into a massive demonstration against the government on 31 August 1959.

Both UCRC and PIFRC were big steps for the left in learning the grammar of making and maintaining coalitions, which proved valuable later in the phase of the United Front governments and, indeed, for the Left Front thereafter. Three typical characteristics of this mode of action were: First, the communists considered their coalition with like-minded parties helpful to expand influence in various segments of the population across different parts of the state. They could now pose their partisan demands as broad-based and universal. Second, in the place of unilateralism of any sort consensus was preferred, creating conditions for joint action irrespective of multiple – often conflicting – political compulsions. Third, in cementing the coalition the regional government became both the target and the cradle of leftwing mobilization generating a mode of politics which, as we shall see, was instrumental both to open new possibilities as well as impose strict limits. However, despite such conciliatory mood, mutual differences between the three communist parties – CPI, CPI(M) and CPI(ML) – persisted.

The distance between the CPI and the CPI(M) widened as the former refused to extend support after the 1971 state election, allowing a frail Bangla Congress government to collapse within months. The CPI now moved closer to the Congress which, under Indira Gandhi, adopted numerous populist measures propelled by a nationalist wave following her successful military campaign against Pakistan. In the 1972 state election, the Congress won an unusually high number of seats, the CPI(M)'s tally shrunk to just 14 with a drop in its vote share by 6 per cent. Losing miserably and arguably unfairly, the CPI(M) and its allies boycotted the legislative assembly for the next five years.[13] Massive state repression set in, reaching its peak in the national emergency, all opposition voices were silenced in the state. The CPI, during most of these years, sided with the Congress.

For the CPI, the Congress now appeared progressively leftwing, so to treat it as an 'enemy' meant undermining the left's own achievements (Gupta, 1972). The party went as far as supporting the national emergency in June 1975 assuming that 'the possibility of ... joint work between the Congress and the CPI has greatly increased'. It urged other left parties to realize 'the gravity of the situation facing our nation' and to 'abandon their line of blind anti-Congressism' which allegedly 'led them into becoming the camp-followers of the worst and most vicious enemies of the left, the forces of the right neocolonialism and counterrevolution'.[14] Over the next couple of years as the emergency lost its sheen the CPI's credibility also got irreparably damaged.[15]

With the Congress in power the CPI(M) lied low to protect its workers from the routine state repressions. In its Madurai Congress (1972), the party described the condition in West Bengal as 'semi-fascist' and predicted its imminent unfolding in other parts of the country. Scores of party workers fled from home and many who remained were formally 'expelled' for their own security. The party saw the declaration of national emergency in 1975 as more of a continuity of the same repressive condition. Many of its workers were incarcerated; several killed. A section within the party got restless demanding that the leadership showed the courage to take on the state. Many felt that Promod Das Gupta and Jyoti Basu, who rose to prominence after the death of Muzaffar Ahmed in 1973 and Harekrishna Konar in 1974, were unduly wary and cautious. To stem any discontent, the leadership responded with firmness. Some members were expelled and a number of local committees dissolved. Under the adverse emergency rule, the party perhaps was keener to preserve its resources than head for a frontal confrontation.[16]

The situation changed dramatically after the emergency. A newly formed Janata Party – a medley of disparate anti-Congress elements ranging from the Hindu-right to the proponents of Gandhian socialism – recorded an extraordinary victory over Indira Gandhi's Congress in the 1977 national election. In the run up to the state election in June that year, the CPI(M) reverted to its coalition *dharma* and attempted an alliance with the Janata Party, willing to concede 52 per cent seats to the latter. Prafulla Chandra Sen, now in charge of Janata in the state, stuck to his demand of 55 per cent seats. With talks failing, the Janata and the left decided to part their ways. In the three-cornered contest that followed, the CPI(M) won 177 constituencies against 20 of Congress and 29 of Janata Party; the Left Front winning 230 of 294 seats. The vote share of the left was 46.3 per cent, slightly higher than the combined share of the Congress (23.4 per cent) and Janata Party (20.5 per cent), bringing home once more the advantage of a solid coalition in a multi-cornered first past the post contest (Kohli, 1987, 107–08).

Jyoti Basu was sworn in as the Chief Minister on 21 June 1977. In its first meeting the cabinet decided to release all political prisoners. In September, an important land reform bill was passed. In mid-October, the Left Front recommended holding the panchayat election early next year, the first of its kind in the country. Within a month the government published a guideline for recording sharecroppers and protecting their rights. Between November 1977 and March 1978, on numerous occasions, the state government highlighted the need for restructuring India's federalism, which was heavily biased to the Centre. In March 1978, the state government took the highly controversial decision to stop the flow of refugees from Dandakaranya.[17] In June, the Left Front recorded a landslide victory in the panchayat election. In September that year, the panchayat played a signal role in rescuing and rehabilitating millions marooned and devastated by a massive flood.

In this period of its making, therefore, the governmental left had internalized some important principles. First, it realized the import of balancing its 'revolutionary' programme with the compulsions of day-to-day functioning in parliamentary democracy. Whenever the balance was disturbed beyond a manageable limit, parties were split. Second, the long United Front months taught the left that a strong coalition was the key operative form not just because it delivered proportionately more seats in the legislature with fewer votes, but also because it helped in keeping the opposition isolated and impeded its consolidation into a formidable force. Third, those on the left, who fully embraced the parliamentary path (CPI) or rejected it completely (CPI-ML), ended up being marginal players in West Bengal for the next several decades. The one [CPI(M)] that used extra-parliamentary rhetoric to maintain a disciplined and hierarchical organization, but followed all the constitutional protocols without any sign of practical dissent received a good deal of electoral approval. Finally, as the train of subsequent events revealed, the object of the mainstream left was now focused on running a government and winning elections, the project of 'capturing the state power', that charged many a communist dreams between 1940s and 1970s, was now eternally deferred. Governing West Bengal, a tumultuous state hopping from one crisis to another, now turned into the core project for the left in power.

Deepening government

Once in charge, the two most important policies of the Left Front government were land reforms and decentralization of rural administration by installing local government, the panchayat, in the countryside. Chapter 2 will discuss land reforms *politically*, what it accomplished and what it did not for consolidating the regime of the left. The panchayat or elected local governments became the epicentre of the left's governmental project in the state, not only bringing far-reaching changes in the organization of political power in rural West Bengal, but also reworking the political mode of the parliamentary left, particularly of the CPI(M) and Krishak Sabha. By offering a concrete institutional form of an embedded, everyday state, the panchayat intended to alter the ways of conducting governmental business in the countryside. The idea was to cut down the hold of bureaucracy and the influence of local elites in matters of policy implementation and open an institutional space for negotiation, participation and interaction between the administration and rural population. While these made up the basic intent, a blueprint of a sort, guided mainly by the CPI(M)'s political ambition of making inroads into the hugely populous rural public sphere, what actually transpired was often different. There were several unintended consequences too, which confronted the left's governmental project with disruptive contingencies. Nevertheless, the structure of rural government elected on party lines, before its introduction elsewhere in the country, created opportunities for the Left Front to gain a unique resilience and depth that deserve a special attention.

In the 1950s and 1960s, in keeping with the rest of the country discussion on the panchayat was common in West Bengal's governmental circles. But the newly proposed structure differed markedly from the one that the Left Front was to adopt later in 1978. The first Panchayat Act was passed in 1957 and the Zilla Parishad Act in 1963, calling for a four-tier system following the recommendations of government appointed Balwant Rai Mehta Study Team. There was no provision for direct election to these tiers except the lowest at the village level. The village was anyway the least powerful stratum, with no autonomy, and – more importantly – with no legal obligation for periodic elections. Consequently, instead of strengthening democracy such decentralized administration, wherever implemented, helped the dominant rural classes consolidate their power with the help of institutional sanctity.

It was the second United Front government, which made an early attempt to arrest such tendencies. A document called 'Basic Ideas about the Reorganisation of Panchayat in West Bengal' was prepared and, subsequently a Panchayat Bill was introduced in 1969. Given the tension within the coalition between the Gandhians and the Marxists, the Bill differed from the 'Basic Ideas' with no explanation given (GoWB, 1969, 4–5; Jainal Abedin's speech). In the debate that followed some argued that the MLAs should also be members of block and district panchayat bodies. Others branded such suggestions as desperate attempts by legislators to secure their formal control over local administration. The Congress, on its part, opposed participation of political parties in panchayat election as proposed in the Bill, arguing that such provision would destroy 'existing peace' in the countryside. The government, however, was toppled before the Bill could be passed. In 1973, the Congress government passed a 'progressive' West Bengal Panchayat Act, which it probably never meant to implement. The Left Front government's Act of 1978 borrowing heavily from this frozen law introduced provisions for competitive elections on party line for three tier panchayat system at the village (Gram Panchayat), block (Panchayat Samiti) and district (Zilla Parishad) levels.

Since 1978, several amendments to the Panchayat Act were brought which, for a quick scanning, can be classified in four phases. The 'first phase' (roughly from 1978 to mid-1980s) was expected mainly to implement land reform policies under the tutelage of either the party or of the bureaucracy. While this indeed made possible the launching of a number of pro-poor initiatives, it was probably little too early to claim 'that the politics of West Bengal is undergoing a fundamental structural change' (Kohli, 1987, 113). Rather, in this period the rural middle classes gained traction within the left party apparatuses at the cost of the poor, as Echeverri-Gent observes, making popular participation skewed. By using the panchayat as an instrument to spread its footprint the CPI(M) now positioned itself as the central figure of West Bengal's rural society. The deepening of the panchayat, therefore, was coeval to the consolidation of the CPI(M) in rural West Bengal and to the rise of the middle classes in the rural power structure (Echeverri-Gent, 1992, 1414). These classes were non-land holding, service dependent, frequently public sector employees, especially school teachers, predominantly male 'often drawn from high-caste Hindu social background' (Basu and Majumder, 2013, 188–89). Chapter 2 will offer a detailed discussion on these connections.

These left-dominated local government bodies in effect differed from what the left claimed them to be. It was common to project the Gram Panchayat as constituted of poor or marginal peasants, agricultural workers and sharecroppers – the left's 'basic classes'. Surya Kanta Mishra, the Panchayat Minister, for instance, claimed that a survey 'revealed that more than 71 per cent of the representatives were small and marginal farmers' holding less than 5 acres each (GoWB, 1991, 19). Benoy Krishna Chowdhury, Minister in charge of land reforms, also made a similar claim: 'It has been found by analyzing the results of the 1978 election to the panchayat that among the members elected 85 per cent did not either have any land at all, or had land below 5 acres' (CPI(M), 1988, 7). A dig into the actual survey (conducted in 1980 on 1466 members from 100 Gram Panchayat) that both ministers referred to, however, reveals a different story (GoWB, 1980f). It shows that the composition of these bodies was overwhelmingly male, majority young (25–39 years), around half owner-cultivators, 14 per cent teachers, 7.5 per cent unemployed and less than 5 per cent agricultural workers. Indeed, more than 70 per cent of owner-cultivators had land below 5 acres. However, when estimated against the *entire* sampled population belonging to different occupation groups, the proportion of landholders below 5 acres was merely 36 per cent. Significantly, of all occupation groups the school teachers made the highest proportion of Gram Panchayat *pradhans* (heads), 14 per cent, while the sharecroppers made only 1.7 per cent.

The 'second phase' (mid-1980s to early-1990s) gave the panchayat some autonomy in allocation of resources, a small part of which was mobilized internally, the larger part delivered from above. That the village panchayat had almost no role in 'planning local development' was now considered a drawback. A Standing Committee was set up in every Zilla Parishad and Panchayat Samiti where the members were encouraged to get involved in the business of 'area planning' along with selection of beneficiaries and implementation of policies (Webster, 1992, 35). While the 'first steps' were taken in this direction, 'there are very few indications that the Left Front parties give priority to furthering this process' (Westergaard, 1987, 110). Doubts were also raised on how far the rural local government, where middle peasants and schoolteachers continued to play an influential role, *represented* the local population. The Scheduled Tribes (ST) and women were found grossly underrepresented and the leading players were almost always from middle ranking families with higher social status (Webster, 1992, 118–21). It was quite obvious that the overall mood of the left now favoured putting up a structure of 'institutional management' rather than opening room for genuine participation of the poor and the marginal (Lieten, 1996, 63).

In the early 1990s, the 'third phase' (early-1990s to 2000) was initiated, when the West Bengal Panchayat Act, 1992 introduced a new apparatus called Gram Sabha (Village Assembly) to be convened twice a year. To make it consistent with the 73rd Constitutional Amendment (1993), the Gram Sabha was later replaced by Gram Sansad (Village Parliament) a body that included all the voters in an electoral booth area. Now representation of the socially and economically backward sections was made mandatory at every panchayat tier in proportion to their share of population in a district and a third of the seats were reserved for women. Early reports of the Gram Sabha meetings, however, were highly discouraging. The Panchayat Minister himself acknowledged that only 8.9 per cent meetings took place in a year, and attendance was less than 20 per cent (Mishra, 1998, 73). Though the number of such meetings increased over the next several years, attendance did not (Datta, 2001, 48). The affluent did not attend since they had little to gain, the opposition stayed away since its voice did not count, the backward groups did not attend as they were insufficiently represented and women did not attend apprehending obvious discrimination (Ghatak and Ghatak, 2002, 50–51).

To make panchayat more accountable and inclusive, two important steps were taken after 2001–02. The government launched the 'Participatory Gram Panchayat Planning under Convergent Community Action' in 2001 with the aim of involving the lowest level of panchayat administration in the planning process (Midnapore Planning and Development Society, 2002). Eventually in 2003 the Gram Unnayan Samiti (Village Development Council) was formed in the Gram Sansad areas mainly to improve the participation of opposition members (GoWB, 2004b, Section 16A[6]). In 2000 a new initiative – 'Participatory Gram Panchayat Planning Under Convergent Community Action' – was taken to make the Gram Sansad a 'genuine forum' for local planning by way of maintaining a village register carrying detailed information on socioeconomic and religio-cultural aspects of every household. Four Panchayat Samitis from four Zilla Parishads were singled out for running a 'pilot project'. Emphasis was placed on planning for small-industry and infrastructure along with agriculture (GoWB, 2002). From numerous field reports and commentaries, it was quite obvious that just like their preceding ones these initiatives also fell much short of their declared goals.

Each of these 'stages', in short, revealed two principal tendencies at play. Top-down policies were made by the government, either by the regional state or the Centre, which, when refracted through layers of divergent social and political interests to the local level, did not quite deliver the results intended. The left, nonetheless, understood the advantage of carrying the government to rural localities rather early for implementing its land reform laws and expanding its popular base. This helped change the highly visible and volatile micro-politics of rural West Bengal, strewn with incessant unrests and violent upsurges, into a more manageable site for planning and disbursement consistent with the principles of rational administration (Williams, 1999). Local governance got largely demystified and turned into a sphere of proximate interaction, rendering the language of rights and entitlement, bureaucracy and law, corruption and malpractice into a popular discourse for daily scrutiny. In this 'deepening' of government, or governmentalization of the locality, a centralized disciplined party – most notably the CPI(M) – played a vital mediatory role, giving West Bengal's local government a unique texture. The 'voice' of the locality, as witnessed in every stage of rural decentralization, could be heard only when amplified by the party. Governmentalization of the locality, as a result, did not quite produce a simultaneous localization of the government. Although the governed now became more familiar with instruments and fields of the government as well as its limits and scope, constraints on public access to critical 'procedures of planning and disbursement' were systematically maintained generating a public apathy in matters of participation and attendance.

Social government

Just as governmentalization of locality was unaccompanied by a localization of government, the left in West Bengal pressed its government into the crevices of the social without socializing the government. The left government – for almost its entire period – received a sustained support from the socially marginal population groups, the Scheduled Castes (SC) and the Scheduled Tribes (ST), which found it least prejudiced of the available options. At the same time, these communities rarely found any place in the top leadership of the left parties or that of the government. Rather, the left preferred not to treat social marginalization as a problem requiring urgent attention. They either handled it as a function of poverty and inequality, resolvable through economic development and distribution, or proposed that 'class' as a collective subsumed every other form of exclusion, segregation or indignity. Thus, even when the left broke the stranglehold of the landlords in rural regions and opened up a more inclusive and deliberative public sphere, it allowed the existing social hierarchies to persist, leaving it largely unproblematized. The most immediate effect of this standoffishness was reflected in the government's poor record in two key areas of human development – education and public health – which should receive maximum focus in the policy agenda of an avowedly leftwing regime.

According to the National Election Survey (NES) that the CSDS-Lokniti conducted over four general (state and national) elections between 2001 and 2009 in West Bengal, the left parties registered a solid block of support from the SC (53.5 per cent on average) and ST (53.25 per cent on average) groups, which far outweighed the support these parties obtained from the upper castes (43.25 per cent), the OBC (49.75 per cent) or even the Muslims (46.25 per cent) in these elections. What was the secret behind such sustained support from these groups? The left claimed that the scheduled communities in West Bengal were among the best served by its land reform policies in the country as a whole. Among the 2.1 million SC families that benefitted from the distribution of land above ceiling in the country, 1.04 million (or 49.52 per cent) belonged to West Bengal. The number of ST beneficiaries in the country was 0.85 million, of whom 0.53 million (or 62.35 per cent) were in the state alone (Government of India, 2007, 255 [Annexure XLVI]).

However, in making the *leadership* of the left parties, the Dalits were either ignored or kept confined only to the local bodies like the ones operating at the village level. By contrast the dominance of the upper castes was firmly established in the higher governmental forums at the regional or national levels. In absence of any data on the social composition of the left leaders, we use here a set of proxy data, comparing the social composition of seven Left Front ministries between 1977 and 2006 with that of the panchayat functionaries in 2008. Though all these state ministers were from the left parties, overwhelmingly from the

CPI(M), not all panchayat functionaries belonged to the left, especially in 2008, the year we draw our data on, as the electoral slide of the left gained momentum since that year. Such qualifications notwithstanding, a simple fact remains; the relative strength of the Dalits in the state level ministry had been incredibly low throughout the Left Front period in comparison with their representation as functionaries in the panchayat bodies. While the combined presence of SC in all seven Left Front ministries was merely 8.75 per cent, and of ST 1.02 per cent, they constituted 40.56 and 10.01 per cent of the panchayat functionaries respectively in 2008.[18] It perhaps can be justifiably argued that this hierarchy between the upper castes and the Dalits across higher and lower governmental bodies turned the latter into 'mere foot soldiers' of the left, who were 'martyred, incarcerated and alienated from their homes and families' helping the 'the upper-caste leaders to flourish, and to establish their complete control' (Rana, 2009, 130, translation by the author).

The Left Front government chose to leave these critical issues unaddressed. It took no special initiative to delve into the 'caste question', which remained politically dormant for decades. West Bengal did not have any large-scale Dalit assertions like some other states, nor was there any upswing in the mobilization of the backward castes over the implementation of Mandal Commission recommendations. Caste-based parties were virtually nonexistent in the state; votes from various caste groups were routinely cast for parties formed on non-identitarian lines. Caste, therefore, appeared 'invisible' in West Bengal, reinforcing the Marxist claim that the politics of 'class' had managed to displace the 'regressive' idea of caste. Indeed, as has been seen, the CPI(M) painted its land reforms that benefited a high proportion of Scheduled Caste and Scheduled Tribe groups as the success *exclusively* of its class politics. Class was the new caste for the Marxists prompting Jyoti Basu, the Chief Minister, to 'remark before the Mandal Commission that in the state there were only two castes – the rich and the poor' (Ghosh, 2001).

Nothing could be far from the ground realities. Caste domination persisted in rural West Bengal with various exclusionary practices. At the same time, however, solidarities along caste lines in the state did not spring up in the form of trans-local associations capable of exerting pressure from below in demand of educational opportunities, employment, or availability of services such as healthcare or public distribution of food and other provisions as happened in Kerala or Tamil Nadu (Desai, 2001; Srinivasan, 2010). In Kerala, caste offered the primary associational form 'in which the peasant masses rose in struggle against feudalism', and locally articulated caste demands could be translated into class reforms for a wider success in delivering education and healthcare facilities (Namboodiripad, 1952, 102; Ramachandran, 1997). Rather, the idiom of 'the party' in West Bengal countryside became the sole channel for almost all social initiatives as it filtered popular demands to suit its purpose (see chapter 4). This, on the one hand, helped the left maintain social tranquility on the surface by diffusing any challenge to its superior organizational position for decades, and on the other it worked as a check on the representation of the marginal social groups in the upper levels of the party and the government, where the upper caste cultural elite, the *bhadralok*, continued to hold forth.

A quick look at West Bengal's records on health and education during the long Left Front years shows how the system 'faltered'. West Bengal's literacy rates, in comparison with 16 major states remained unchanged over two long decades of left rule: sixth (48.65 per cent) in 1981, seventh (57.70 per cent) in 1991 and sixth (69.22 per cent) in 2001 (computed from Government of India, 2002, 186, Table 4.1). In the school enrolment for girl students, a key indicator to measure educational well-being, the state remained below the national average for the first 16 years of the left government (Government of India, 2002, 200–03). A Planning Commission document compared 20 Indian states on a select set of indicators to assess the level of infrastructure available for primary education. West Bengal ranked third from the bottom, only above Jharkhand and Bihar (Government of India, 2010, 137–38). In healthcare, West Bengal showed remarkable results in lowering infant mortality, raising longevity and bridging the gender ratio (Guruswamy et al., 2005, 2155; GoI, 2010, 121). However, the existing strength of medical and paramedical staff and their growth in West Bengal remained low rendering the healthcare received by the poor in the state unsatisfactory (GoI, 2010, 130). Those capable of purchasing private facilities tended to avoid government hospitals due to overcrowding, poor sanitary conditions or lack of care. As a result, government facilities were meant mainly for the underclasses, causing a further deterioration in their accountability and service quality. A study using the 60th Round NSS data found that patients commonly avoided government facilities for outpatient care on grounds of 'bad treatment', 'poor accessibility' and 'long waiting period' (GoI, 2010, 130). West Bengal's ranking on the scale of Human Development Index among 16 major states remained ninth, showing no sign of improvement between 1981 and 1991 (GoI, 2002, 140–41, Tables 1.1–1.2).

The complex caste/class dynamics at the ground level and the effects of left intervention on them were taken up by some ethnographic studies of rural change. One such study, for instance, observed that the Left Front reforms made possible a greater participation of the lower castes in the rural public sphere, which they were denied in, say, the 1960s. Earlier the 'wealthy' village notables routinely had evening meetings in their *baithakkhana* or private 'discussion house' to deliberate on important village matters. There was no place for the lower castes in these meetings. With the onset of the left the format changed. Such meetings were now called in the name of some 'committee', held at a public place enabling the lower castes to participate in good numbers. Though they were presented as 'formal' or 'official' there was no bar to engage 'in the kind of particularistic activities required in the informal arena'. The CPI(M) workers in the early 1990s were 'very aware' of the liminal potentials of these meetings cutting across public and private affairs, which they 'fully exploited' to enhance their 'legitimacy and entrenchment' (Ruud, 2003, 153). The lower castes, on their part, expected not just material benefits from the newly emergent left. In their aspiration for recognition, for 'symbolic power', they aligned with the left as an alternative channel for mobility. Thus, a low caste agricultural worker, frequently looked down as a 'criminal', could find in his association with the middle class culturally equipped upper caste left activists (often from outside the village) a useful 'enabler', a handle to upset the social and economic grip of the *local* elite (Ruud, 1999, 689–732, especially 700–05). From its inception the left-dominated panchayat was sought to be employed by the rural subalterns to cut into the normative arrangement of the old social order (Ruud, 1994, 357–80, especially, 374–78; Ruud, 2003). That the left received a solid and enduring electoral support from the Scheduled communities for more than three decades was a validation of this point.

What, however, remains to be explored is the *limited* character of mobility that the upper caste left leadership opened for lower caste peasants in rural West Bengal. True, the shift from the private 'discussion house' to the public 'committee' was a step in the direction of democratization of the local deliberative mechanisms. However, while the 'discussion house' of the upper castes lost its eminence, its doors remained shut for the lower castes. The left did not launch any project for social reorganization to break the exclusive grip of the upper castes over all relevant channels of political and cultural mobility. By associating with the upper caste leaders in the hope of altering the social geography of power, the lower castes in effect reinforced the latter's cultural hegemony. Attempts were made only to jettison the hegemony of the local/rural elite by the outsider/urban elite, substituting one form of domination with another. There was scarcely any mood of defiance, or any move to refute the social hierarchy based on what Pierre Bourdieu in another context called 'misrecognition' of 'arbitrary' as 'essential', a clear act of 'symbolic violence' (Bourdieu, 1984, 175). Instead, the inner domain of the rural society, its own manner of ordering status and privileges, was left largely unaffected by any systematic intervention.

This distinction (not to be confused with separation) between the formal-institutional domain of the modern state and the constituted 'self' of the community perpetrated conditions in which, as Partha Chatterjee points out, caste or a tribal community,

> still regards the state and the various organizations or personalities vying for state power as external entities which are either benevolent or malicious, and accordingly worthy of veneration or resistance, but never as the products of a set of social relations of power and authority of which it is itself a part (Chatterjee, 1997, 86).

'Even after the introduction of panchayati raj and mass mobilization', as an ethnographic account informs us, 'villages retained a large degree of internal self-rule' (Ruud, 1995, 286–87). Others, however, rejected this arguing that the peasants are located within both class and caste matrices and 'the broader structures of power, particularly in a Panchayati Raj where they can use it for their own empowerment' (Bandopadhyay, 2004, 35–36). Whichever view one accepts – of articulated autonomy or systemic incorporation into the modern institutions of power – there perhaps is little doubt that the parliamentary left in rural West Bengal expanded its political base either by leaving the 'deep structure' of society undisturbed, or by keeping the higher institutions of power out of bounds of the social outcastes. Either way, any possibility for the lower castes to emerge as leaders of the left parties or ministers in the Left Front government got thoroughly undermined. The left's social project, therefore, stood for a formalization of local politics short of politicizing the institutions internal to the communities or facilitating genuine mobility ('empowerment') of the marginal groups within the formal structures of government.

Political government

From the left's local and social governmental practices, we move to its political aspects. Both the unusual pro-incumbency pattern of elections for decades in West Bengal and the sharp decline in popularity of the left parties demand an appropriate explanation. Was the left's long innings a result of 'good' governance, a systematic pruning of its radicalism, of judicious patronage that avoided any obvious favouritism? Or was it, instead, an effect of strategic clientelism, of sustaining a massive network for delivering material benefits in lieu of electoral support? Or, on a different plane, did the left's long stay result from a durable compact with its 'basic classes' that carefully balanced its pragmatic maneuvers with an emancipatory ideology? And, by default, did the left regime collapse when its capacity to deliver was lost, its clientelist network waned, or it strayed from its core classes?

Some suggest that the left stayed in power because, and as long as, it offered 'good governance'. Good governance basically implies using administration to its potentials for delivering resources to targeted population without disturbing peace and order.[19] On this view, the CPI(M)'s disciplined and organized network made possible a smooth functioning of the administration for an unbiased and legitimate implementation of policies. The left's greatest success in West Bengal, it is suggested, was to transform an 'unruly' state into an eminently governable one with the aid of a highly determined and cogent political actor. Atul Kohli claimed that 'West Bengal under the CPM probably is India's best governed state' (Kohli, 1990, 268). The left's defeat, therefore, is seen as a result of its growing failure to deliver, its inability to meet the changing aspirations of the electorate, its slide from 'good' to 'bad'. From this point of view political consequences (such as electability of a regime) followed the logic of its government which, in turn, is judged by a set of politically neutral criteria.

From a somewhat contrasting position treating the Left Front's electoral durability as 'an intriguing question', Pranab Bardhan, Dilip Mookherjee *et al* feel that it resulted from 'a strategy of clientelism' driven by preferential treatment to particular groups. Citing an elaborate system of patronage they suggested that the regime encouraged clientelism and elite capture in top-down delivery of public goods for a politically-targeted population (Bardhan *et al.*, 2011, 4). A large sample survey they conducted in several rural districts indicates that voting preferences of the beneficiaries remained sensitive more to recurring, personalized and short-term benefits than one-time benefits or improvement in the local infrastructure (Bardhan and Mookherjee, 2012b, 24). A peculiarity of West Bengal's clientelism was that while it allowed political considerations to influence the delivery of public goods from higher to lower bodies of the local government, such political favouritism was generally discouraged for distribution within a village irrespective of the party in power (Bardhan and Mookherjee, 2006, 325; Bardhan *et al.*, 2011, 40).

So the left's electoral appeal on this view was explained by a combination of three governmental processes: emphasis on short-change recurring benefits over programmatic benefits of lasting value, priority of political clientelism over legal-rational considerations in the descending flow of public goods, and maintenance of a broadly non-partisan formula for lateral allotment within the village. In a repeat survey conducted *after* the defeat of the left in 2011, it is found that support for the left in its core constituency eroded in the countryside not because clientelism became ineffective, but because the voters got increasingly unhappy with the local leaders, especially with the latter's excessive interference in public matters and indulgence in corruption. The unhappiness was more pronounced in left-ruled villages than the non-left ones and so dealt a decisive blow to the regime when supplemented by a general resentment with the government's inept handling of land acquisition in Singur and Nandigram (Bardhan *et al.*, 2014). Beset with micro-corruption on a daily basis and gross strategic miscalculation, the left's time-honoured 'machinery' for winning election came to a grinding halt.

A third major perspective on the political dimension of the left's government is that of Prabhat Patnaik, for whom the regime of the left received electoral approval as long as it maintained an ideological linkage with its 'basic classes' by balancing its existing compulsions with 'a politics of transcending capitalism'. The government collapsed when the balance got irrevocably disturbed, when the left found itself detached from its basic classes. 'I shall call this process which has caused the decline, a process of "empiricisation", by which I mean the pursuit of a political praxis that is uninformed by the project of transcending capitalism' (Patnaik, 2011, 12). 'Empiricisation' is the other name of 'mundane and pedestrian' politics, which Patnaik quotes the veteran CPI(M) leader B. T. Ranadive to describe as nothing more than 'the small change of politics'. Such quotidian action delinked from any transformative project had a corrosive effect on the party. The problem was not in the CPI(M) being a parliamentary party, because rejecting parliament also amounts to imputing a mystical power to the institution, to its fetishization. The signs of empiricization were in the CPI(M)'s failure to generate a new normative politics after the collapse of the Soviet Union and the initiation of market reforms in China, its inability to set a clear follow-up agenda to back the initial success of land reforms and decentralization. Instead, some 'comrades' suffered from a misconception that promoting industrialization by attracting investments was their responsibility. They failed to realize that such attempts decoupled the party from its 'basic classes' and the 'jobless growth' of capitalism did not either produce a proletariat free from old community ties (Patnaik, 2011, 15).

These three critiques of the government of the Left Front, its unusual continuity and eventual collapse, are by no means exhaustive; they only stand for a spectrum of longstanding research and in-depth analysis in the area. For the sake of simplicity, we can name the three as 'functionalist', 'structuralist' and 'ideological' critiques of the governmental left. From the 'functionalist' point of view, the left regime was 'well governed' as long as it ran an efficient institutional order with minimum extraneous interference for delivering resources in a stable and rational manner to the poor, the bulk of the state's population and the building block for the left's electoral support. The collapse of the regime, therefore, is traced to the *dysfunctionality* of the order due to its inability to adjust to some vital internal and external changes. The 'structuralist' view, by contrast, assumes that a reciprocal arrangement between the government and the population, which helped the left to reap electoral rewards for an exceptionally long duration, was vitiated in the recent past by the rising corruption of the regime's local agents, the most proximate patrons for a large group of clients. And for the 'ideological' critique, the regime was sustainable as long as it valued its commitment to its core classes by covering the distance between the compulsions of operating within a capitalist reality and the goal of transcending that reality. As the confines of 'politics of small change' weakened the will to link the empirical present with an idealized future, 'false' beliefs in capitalism's capacity to bring real changes set in and the left's contract with the poor, the principal source of its appeal, was annulled.

Curiously, the entire range of these critiques, each of them, operates within a framework of logical binary in which certain conditions are accepted as desirable or 'pure' while certain other as unwanted or 'polluted'. It is the slide of the government from the one to the other which offers them an explanation for its collapse. For the first it was the triumph of 'bad' government over 'good', for the second, disruption of a sound structure by some corrupt agents, for the third, substitution of revolutionary transcendence with crass empiricism. The duality remains, and the possibility that 'good' and 'bad', 'structure' and 'agency', 'transcendence' and 'empiricism', instead of being polar positions can both be simultaneously present as tendencies on a continuum is left unexplored. The political form of government, for each of these positions is an institutional order, a system of exchange, or an ideological formation, finite and given, the analytical territory of which is neatly bound and visibly outlined. In contrast, I propose here the idea of government as a process that evolves with practice and that defies any functional, structural or ideological bipolarity between attributes that are 'positive' or 'negative'. 'Government as practice' works its way through the messy terrain of myriad contradictions.

Government as practice

These contradictions, we argue, rather than being disruptive or upsetting, can actually be productive or constitutive in a government's engagement with diverse population groups. The West Bengal experience shows that a government can work its way through these contradictions as long as it productively connects the ground realities with policymaking at the top. Only the mediation of a coherent reformist agent (in this case 'the party') makes such linkages – necessary to constantly renew an elected government's relevance for heterogeneous social groups in a fiercely competitive polity – possible. These groups throw up demands that are frequently at loggerheads, requiring the government offset one set of demands in order to meet another. Government as practice, we show below, demands a full recognition of these contradictions, which make the process of governing unwieldy, demanding a dynamic use of tools for working daily through unknown, uncharted and unexpected contingencies. That is, a populist government cannot afford to be unilateral or unequivocal in its orientation, be as a rational-bureaucratic actor, a strategic patron, or an instrument for specific class interests. Paraphrasing Ernesto Laclau's logic of populism one could claim, the language of governmental discourse – 'whether Left or Right – is always going to be imprecise and fluctuating not because of any cognitive failure, but because it tries to operate performatively within a social reality which is to a large extent heterogeneous and fluctuating' (Laclau, 2007, 118). We can now recall some key contradictions from West Bengal's 'heterogeneous and fluctuating' social reality as constitutive of the government by the left.

First, governmentalization of locality without localization of government: We noted that the project of governmentalization was never smooth – it involved obvious disruptions by forces internal to local society. As a counter-measure, the left pushed the project by means of a disciplined organization – the 'party' – to maintain the communication between the higher and the lower rungs of administration going as smoothly as possible. While the party's mediation made the local government in rural West Bengal work, it seriously undermined the autonomy of the village localities. Thus, every attempt by the regime to 'deepen' its governmental structure paradoxically was foiled by its own 'success'.[20]

Second, benefits to the socially marginal groups without facilitating social mobility: The left gained local access by leaving the inner dynamics of social identities undisturbed. It chose not to interfere in self-organization or subjectification of social groups, such as caste. The left's reluctance to intervene in the deeper structures of the society worked like a double-edged sword. It protected the left workers from social resistance at the ground level, but at the same time, it exposed the inadequacy of 'class' for expressing the idioms of exclusion and injustice, indignity and humiliation, both between and within the social groups. Thus, the left maintained a stable electoral constituency while keeping the political project of transformation confined only to the 'surface' of the society.

Third, contingent action but avowal of 'vanguardism': in implementing its reforms, such as land reforms, the parliamentary left made use of both idealism and realism. Its rhetorical idealism was on display in validating a formal programme for, say, 'radical' land reforms or 'all land to the tiller'. Its actual practices nonetheless were limited to legally plausible limits of reforms. Tenancy, for instance, was not abolished. It had promised to intensify peasant unrest in the fields, yet it took little time to deploying the police for reinstating public order. In theory the left was vanguardist. It was expected to provide leadership to 'the majority of men [who] were fundamentally honest and upright, but prey to and victims of ignorance of their own real interests and the goals that they could more usefully aim for' (Gramsci, quoted in Davidson, 2002, 186). In practice, however, it realized that 'governing is not the realization of a programmer's dreams', that the 'real' always 'insists in the form of resistance to programming and the programmer's world is one of constant experiment, invention, failure, critique and adjustment' (Miller and Rose, 2008, 39).

Fourth, an ideological cover and intellectual vulnerability: Despite its ad hocism and hands-on action, the left – the CPI(M) in particular – was 'bound' within a version of Marxism that proclaimed 'people's democracy', maintained a 'democratic centralist' organization and asserted the aim of establishing 'dictatorship of the proletariat'. Splits in the communist movement, as noted above, resulted from bloody factional fights over 'authenticity', over what constituted the 'right' ideological line unblemished by so-called 'revisionism'. While this protected the left and helped it build and keep up a disciplined outfit suitable for cogent action, it also weakened the left, made its political conduct within the confines of constitutional democracy increasingly incongruous with its formal ideological pronouncement.

In the first decade of the Left Front government when a series of reforms were undertaken, 'government as practice' encompassed the interstices of these contradictions, the edgy, risky, eternally shifting points of encounter for these disparate tendencies. In a single breath it displayed the left's delicate skill to balance its necessity to have a long-term programmatic stability with its everyday compulsion to find pragmatic solutions for pressing contingencies. It required the higher or 'elevated' level of policy to have a dynamic exchange with the implementing agents at the local or 'embedded' level, which the CPI(M) did better than others by its multi-level mediation as a disciplined, pro-reform party.

From a descriptive viewpoint, government as practice appeared as a mode of administering power that worked with and through a series of antinomies, of disruptive tendencies in which good coexisted with bad, benefits with corruption and crass empiricization with transcendental ideology. The passage from one to the other, from purity to pollution or back, was made irrelevant by the continuous contamination of the congregated opposites, entangled, interspersed and unrecognizably intertwined. Popular approval or appeal of such practices depended largely on how far they facilitated changes in the oppressive status quo, in the ongoing injustice and exclusion, evaluated not by any abstract moral principles, but by the experience of everyday lives of the multitude. In concrete terms, the left's early government as practice can be judged by the extent to which it moulded the juridical authority of the state with the organizational mediation of the party for a tactical use of law so that the material resources could be regulated to maximize both productivity and security of the poor and the marginal population groups.

Analytically, the 'practice' is akin to what Michel Foucault called 'the problematic of government in general' as distinct from 'the political form of government'. For him the political form represented 'the actual definition of the government of the state'. By contrast, a general problematic of the government arose at the meeting point of two opposing movements: the centralization of the state (which he traces following the dismantling of the feudal structure in sixteenth century Europe) and religious dispersion and dissidence. 'How to govern oneself, how to be governed, by whom should we accept to be governed, how to be the best possible governor? It seems to me that all these problems, both in their intensity and multiplicity, are typical of the sixteenth century and, putting it very schematically, are the point of intersection of two movements, two processes' (Foucault, 2009, 127). While 'the political form of government' treats organization of the society as distinct from governing institutions of the state, 'the problematic of government in

31

general' seeks to place the government of the self, the community, the society or the state on a continuum of interplay involving centralization and dispersal, regulation and dissidence.

This marked a departure from Foucault's early interest in the diffusion of disciplinary norms by various institutional and epistemic mechanisms. In the late 1970s and early 1980s his focus shifted, as his Collège de France lectures testify, on the reflexive subject who exercised choice in questioning, challenging and resisting such norms. A recent study in Foucault's epistemology, for instance, points out that his 'early scholarship on governmentality represents actors as unconscious of the regulatory framework with which they implicitly are complicit, but his later work on resistance emphasizes reflexivity and the proactive constitution and transformation of the self' (Ettlinger, 2011, 537; also Brockling, Krasmann and Lemke, 2011, 4). The four contradictions listed above triggered off a similar process of reflexive transmutation that the left government had recognized and facilitated. It involved, in the main, pressing a range of disciplinary and epistemic norms to absorb the population within a set of governmental rationalities, and simultaneous resistance of the governed to acquiesce to any prescribed norms. This contradictory mode of power, managerial and resistant, constitutes a continuum upon which the 'mythicized abstraction' called 'the state' gets governmentalized. 'What is important for our modernity... is not then the state's takeover (*étatisation*) of society, so much as what I would call the "governmentalization" of the state' which offers 'the only political stake and the only real space of political struggle and contestation' (Foucault, 2009, 144).

From here, again, the left's early government as practice cannot be read through the prism of good or bad governance, because disruption is the order and the presumption of a status quo that informs such a reading can only be illusory. Nor can it be treated as a transaction between a party and its constituency for actual or expected transfer of benefits, because reflexive popular politics is too agile and unpredictable to conform to a stable arrangement of material quid-pro-quo. Also, the object of transcending capitalism is not a matter of finding *the* right direction on an ideological compass derived in a modular form from elsewhere, because the local meanings of transcendence embedded in the everyday relations of power are by no means theoretically inferior to the goal of a distant revolution. They appear as so from a static or idealized analytical point focused narrowly on the left's 'political form of government'. Instead, the purpose here is to build a critique of the left government upon its actual practices, upon the contextual contradictions of its 'government in general', upon the lived experiences of the governed.

The 'lived experience' of various social groups, as Michael Burawoy reminds us, marked the point of departure for variants of 'sociological' Marxism. Elements of this intellection can be drawn from both Antonio Gramsci's and Karl Polanyi's works. Gramsci is critical of any attempt to import an ideological or 'vanguardist' notion of transcendence, something he views as 'cultural messianism'. Karl Polanyi's critique of the 'free market', likewise, is premised on moral impulses deeply embedded in society (Polanyi, [1944] 2001, 79).[21] For this Marxist standpoint 'society is Janus faced, on the one hand acting to stabilize capitalism but on the other hand providing a terrain for transcending capitalism'. Gramsci begins by interrogating ways in which the civil society, through its linkages with the state, enlist consent and restrict struggle between classes ('passive revolution'). Polanyi takes his cues from the manner in which an active society seeks to counter the dehumanizing effects of market economy. Suspicious of universal abstractions such as the state or the market, they both 'end up asking how society can found an altogether new order of socialism – an order that subordinates both economy and state to a self-regulating community' (Burawoy, 2003, 199).

In fact, this Marxist enunciation not only shares a normative focus on self-governing society/community, it also rejects any suggestion that capitalism expands or contracts along a linear trajectory where each country follows a leading model in toe. Rather it reads capitalism as a multidirectional process, producing different arrangements of state, society and economy. Though it embraces a global analysis, it never loses sight of the concrete lived experiences 'that propelled classes into action'. Gramsci theorizes the lived experiences as 'common sense', which encloses a kernel of 'good sense' representing the emancipatory potentials of different classes. Similarly, 'Polanyi was no less interested in the lived experience of different subordinate classes' either (Burawoy, 2003, 206). Taking a cue from Michel de Certeau one may suggest what makes Gramsci, Polanyi and Foucault talk to each other is their common appetite to absorb 'insignificant', 'ordinary' or 'non-discursive' lives, the 'tales of the unrecognised' immanent in everyday practices, their enthusiasm to fit these 'ethnological particularities' into an 'empty space' of theory (Certeau, 1984, Part II).

The global project of 'transcending capitalism', therefore, can be understood only in its disparate local meanings. A 'social control of economy' (Polanyi) or a 'regulated society' (Gramsci) can have a range of meanings, each no more valid than the other and the task of theory is to recover them from the prevailing social hegemony. For Gramsci, therefore, revolution ought to begin *within* subaltern common sense – under the hegemonic spell of the ruling classes – not outside it. For criticism and philosophy to go beyond common sense 'the starting point must always be that common sense which is the spontaneous philosophy of the multitude and which has to be made ideologically coherent' (Gramsci, 1971, 421). This he contrasts with 'economism' or esoteric 'scientific' analysis that reduces political struggle to a series of personal affairs between those with a genie in the lamp who know everything and those who are fooled by their own leaders but are so incurably thick that they refuse to believe it (Gramsci, 2000, 217). Revolution, must draw from real popular beliefs in their everyday occurrences. Politics here and now, politics of empirics, does not impede transcendence; it only demands a *theory* for emergence.

Some reasoning of the left's debacle in West Bengal, discussed earlier, can be briefly revisited from this 'sociological' perspective. For instance, what went wrong for the left does no more seem to be its 'failure' to evolve a theoretical understanding that could 'span the distance' and 'establish a link' between its politics of small change and the task of transcending capitalism. Rather, the task of transcending ought to have begun in the politics of small change itself. The problem, therefore, was more in the left's inability to make an adequate sense of its politics of small change, of the true worth of its everyday, mundane, contingent social exchanges. As a result, the left failed to tune its formal ideological position to the concrete reality of its pragmatic politics. It made no attempt to make an ideological sense of its practice aimed primarily at the critical task of making and maintaining an electoral majority. Instead, it valorized a derived corpus of orthodox Marxism as universal 'truth' which carried little reflection of its experiential world. This in the long run offered a sure recipe to derail its government as practice, to snap the organic link between policies and politics, leaders and workers, which was so meticulously built – as we have seen – through the popular alliances in the 1950s and 1960s, and during the pro-poor reforms of the Left Front government in late-1970s and early-1980s.

Similarly, from the 'sociological' point of view one can reinterpret the results of a survey we mentioned earlier that shows a certain shift in the perception of rural respondents in the closing days of the left rule in West Bengal. The withdrawal of popular support for the left, it was observed, was coeval with the rising unhappiness of the respondents with the local left leaders in contrast to both the local non-left leaders as well as the left leaders who were not local in origin. True, popular discontent may frequently have local reasons which, in turn, may also reflect a uniform pattern across localities due to their common structural origin culminating in a larger change at the macro level. However, in this case the reasons for change might not have been adequately captured by contrasting the respondents' attitude toward the local leadership of the left as against non-local leaders, and the local left leaders against the non-left leaders. Several ethnographic accounts as well as media reports indicate that the new leadership of the non-left parties frequently was made of those who switched sides from the left parties when the public mood started to change post-2007. It could well be the case that the survey registered growing unhappiness with the local left leaders because now, with the perceived shift in the political climate, the respondents – having their experiences rooted in the local ambience of power – could *afford to be* fearless and expressive about their disapproval of the local left leadership than ever before. Large scale quantitative surveys, despite their tremendous importance in explaining broader trends, often remain blind to the delicate ambience that colour the 'lived experience' of their respondents.

To return to the early years of left government, at least three factors were responsible for creating a condition conducive to an intimate connection between the programmatic and pragmatic activities of the coalition in power. First, the government was bent on implementing a host of distributive reform policies, which were triggered more or less by a series of class-based movements in the preceding decades. As these policies required popular monitoring at various stages of implementation, they acted as a deterrent for the left's governmental practices to congeal into a rule-bound bureaucratic routine. Second, the left was still very edgy and uncertain about the longevity of its tenure given the bumpy ride of two United Front governments in the late 1960s, and the authoritarian trends in Indian politics peaking in the national emergency in the mid-1970s. So the coalition was still chary of abandoning the popular logic of mass action in favour of the institutional logic of governmental policies, and continued to push the limits of law with popular pressure from below. Third, as an antidote to its overall insecurity, the Left Front opted to forge a larger alliance of regional parties in its initial years of existence to protest against the 'centralizing tendencies' of Indian federalism, which allegedly made the Centre disproportionately powerful – especially in fiscal and administrative matters – at the cost of the states. The campaign, in a peculiar way, projected the Centre or the Indian State as a coercive authoritarian mechanism pitted against a deprived yet democratic regional government, responsible primarily to provide social welfare (or 'relief') to the people. Such a strong federalist stance, coupled with the left's pioneering administrative decentralization in rural West Bengal, underscored its dispersed practices of 'government in general' in contrast with the concentric instrumentalities of the 'political form of government'.

The person who seemingly embodied the left's logic of government most comprehensively in this period was Jyoti Basu, the Chief Minister of West Bengal. Basu joined the Communist Party of Great Britain in 1937 and, upon returning to India, as a CPI member worked his way through the All India Railwaymen's Federation which elected him from the Railway Workers' Constituency to the Bengal Assembly in 1946. Known for his hardnosed pragmatism, an immense negotiating skill, and positional dexterity, Basu became the bridge between the ideological compulsions of his party and the daily demands of practical politics in the state. Writing on his rise in the state's messy battlefields in the 1950s, a historian observes:

> Unlike the usual Communist party leaders, he developed into a charismatic public personality and although remained firmly rooted in the Party... he could not easily shed his outsider character among the organizational cadre, largely controlled by Promode Dasgupta, because of his patrician background. He was exceptionally skilful as a parliamentarian. He could have easily established himself as a theoretician in the Party. But he preferred not to do so. He was too pragmatic, too alive to complex character of the political situation in India, particularly in West Bengal, to formulate and stick to a political line of his own... He was the classical middle-of-the-roader and still remains so. He always chose to remain in between two extreme positions whenever such situations developed within the Party, which gave him room to manoeuvre... Finally when he had chosen, he softened the position he had opted for by the sheer weight of his presence and by the day-to-day working out of the party programme... He was the invariable mediator... was eminently fitted to work out and lead a united Left Front... He alone among the Left leaders could work out the delicate power equations of the day... [I]t became evident to the people of West Bengal that he could not be identified with the Left-sectarianism of his own Party... There were no fire-works (in his speech). He was coldly logical, persuasive and incisive and capable of a biting sarcasm, which... made him inimitable' (Chakrabarti, 1990, 376–77).

Popular yet distant, partisan yet malleable, resolute yet mediating, oppositional yet authoritative, long ranging yet quotidian, populist yet calibrated, Jyoti Basu was both a purveyor and a product of the emerging governmental logic. He personified the left's predicaments over a period when it faced various encumbrances despite its electoral endorsements, and when it harboured a reformist zeal critical of the state power although it was reluctant to breach the legal parameters of the system. He was so completely identified with the government that the Left Front's unusual stint also made him the country's longest serving Chief Minister ever.

As the left got ensconced in power, its reformism gave way to bureaucratic moderation and its insecurity waned with repeated electoral success. As the commanding state was overtaken by the neoliberal economy its critique of sovereign allocations of resources was replaced by an aggressive, and somewhat un-reflected, competition for private investments. With the growing level of comfort, the left's antinomies with the Indian state mellowed; as it began to see new opportunities in the market, its earlier logic of government became unsustainable. On the one hand the left's reformist campaigns, which generated huge populist appeal in the early years, were now pushed aside as winning elections became the central object of the government. Legislative innovations (or tactical use of law) were overshadowed by administrative routines; popular participation was reduced to token endorsement of official decisions.

On the other hand, the left chose to reify a rendition of Marxism as *the* scientific truth that had a limited interface with its actual practice, its 'politics of small change'. Little attention was paid to absorb 'the concrete lived experiences' into the 'empty space' of theory, which could have been its unique contribution to Marxian praxis. As a result, its 'small' political actors, dedicated and sincere foot soldiers working tirelessly at the grassroots level, were condemned to remain as 'ordinary tales of the unrecognized'. Any possibility of the lowest and the most marginal rungs of the society to emerge as the top leaders of the left was jettisoned. We have seen how the mainstream left's social politics in West Bengal was deliberately kept thin. Here it can be argued, that the inability (or refusal?) of the left to theorize its contradictory practices and move beyond 'economism' strengthened its middle class, upper caste and overtly male leadership. Since the late 1980s, as the left was rapidly spreading across the political fields of West Bengal on the wave of its successive electoral triumphs, its early moment of government, government as practice, ironically, was slipping off its balance.

Lineages of the 'crisis'

The left's initial mode of government, to repeat what discussed earlier, was based on a reciprocal relationship between its pragmatic and programmatic concerns held together by a disciplined party that enabled the poor and the marginal groups to receive benefits from various economic packages of the state and central governments. This was further reinforced by the left's policies of decentralization and distributive reforms, which gave the poor some economic security and representation. In the early years of the Left Front, a good deal of popular approval could be generated within this interplay of a commanding state economy, a reformist party and a representative local government (a triangular arrangement of the sovereign, the disciplinary and the regulative).[22] The interplay seemed durable (based on expected norms of reciprocity), was genuinely productive (unleashing growth in the peasant economy) and security enhancing (especially for the sharecroppers and the industrial and agricultural workers against the deceits of the *jotdars* and owners of capital and land). It produced a good deal of consent in the population *viz a viz* the regime, a source of the left's early influence in rural West Bengal.[23]

The balance got tipped since the late 1980s due to a number of reasons. The left failed to follow up its policy of distributive reforms. Within a short time land reform lost its steam and, with demographic pressure on land mounting, a good number of people found themselves as uneconomic burdens on land. The country's economy took a pro-market turn in the early 1990s reducing the state's role in incentivizing agriculture. With the rising input costs and inadequate institutional support, West Bengal's agriculture entered an impasse by the middle of 1990s.[24] The new economy demanded changes in the local government's orientation

– from managerial to entrepreneurial – to hone new skills and seize the opportunities in the rising market. The need was to tap the collective spirit of the people and imagine a new set of innovative reforms to enable the rural poor to tide over the emerging uncertainties. In short, the left now had to evolve a regime of new practices supported by an updated theory of ongoing empirical changes, so that its committed grassroots workers could get recognition for their isolated everyday struggles within a coherent and intelligible policy. This, however, did not happen. Instead, a class of petty capitalists, owners of 'non-corporate capital', increased their control over both the local economy and the local government. The new leadership in rural West Bengal emerged from local traders of fertilizer and pesticide, agents of ponzi companies, local transporters, suppliers of building materials, owners of brick kiln or rice mills, labour contractors, and ration shop dealers.

These operators in the high-risk zones of small-scale commercial capital had to maintain a friendly tie with the locally influential political party on purely instrumental, pragmatic grounds. With the waning influence of traditional leadership in the remote villages – typified in the figure of the rural school teacher – these men slowly but steadily captured the nerve centres of the local geography of power – the cooperatives, the school boards, the sports clubs, the panchayat bodies, the party committees and so on (we will return to this in chapter 3). This altered the thrust of the left parties, including the CPI(M), further widening the gap between these parties and their basic social classes, poor peasants, sharecroppers, agricultural workers etc. The state's indifference to the agricultural crisis, the local government's failure to reinvent itself in the new economy, and the rise of petty entrepreneurs – who were described in the local parlance by the generic term 'promoters' – irreparably disturbed by the mid-1990s the working triad between the state, the party and the government.[25]

In the changed circumstances pragmatic or instrumental politics overshadowed normative or programmatic concerns especially in the lower rung of the CPI(M). For the new grassroots leadership, the party's ideology was of little relevance; they found even a rhetorical conformity to the party's long-term programmes (such as 'people's democracy') as a pointless exercise. Many used the party as an instrument for private gains, and exploited its vast network for advancing personal interests. True, these men did not represent the *entire* local leadership of the party, but they indeed were key political managers with a band of followers – a clientele of mostly unemployed young men – around them. As they populated the branch committees and local committees of the CPI(M), the district and higher leaders began to depend on them for maintaining local 'peace' and for mobilizing support during elections. They supplied the cogs and wheels in the CPI(M)'s legendary 'election machine'.

Government as practice, as we knew it at the beginning of the left rule, transformed rather irreversibly with the change in the grassroots custodians of left politics affecting profoundly both the disciplinary regime of the party and the regulative apparatuses of the local government. While the outer shell of the party's disciplinary hierarchy (formally, 'democratic centralism') remained unchanged, its core got hollowed out. Contingent and pragmatic politics now lost its impetus to evolve any ideological/normative concern. The trend became more obvious at local level where the new leaders called the shots and edged the poorer classes out of decisive committees. The panchayat was turned into an instrument for bureaucratic endorsement of skewed political interests. The party now started losing grip over the spontaneous consent of the multitude. Rising corruption, graft, rent-seeking and associated depletion of values competed with the refinement of its coercive mechanisms. The party, in the main, remained a colossal machine to maintain the status quo and routinely deliver electoral renewal for the regime. The top leadership of the CPI(M) had little interest to make intellectual investments in analysing the realm of the party's everyday practices, or to encourage questioning of social and cultural norms in relation to religious, caste-based, gender-related, environmental or sexual domination. Now with a diminishing ability to influence the course of events at the ground level, the leaders chose to cast a blind eye at the organizational atrophy underway as long as the left retained its numbers in the assembly and in parliament.

Despite such disconnect within the party, the left retained a minimum level of efficiency in maintaining peace, delivering public goods, running a clientelist network and administering the state bureaucracy. Although 'government as practice' was rapidly losing its relevance after the first decade of the Left Front rule, and there was a dearth of innovative policy after the initial agrarian reforms and decentralization programmes, there was no apparent deficit in the left's capacity to provide 'good governance'. The left's credibility for the next two decades (roughly, 1987–2007) relied by and large on its ability to run a stable government that maintained a level of security for the socially marginal, economically poor and the religious minority groups, its basic constituencies. This, however, followed a routine and repetitive course in which governance turned into more of a technical conduct, measuring the demands of different population groups mediated through the local leaders and offering policy-responses through bureaucratic channels in equally calibrated forms. Governance, depleted of the ideological or normative concerns of traditional leftwing politics and withdrawn from genuine social or economic movements (which were often suppressed by the left in power), now turned into an exclusive exercise in pragmatic contingencies. Yet, the continued electoral triumphs of the left created an aura of its invincibility, which helped conceal the massive entropy eating into the very foundation of its regime.

In the post-liberalization period, the federal government dismantled its industrial licensing regime and ended the freight equalization policy (we will discuss these shifts in chapter 5). A section of the Left Front, anxious to overcome the agrarian slowdown and enlarge the state's economy, considered it necessary to invite big investments in infrastructure and industry. 'Agriculture is our foundation', a state government advertisement announced, 'Industry our future'. Following the state election of 2006, in which the Left Front recorded an emphatic win, the government started a process of acquiring agricultural land in the countryside. This was a major policy shift, perhaps the most important since the early days of land reforms and decentralization. Unlike the early Left Front, however, a political-consultative process was no more available for the present leadership as powerful interests and politics of exclusion had already established their control over both the party and the panchayat. The government now depended entirely on state bureaucracy and party chieftains. It moved to break the status quo by a pro-market unilateralism from above, by way of enforcing a severe programmatic dictate on a polity that for decades only experienced predictable patterns of pragmatic exchanges.

Not surprisingly, the initiative soon faced massive popular resistance, galvanizing a broad opposition from the extreme left to the right. The government, in response, activated the police, the coercive arm of the state. This caused violence and deaths of ordinary villagers, and images of bloodshed started to circulate through print, electronic and social media in the state and beyond. Regulative governance, a veneer of which the regime managed to wear for the last two decades despite obvious erosion in its foundation, was now replaced by a widely visible sovereign power, out to destroy any opposition. In a civil war like situation the government lost space for tactical manoeuvres and found itself on the 'wrong side' of history. It was perceived as defending the indefensible: moneybag against multitude, profit against people, dominance against dialogue. Within months the regime lost its moral force to govern.

As soon as any moral recovery appeared improbable, segments of the left's structured support base, which was now attached to its organizational network not by any social or ideological bonding but mainly by instrumental quid-pro-quos, started switching sides. These aspiring segments of workers and upwardly mobile petty entrepreneurs had little choice but to look for alternative political protection in the messy and dangerous world of informal economy. They changed their affiliation almost overnight from the left to the opposition, mainly to the Trinamool Congress (TMC), and carried with them the left's fabled 'election machinery'. A large segment of peasants now perceived the left, which had once given them land and security of tenure, as a force that wanted to take that land away without consultation or compensation. The left now lost its moral compass, and appeared as a force that colludes with injustice. In no time the electorate of West Bengal unseated the Left

Front from power after more than three decades of uninterrupted rule. A left coalition, focused primarily on electoral competition, found itself debased from its basic political constituency.

'Retrieval' of the governmental left

The decline of the left as reflected in the steady drop of its vote-share in every successive election had, in fact, continued for no less than a decade since 2004. In the 2014 parliamentary election, as mentioned at the beginning, the left parties registered win in only 12 electoral constituencies in the country, its lowest tally since the first general election in 1951– 52. The CPI(M) won in 9 of the 93 constituencies where it contested, securing merely 3.2 per cent popular votes, the lowest since the party was formed some 50 years ago. In West Bengal the party had obtained 38.56 per cent popular votes in 2004, which shrunk to 33.11 per cent in 2009, and slid further to 22.7 per cent in 2014. There was little doubt that the left in general, and the CPI(M) in particular, was facing its most difficult crisis in the country's, and the state's, electoral battlefield. With the rise of the right in the country, with its 'developmental' rhetoric clothing a sustained attempt for communal polarization, the fragility of the left looked particularly exasperating.

In the light of this poll debacle 'reclaiming the left' has become a recurring theme for a group of intellectuals and activists, particularly those who are, or had at some point been, inside the party or any of its mass organizations. Some of them now demanded an immediate change in the CPI(M)'s top leadership, updating of its ideology to suit contemporary concerns, unqualified rejection of 'neo-liberal' capitalism, renunciation of the Left Front government's land acquisition policies, and a tactical rethink of the left's place in the Indian political conundrum.[26] For them the 'fundamental strategic mistake' of the left was its adoption of the neo-liberal agenda for industrialization as its own. 'It is impossible to distinguish the CPI(M) leadership's idea of development', they pointed out, 'from the neo-liberal developmental model that the Indian ruling class has brought in the public domain over the preceding decade'.

They also alleged that the left's tactical moves in the run up to the Lok Sabha poll were indecisive and ambivalent. Though the CPI(M) party congress in 2012 decided to keep both the Congress and the BJP equally at bay, the party started to swing between the two poles as the election approached. It supported the Presidential nominee of the Congress (whom the TMC opposed) in the hope of driving a wedge between the Congress and the TMC. Yet, the move backfired as the latter came round supporting the Congress candidate and the left was widely perceived as improperly eager to stand by a political party immersed in graft and corruption. Thereafter, in its anxiety to appear as equidistant from both the BJP and the Congress, the CPI(M) mooted the idea of a 'Third Front', a concept that the electorate had roundly rejected in the 2009 Lok Sabha election. Moreover, the left's Third Front included the Samajwadi Party, which many believed had a hand in orchestrating a religious riot in Mujaffarnagar, and Janta Dal (United), which was integral to the BJP-led National Democratic Alliance (NDA) for more than a decade. Despite the rising nationwide tide for the BJP in the election, the CPI(M) in West Bengal kept its anti-BJP invectives surprisingly taciturn, way mellower than the TMC chief Mamata Banerjee's volley of vitriolic assaults on the communal brigade. It seemed that the state leadership of the CPI(M) expected that a rising BJP would rattle the TMC, leaving its own house intact. The results were otherwise: the CPI(M) lost bulk of its Muslim votes to the Congress in the north and to the TMC in the south, and a large segment of its middle class votes migrated to the BJP in urban and semi-urban constituencies.

For the present analysis, what is more important than these alleged 'blunders' of the left is its strategic concurrence with 'neo-liberal' industrialism and tactical inability to adopt an independent line of action – is the *framework* within which such strategic options were exercised. A mere change of guard is unlikely to alter the course of the party: in the absence of a systematic popular mobilization from below a new set of leaders can only be appointed *from above*, signifying a continuity of the same albeit in a different mould. Similarly, a governmental left simply cannot wish away corporate capital if it intends to industrialize a grossly agrarian economy stuck in a chronic impasse and, therefore, cannot oppose land acquisition (which doubtless involves displacement and loss of subsistence for the rural poor) *in principle*. On the tactical side, as seen between 1950s and the 1970s, the left always dithered over its stance on the Congress, changing its posture in tune with the overall political dynamic in the country. What marks the present departure, I argue, is the left's consistent failure over more than a decade to *justify* its action within a set of transformative agendas without compromising its *distinction* as left. And this, in turn, is an effect of the left's inability to imagine a new politics, its failure to tune its ideology to the dynamics of real political conduct at the ground-level, to reinvent a government as practice suited for the massive economic changes underway in the country.

This new political imagination would require, among myriad other things, an appropriate treatment of two vital politico-economic entities: labour and capital. A more extensive discussion on them will be taken up in chapter 5, while engaging with some current debates on 'primitive accumulation of capital'. The form and composition of labour in post-colonial capitalism – that combines post-Fordist production processes in which a rising private capital takes advantage of a fragmented body of cheaply available spatially dispersed, insecure and casual labour force – need be identified both within capital (as dependent and antagonist) as well as autonomous (having independent life forms). The earlier imagination of 'the working class' – typical of a proto-socialist import-substituting mixed economy marked by low productivity of a small industrial base in a vastly agrarian economic landscape does not hold any longer. As recent studies show, a growing number of India's workforce is engaged in the tertiary sector consisting of both urban and non-agrarian rural labour, and a vast majority of the entire workforce is in the informal economy. It is impossible to devise a new working class politics without understanding the reality of this new labour in the country's changing economy.

On the other hand a multivalent left, that seeks to combine democratic representation with extra-parliamentary mobilization, cannot join a choral opposition to capital in general, nor can it offer a blanket resistance to acquisition of agricultural land for setting industry or urban infrastructure. True, India's economic growth in the last two decades has failed to create adequate jobs or contain the expanding inequality between classes (Dasgupta and Singh, 2005, 1035–57; Dreze and Sen, 2013; Kohli, 2012). It is no less true that there cannot be any economic growth without investment of private capital, and within the existing parameters only a growing economy can ensure sources of adequate revenue for governmental spending on various welfare programmes. The mainstream left, therefore, has to find ingenious ways of calibrating its theoretical opposition to the regime of capital and, in practice, of managing capitalism's adversarial consequences of inequality and jobless growth. Equally, it must stand in solidarity with popular movements against corporate encroachment upon livelihoods and habitats of the multitudes without an agreeable compensation or rehabilitation. The point, therefore, is not to prevent capital investments in projects with potentials for income enhancement, but to negotiate with the forces of capital aimed to keep them on the edge, to keep a constant vigil so that popular interests do not lose traction under the pressure of private profit.

A unity of these apparently conflicting moves – of moderation and incitement – ought to be searched in a new ideological orientation at the frontier of Marxism that identifies modern forms of governmental power as one that seeks to manage population rather than discipline individual bodies or dominate economic classes, and employs 'preventive' rather than punitive techniques for maximizing productivity. Labour (and the left), therefore, should adopt a proactive dynamism rather than imagining itself at the receiving end of capital, it should push equality's limit without compromising productivity (Negri, 2008). The need is to perceive both labour and capital as constitutive of an economic continuum placed within a framework of 'government in general', in which private capital tends to pull in the direction of oligarchy and kleptocracy, and labour ought to counterweigh in the direction of equality and democracy. Should the Indian left reboot its politico-economic understanding of global capitalism in the twenty-first century, it would discover a minefield of resources in myriad disruptive forms of life and power intertwined with, yet unabsorbed by, capital.

Such a discovery of disruptive resources, in turn, would largely depend on the left's ability to devise a new political practice. In the manufacturing sector, a spatially dispersed labour working under conditions of temporally disjointed lines of operation and no legal security of tenure can scarcely evolve a common proletarian 'class' interest. In the rural economy, non-agricultural petty services offer the only option for subsistence in the context of agricultural impasse and absence of any large-scale absorption into industry. Older forms of labour unions – trade unions and agricultural workers unions – are of diminishing value to satisfy the demands of this new labour. Informal workers tend to compensate their lack of protection as a class against capital less by uniting as a class, a 'class for itself'. They rather deploy other protective mechanisms available in community networks such as caste affinity, religious bonding, neighbourhood solidarity, place-bound commonality or linguistic empathy. In this, the workers do not necessarily perceive the owner of capital or of land as their main antagonist; instead a host of everyday concerns such as injury, illness, illiteracy, skill-deficit, arbitrary legal sanctions, police brutality, coercion by local chieftains, violation of women, addiction to drugs and alcohol, loss of livelihood etc. constitute their battle for survival. The more individuated the workforce, the more lurking their vulnerabilities, the higher the seduction of a moral community of affect. The left would fail to evolve a new politics if it remains blind to the mobilizational resources available in this 'new communalism'.

The need, therefore, is to conceive 'class' as a category bound to a communal mode of power, inextricable from its social and cultural dimension by any economistic or historicist abstraction. This is particularly relevant in the global South where capital fails to undertake a complete subsumption of pre-capitalist social forms and to universalize itself as a replica of industrially advanced economies. There is no escaping for the left, if it wants to be relevant, from a deep engagement with what can be called the society's 'inner domain'. It has to stand in solidarity with struggle for recognition against all forms of exclusion, for minority rights of the religious, cultural, linguistic and sexual groups against all varieties of majoritarianism, for ecological balance against hyper-productivist ideologies, for gender equality against brazen and implicit patriarchy, for moral claims of the deprived against arbitrary legal regime, for free flow of information against bureaucratic opacity, for improving the conditions of health, hygiene, education and nutrition against a skewed idiom of economic growth. If the left continues to fail in playing a role of 'vanguard' in these everyday issues of popular politics, it will be of little use for a working class that is incessantly mobile yet intuitively rooted through modern technologies of communication, cellular telephony and satellite television, a class that is palpably deprived yet increasingly alive of its rights and entitlements in relation to a global governmental order. It is only by politicizing the 'social', by destabilizing the status quo, by redrafting its 'contract' with its basic constituencies, and by ideologically reinventing its understanding of the 'everyday' in a rapidly transforming world that the left can hope to inaugurate a new dialogue between its programmatic goals and pragmatic conducts, a new 'government as practice'.

Endnotes

1. E. M. S. Namboodiripad, the world's first elected chief minister of a communist ministry (in Kerala) who was deposed by Nehru was to reminisce many years later: 'If the "experiment" in Kerala showed anything, it is this: the struggle on the parliamentary arena, including the formation of state governments when a majority is secured, is one specific form of class struggle in which the struggle on the parliamentary arena would have to be subordinated to, though being integrated with, the extra-parliamentary struggle'. See Namboodiripad, 1987, 177.

2 West Bengal's increase in productivity of foodgrains between 1952–53 and 1964–65 was merely 0.9 per cent, far less than the all-India average of 1.6 per cent. During 1965–67 the number of people employed in factories in the state fell from 9.1 to 8.6 lakhs, while the number of registered factories actually increased from 5,878 to 6,133. On the top of it, in respect to the per capita share of total central devolution, the position of West Bengal had gone down from the second position in 1957–58 to the ninth place in 1962–63 and tenth in 1966–67. See Government of West Bengal, 1968, 5.

3 The tussle in the Congress party was between Ajoy Mukherjee – a rural satrap with base in southern Medinipur – who was ousted by the Prafulla Chandra Sen–Atulya Ghosh faction of the Congress in a leadership wrangle. Mukherjee drew considerable

support from the agrarian rich – the rice mill-owners and food grain growers – who were getting critical of the Congress government which had imposed levy to tackle the food shortage. See Franda, 1971a, 207–9.

4   Constituents of the PULF were the CPI, Bangla Congress, the Forward Bloc, the Praja Socialist Party (PSP), Lok Sevak Sangha, Gorkha League and Bolshevik Party. That of the United Left Front (ULF) were the CPI(M), Revolutionary Socialist Party (RSP), Socialist Unity Centre (SUC), Revolutionary Communist Party of India (RCPI) and the Forward Bloc (Marxist).

5   On 29 November Ghosh was asked to prove majority in the House; the speaker Bijoy Banerjee dramatically adjourned the House *sine die* before a voting could commence. This pushed West Bengal into a limbo, a government dismissed and another hurriedly installed with untested majority. Severe factional feuds ensued within the new ruling coalition and after the adjournment of the budget session by the speaker once again it was quite apparent by the second half of February 1968 that Ghosh did not have the requisite numbers on his side. Now the United Front could forge a majority with the assistance of some members defecting from the Congress-PDF alliance, if it were given an opportunity. Instead, the union cabinet recommended presidential rule on the midnight of 19–20 February.

6   A new equation now emerged between the United Front and the union government under an increasingly besieged Indira Gandhi who was fighting the rightwing Syndicate within her party to establish her own authority. She invited support from the Communists. The CPI was unequivocal in offering its support. The CPI(M) was cautious and conditional, and played a critical role in getting Indira Gandhi's presidential candidate V. V. Giri to win against the Syndicate-backed Sanjeeva Reddy. In return, the CPI(M) bought assurance of the union government's non-interference in the workings of the United Front.

7   Two of the most momentous peasant movements in Bengal in the twentieth century were *Tebhaga* and *Naxalbari*, and they complemented each other in many ways. Both these peasant struggles are extensively studied and their links with leftwing political mobilization well documented. *Tebhaga*, which meant a third of the share, became the demand of impoverished sharecroppers who were forced to transfer half of their produce to the landlord or *jotdar* even when the latter did not invest in production inputs. The peasant wing of the CPI, the Krishak Sabha, carried out a prolonged campaign among the poor peasants and sharecroppers (or *bhagchashis*) highlighting the injustice involved. The movement demanded that the crop sharing arrangement be revised, and the *jotdar* retain only a third (or *tebhaga*) of the produce. According to an activist of the movement 'Between December 1946 and January, 1947 the Tebhaga Movement spread to 19 districts of undivided Bengal' (See Sen, 1991, 106). For a detailed chronology of *tebhaga* movement across undivided Bengal, the interplay between 'spontaneity' of peasant action, scale of

Krishak Sabha organization, variety of forms of struggle, the nature of leadership and the influence of community identities see Cooper 1988 (especially chapters 5, 6 and 7). Also see Majumdar, 2011. The leading role in Naxalbari peasant uprising was taken by the 'Siliguri Group' of the CPI(M) in the mid-1967. The peasants were up in arms against the exploitative land relations perpetrated by the *jotdars* for several weeks. The United Front government first tried to pacify the peasants, and then resolved to quell it. In May that year the police fired on groups of protesting peasants killing six, including women and children. In June, the struggle intensified in three subdivisions of Darjeeling district, Naxalbari, Kharibari and Phansidewa. On 28 June Radio Peking declared in a broadcast 'A phase of peasants' armed struggle led by the revolutionaries of the Indian Communist Party had been set up in the countryside... This is the front paw of the revolutionary armed struggle launched by the Indian people'. Although the movement met with suppression, the Naxalbari peasant upsurge had a lasting impact and continues to be a moment of inspiration for rebellious political mobilization across the subcontinent. While the parliamentary communists align with *tebhaga*, which was part of anti-colonial struggle, they mark their distance from the *Naxalites*, attributing the latter as victims of 'ultra-left deviation'. For two contrary viewpoints see Dasgupta, 1974 and Banerjee, 1980.

8   See the '18-Point Programme of The UF Government 1967'. In March 1967, the Government decided that the police must obtain orders from the labour ministry before arresting workers or peasants participating in 'democratic movements'. See H. C. Hart, 1988, 23.

9   'The victory for the (peasants') demands depends upon the extent to which we can strengthen the United Front government by waging movements of the peasants and the masses'. (WBPKS, 1968, 47).

10 In its statement the politburo claimed that 'certain individual party members, especially in West Bengal ... were no more a political trend in the party, but have grouped themselves into an organized anti-party group advocating an adventuristic line and actions, challenging the party programme and resolution and directive, passed by the Central Committee' and directed the 'State Secretariats, especially ... the West Bengal State Secretariat, to immediately expel them from party membership'. *People's Democracy*, 25 June 1967.

11 *Central Committee's Draft for the Ideological Discussion*, Calcutta, CPI(M), 1967, 47–48 (quoted in Sen Gupta,1972, 324, footnote 4).

12 *Central Committee Draft for the Ideological Discussion*, Calcutta, CPI(M), 1967, 51 (quoted in Sen Gupta,1972, 325). The *Draft* was rejected by the Andhra Pradesh state plenum where counter resolutions were places by T. Nagi Reddy, C. Pulla Reddy and Kolla Venkiah. The Andhra comrades carried the fight to the CPI(M)'s Burdwan plenum in May 1968. They referred to the peasant uprising in Srikakulam and other places where the landlord and their *goondas* had brought down heavy repression but

the party, without a clear line of action and anxious to remain legal, was incapable of standing by the rebellious peasants. The Bardhaman plenum retained the *Draft* with minor corrections, resulting in large-scale defections from the CPI(M), bulk of them in Andhra Pradesh, where the party membership shrunk by 60 per cent. The Andhra communists set up a state level committee for the communist revolutionaries. Similar committees sprung up in other states within the CPI(M). The West Bengal committee was given the responsibility of coordinating between them, thus the AICCCR was established. Charu Mazumdar, the ideologue of the Naxalbari uprising, called for the formation of a Maoist party to build bases for armed struggle in the countryside. 'Such a party', he said, 'will not only be a revolutionary party, but it will be at the same time the people's armed force and the people's State power'. Once the AICCCR was formed, differences broke out at several levels. There were differences between the Andhra state CCCR and the district CCCR, which was heading the Srikakulam peasant movement. The AICCCR supported the district leadership at the cost of the state committee. The district leaders contended that the time was ripe to take the peasant movement to the next level – that of capturing the state power and alleged that the state leadership was revisionist for not acknowledging the necessity. In February 1969, the AICCCR resolved that a separate communist party was needed to lead the peasants. On 22 April 1969, the AICCCR converted itself to the CPI(ML) and the party was formally launched on 1 May 1969 (Sen Gupta, 1972, 326–332).

13 The 1972 election is widely viewed as a rigged election. 'Though a certain amount of rigging and bogus voting is common in Indian elections, the magnitude of the 1972 election rigging was much greater.' Analysing the share of popular votes in some key constituencies shows 'that the Indira wave of 1972 was restricted to CPM strongholds while a CPM wave took place in Congress areas, thus indicating that the CPM might have increased its votes and probably formed a coalition government had the election been fair' (Mallick, 1994, 134 and 138).

14 *National Emergency and our Task*, Communist Party of India, New Delhi, July 1975, 5, 8 (quoted in Mallick, 1994, 149–50).

15 The CPI's support for the emergency was partly prompted by the CPSU which aligned with Indira Gandhi in its Cold War calculus to restrain US influence in the subcontinent. It was also in part necessitated by its own organizational compulsions. The CPI was terribly shaken by a large-scale exit of its ground-level workers to the CPI(M), that made it lose organizational strength in traditional left strongholds. (For a detailed account of how the CPI fared poorly compared to the CPI(M) in West Bengal's closely contested elections between 1969 and 1971 see Field and Franda,1974, 45–51.) So to offset the CPI(M) and emerge as the most influential left organ in the country, it decided to get closer to the Congress. The Congress, on its part, facilitated the proximity through its Forum for Socialist Action consisting

of a group of former communists and Congress progressives. It was accumulation of power without any authority that pushed the CPI in an unenviable position. In Kerala its support was at least crucial for the survival of the state government; in West Bengal, however, it acted as a redundant tail of a massively repressive government sharing its culpabilities without any control over its conduct. Discontent in West Bengal unit of the CPI started brewing against the party's official line during the final years of the emergency. In 1977 election the party failed miserably, in contrast to the CPI(M)'s stellar performance.

16 CPI's Mohit Sen and Bhupesh Gupta were livid in their criticism of the CPI(M)'s 'inaction' during the Emergency. As if to cover their own support for Indira Gandhi's excesses, they asked in a pamphlet: 'Where were the struggles against the Emergency and action calling it to be lifted by CPM? What and where did it do anything against sterilization and the savage demolition operations aimed at the urban poor? What did it do to battle against the caucus and the repulsive Sanjay built-up campaign? What is its answer to P.C. Sen's public statement that the CPM turned down his proposal to launch a Satyagraha against the Emergency in West Bengal?' (Sen and Gupta, 1978, 8).

17 For the ambivalence, if not 'insensitivity' and 'hypocrisy', of the Left Front government on the refugee question see Pal, 2009; also Gupta, 1994 (especially, 'Prosongo Dandakaranya', 121–29, and 'Seemaheen Oggwota', 130–34).

18 Sources for these figures: For the social background of state-level ministers see Rana and Rana, 2009, 131. Figures for elected panchayat functionaries after the election of 2008 at Gram Panchayat (Pradhan and Upa-pradhan), Panchayat Samiti (Sabhapati and Sahakari Sabhapati) and Zilla Parishad (Sabhadhipati and Sahakari Sabhadhipati) have been computed from Government of West Bengal, 2010, 115 (Table 9). The document collected information from 6987 out of 7180 (or 97 per cent) elected functionaries. I have deliberately removed the *Karmadhyakshas* for computing purposes because they are not elected representatives and so cannot be compared with the ministers of the state government. It is also evident from the available statistical details that the panchayat functionaries are significantly in sync with the local population in several other capabilities, such as literacy and period of formal schooling.

19 For a discussion on the concept of 'good governance' as determined by the priorities of the World Bank and International Monetary Fund, and the lack of any objective criteria for determining what it constitutes (political stability, rule of law, control of corruption, accountability etc.), see Nanda, 2006, 269–83. In the initial stage of its emergence, the concept had its emphasis on economic aspects of development. When political considerations were included, the emphasis was not so much on the legitimacy of a regime, but its capacity to undertake administrative reforms for efficiency, rule of law, accountability and transparency. The standards for judging what constitutes 'good governance' continued to be determined by the objectives of

the donor countries or institutions, with little regard for the cultural and historical specificities of the countries receiving monetary aids or loans for development. For an internal critique of the concept and a proposal for its substitution by a more practicable agenda see Grindle, 2004, 525–48.

20 It perhaps will not be out of place to show how successful the 'party' was in the local government elections until 2003, after which the slide of the left started. The minimum and maximum seats polled by the Left Front in different tiers of the Panchayat are: 60 per cent (1998) and 73 per cent (1988) in Village Panchayat; 74 per cent (1983) and 79 per cent (1988) in Panchayat Samiti; 74 per cent (1983) and 92 per cent (1978) in Zilla Parishad. In the 2003 elections, the Left Front's share of total seats stood at 65.75, 74.05 and 86.82 per cents in the Village Panchayat, Panchayat Samiti and Zilla Parishad respectively (CPI(M), 2004). The rate of success of the CPI(M) was far greater than other political parties. For instance, in 1988 the CPI(M) contested in 44,803 gram panchayat seats and won 33,834, its degree of success being 75.51 per cent, much higher than the Congress(I) (28.46 per cent), RSP (25.60 per cent), Forward Bloc (18.16 per cent) and CPI (54.34 per cent) (GoWB, 1988, 6). The panchayat polls were also the occasion when the parties belonging to the Left Front coalition could mutually contest to measure their respective strengths in different localities, an opportunity, which was not available for general elections. In 1988 the Left Front partners had an internal fight in 10.96 per cent seats. In 2003 this happened in 14.02 per cent seats. On both occasions, the rate of success (the ratio between seats contested and won) of the CPI(M) exceeded that of its major coalition partners (CPI(M), 2004).

21 The economy, Polanyi argued, has always been embedded in society and capitalism attempts to disentangle it by reducing labour and nature to commodities. This, he reckoned, was bound to invite severe social reactions – or 'double movement' – for reclaiming what the society regarded as ethically its own. In fact, a wide range of social democratic attempts to re-inscribe the social into the economic in the present world draw their inspirations from Polanyi's work. For a recent analysis of social movement in India through Polanyi's formulations see Levien, 2007.

22 This formulation, in fact, resonates with Foucault's attempt in *Security, Territory, Population* to dissociate his project from a historicist attempt to 'see things as the replacement of a society of sovereignty by a society of discipline, and then of a society of discipline by a society, say, of government'. Rather, he says, 'we have a triangle: sovereignty, discipline, and governmental management, which has population as its main target and apparatuses of security as its essential mechanism'. His analysis has shown how the problem of population 'as a given, as a field of intervention, and as the end of government techniques' 'overturns the constants of sovereignty'. See Foucault, 2009, 143. In this context also see Erlenbusch, 2013, 44–69, especially 56–62.

23 Timothy Mitchell, in his critique of James Scott's *Weapons of the Weak*, distinguishes 'consent' from 'consensus'. Consent, he says, 'reduces the need for the use of violence' but cannot be equated with consensus 'in the sense of harmony'. 'Consent', according to him, is closer to what Gramsci called *consenso*, 'which refers primarily to the 'consent' given by the exploited groups to their exploitation'. This distinction helps us reiterate that hegemony is always placed on a *tentative* and *narrow* outlay of institutional power (Mitchell, 1990, 554).

24 It was observed that there was a general decline across a number of variables such as area cropped, production achieved, gross yield, consumption of fertilizer, proportion of high yielding variety seeds, cropping intensity, institutional credit and land reforms from the 1980s to 1990s (Bhattacharyya and Bhattacharyya, 2007, 65–71).

25 This transformation of the CPI(M) was deeply resented by Benoy Krishna Choudhury, an octogenarian peasant leader who masterminded Operation Barga, next in seniority only to Chief Minister Jyoti Basu in the Left Front cabinet, and a man known for his impeccable integrity. Choudhury was reported as having remarked on 17 December 1995: 'This is a government of contractors, by contractors and for contractors'. Cited in Chanchal Sarkar, 'He was a man of the masses', *The Tribune*, Spectrum (Sunday Magazine), 25 June 2000. Soon after, Benoy Krishna Choudhury took retirement from active politics and died a lonely death in 2000.

26 For a representative sample of these new criticisms see *Arek Rakam*, Volume 2, Number 11 (1–15 June 2014), and *Arek Rakam*, Volume 2, Number 12 (16–30 June 2014).

2

CONSOLIDATION: LAND REFORMS

After forming the government, the parliamentary left in West Bengal implemented some of the country's most effective land reform laws that had a long-term impact on the structure of rural property and power. Although the stated intent was to reduce poverty and encourage a just sharing of agrarian assets by reducing age old exploitation of poor cultivators by a handful of landlords, these reforms also helped the left build a solid constituency of support that stood by it in every election for decades. The use of an economic policy as a political tool for organized support required skilful manoeuvring since land reforms could also split the rural classes and pit one against the other. To garner a composite electoral constituency from the rural population that included its 'class-friends' as well as 'class-enemies', the left modified its radicalism and mellowed down its rhetoric. The shift in the left's ideological position was attempted in a strategic and calibrated way so as not to appear 'revisionist' or 'class collaborationist'. While it helped the left's electoral prospect in the state, it also created some long-term insoluble problems.

Land reforms had been a demand of the nationalist bourgeoisie in its attempt to enlist support from the peasantry during the anti-colonial mobilization. A resolution of the Agrarian Reforms Committee of the Indian National Congress in 1935 stated that a 'fundamental method of improving village life' was to introduce 'a system of peasant proprietorship under which the tiller of the soil is himself the owner of it and pays revenues direct to the government without the intervention of any zamindar or taluqdar'. Post-independence, the First Five Year Plan (1951–56) echoed these concerns despite its care not to hurt the property rights of the intermediary classes. In some states, policies were made to eliminate big tax-farming zamindars which effectively ended up increasing the power of the rich peasants and the intermediary landlords. The demand for 'land to the tiller' figured in Congress party's agenda only until the mid-1950s (Harriss, 2012). The party put land reforms to rest in its annual meeting in Nagpur in 1959, when Charan Singh – a North Indian leader of rich farmers – made sure that a reformist draft entitled 'Resolution on Agricultural Organisational Pattern' was rejected. A decade later the Indian state launched 'Green Revolution' with the intention of fighting food shortage in the country that left the existing property relations undisturbed.

The Congress party was, in fact, dependent on these intermediary classes to maintain control over the vast popular segments in the countryside within a reciprocal system of sharing power and patronage. In West Bengal these rich peasant classes – the jotedars – soon became a target of violent protest of the sharecroppers and agricultural workers in the course of Tebhaga and Naxalbari uprisings for over two decades since the late 1940s. After defeating the Congress in 1977, it therefore made good political sense for the Left Front to press the state's administrative apparatus for implementing a series of distributive reforms to alter property and labour relations in rural West Bengal. It also made good economic sense in a state that had a very low land-man ratio: about 40 million people depending on barely 13.6 million acres, less than 0.34 acres or 0.14 hectare per capita (GoWB, 1989a).

The leftwing consensus in the 1970s favoured land reforms over Green Revolution, which was perceived as a capital-intensive production strategy partial to the rich and biased against sharing of benefits. A number of empirically grounded studies in the 1950s and 1960s suggested that the country's stagnant agriculture was a result of an archaic production relation, which needed a serious institutional reworking. Daniel Thorner, for instance, called the unequal landholding and wealth distribution a 'depressor', rendering investments in agriculture for the land-rich unnecessary and for the land-poor impossible (Thorner, 1956). In the 1970s, after the beginning of Green Revolution, economists Ashok Rudra and Amit Bhaduri added a theoretical edge to their empirical findings on class domination and agricultural productivity. While Rudra focused on the development of capitalism and resultant differentiation of the peasantry, Bhaduri worked out an elaborate analytical model of agrarian political economy in which semi-feudal exploitations based on land and usury produced a disincentive for capitalism, and therefore growth (Rudra, 1975a; Rudra, 1975b; Bhaduri, 1973a; Bhaduri, 1973b). Eventually, there was a shift from the meta-theoretical explanations to more localized studies that implicitly recognized the importance of both land reforms and Green Revolution for the country's agro-economic diversity (Desai et al., 1984).

Agrarian conditions

In 1982, a whopping 81.6 per cent of West Bengal's agricultural households held less than 5 acres. Ownership of agricultural land went through some changes between 1960s and 1970s. The number of 'marginal' households, i.e., those holding less than 0.01 acre, fell by 22.1 per cent in the 1960s before shooting up by 76 per cent in the 1970s. Over the same decade, concentration of land ownership increased among all landed classes, most significantly among the 'large holders' of 5–10 acres (by 67.6 per cent) followed by the 'middle-peasants' 2.5–5 acres (by 62.3 per cent). The number of landless households also grew and the trend continued even into the first five years of left rule despite steps to arrest it (Bhaumik. 1989, 156; Lieten, 1990, 2265).

In a state that had significant land under shared tenancy (some claim 20 per cent of cultivated land), the pattern of 'operational holding', that includes the land leased-in, offers a more accurate picture. Here also the concentration of operational holding for each size class followed the trend of ownership-holding during 1960s and 1970s, albeit at a slower pace (see NSS 17th Round for 1961–62 and 27th Round for 1971–72).

Both the area operated by and the share of households in the lowest size class (less than 2.5 acres) grew in this period indicating a remarkable rise in lease-in by the poor peasants. The average size of operational holding in 1982 stood at 1.9 acres. In short, the land economy in the state had a preponderance of small/medium tenants cultivating land belonging to small/medium landowners.

West Bengal's parliamentary left, therefore, worked upon a changing agrarian economy in which the small cultivating peasants – landowners as well as sharecroppers – constituted the majority. For its flagship reform programme – Operation Barga – it was important that the government had an accurate estimate of the number of sharecroppers or bargadars in the state. Early on, the Floud Commission in its report on undivided Bengal had an estimate that 21.1 per cent land was under fulltime share tenancy, and 12.2 per cent under part-time (GOB, 1940, vol. 2, 117–19). The Census of 1951, that included the category 'bargadars' (discontinued since), gave two different estimates. According to revelations by landlords, there were 300,000 sharecroppers, according to self-declaration by sharecroppers, 750,000. Although the official estimates in the early 1980s ranged from 2 million (Chowdhury, 1985, 30–31) to 2.31 million (GoWB, 1981b, 9–10) sharecroppers, the peasant leaders put the figure at 1.5 million and a survey estimated 1.37 million (Bandyopadhyay et al., 1983, 25–30). By early 1990s, however, the number of recorded bargadars crossed 1.4 million and was still counting. The irony was, these sharecroppers most frequently leased-in land from the 2.5–5.0 acres size-class households (the 'middle' peasants), who constituted 'about 15 per cent of rural population' and exerted 'considerable... influence over the peasantry, being educationally and otherwise more advanced'. Much of the left's political attention was spent 'in setting disputes between this section and the sharecroppers' (Dasgupta, 1987, 30)

Landlord violence

In the pre-Left Front period, the big landlords routinely flouted the existing land reform laws (such as Estate Acquisition Act) to maintain

59

extra-constitutional advantages in their area of dominance. In 1973, a report of a government appointed land commission detected that a landlord in the 24 Parganas district managed to retain more than 1,700 acres over 18 maujas falsely claiming the land above legal limit as belonging to fisheries or orchards (GoWB, 1973a, 12).[1] The landlord, according to the commission, had an absolute control over the local society with 'tyranny' and 'oppression'. 'Correctly speaking his administration in the area is of the 'Perso-Arabic' type of Mughal administration... essentially military in nature and a centrally controlled autocracy and his power is unlimited... his word is law and his will none can dispute'. Pointing out that no 'modern civil administration' existed there, the commission noted, the villagers made some attempts

> during the land grabbing movement of 1969-70, for asserting their rights and privileges but this could not, in the long run, be successful due to filing of several criminal cases against some of the pioneers who came forward to help the villagers in asserting their rights (GoWB, 1973a, 37–38).

The report indeed draws a stark picture of absolute coercion by the landed power.

Rather than any 'absence' of civil administration, the ongoing tyranny in fact reflected a collusion of some state officials with the big landlords. A study by the Directorate of Land Records and Survey covering 24 maujas in the mid-1970s suggested that the land reforms administration 'reeks with graft and corruption'. Only a third of the land vested in the government and officially distributed was actually in possession of the assignees. Even those who possessed did not receive the patta or the deed in 65 per cent cases and in only 30 per cent cases the land received was being cultivated. When the recipients were asked whom they wanted to give credit for the land they got, they referred to three factors: 'the strength of their purse, the accident of belonging to a particular group or the good offices of a local big gun' (GoWB, 1976). In other words, the poor landless peasants could get what they were entitled to either by bribing the officials, or mobilizing their caste/religious identity, or by appealing to the generosity of the landlord.

The sharecroppers were also not any better. One can refer to a number of studies from the 1970s that described their condition in graphic detail.[2] The findings, when brought down to essentials, show that in every observed case the sharecropper got 50 per cent or less of the produce which was below what was legally due (60 per cent), and in cases where the landowner shared inputs, the share was even less (legal share 50 per cent). The bargadars were constantly under the threat of eviction most frequently on the plea of 'self cultivation' by the landowner. Moreover, usurious practices were found rampant in the villages as professional moneylending was gradually being replaced by borrowing from the landlord. Inadequate information, opposition by the landlord, or non-cooperation by the corrupt bureaucracy were frequently found responsible for dissuading the bargadars from recording their names in the government's registrar.

Some unpublished state government reports from the early to mid-1970s offer a peek at some cases of resistance by bargadars, and also indicate the limits of their defiance. In Salihan, a small village in the Bankura district, bargadars led by a local school teacher demanded their legal dues. In response, landlords with the support of the local police and the Sub-Divisional Magistrate slapped false criminal charges against them.[3] An enquiry into the incident by the Director of Land Records and Survey put the blame squarely on the lower rung of the bureaucracy for frequently colluding with the landlords in the pretext of maintaining law and order.[4] Such incidents took place despite the ruling Congress government adopted a formal position in support of the bargadars. '[I] n order to maintain law and order', a government circular had stated, 'protection should be given to the party in possession of the disputed land [that is, the tenant] by growing crops therein and anyone attempting to disturb his possession should be legally restrained, where necessary'.[5] In Salihan, the opposite happened. Clearly, directives from the top were ineffective at the local level where the officials were complicit to violations by the propertied classes, and the party in power had no will or instrument to change the situation.

A similar incidence of heroic defiance by a poor bargadar, and his eventual capitulation in the face of brutal machinations by the landlords and the bureaucracy was recorded graphically in an official document. In order to prove his devotion to the landlord, Indra Lohar, the bargadar, chose not to get recorded by the government, to join any political party or to annoy his master for whom he worked for two decades by refusing to pay up in excess of his legal dues. At the end of the winter harvest in 1971–72, however, he was asked by the landlord family to give up all his claims as a tenant and move out. Indra first offered to pay more, since he had no other source of livelihood, but got rebuffed. Then with the help of a lawyer belonging to a leftwing party, he lodged a complaint at the Sub Divisional Executive Magistrate's court, appealing for his claim. In the days before the state election in 1972, the police raided Indra's house without a warrant and looted his granary. As court order was pending, the landlord's men visited him once more, beat him up badly, and forced him put his thumb impression on a white paper, which they later produced at the Munsif's court as a 'proof' of Indra's abdication of all claims. At the time of filing the report, the Executive Magistrate supported Indra's claim, which the Munsif's court turned down, and the case moved to the High Court in Calcutta. The document concluded with the following lines:

> Indra Lohar lost his will to fight for his right. He paid rather dearly for his temerity to assert his notional rights embodied in law. Maimed and feeble, defeated and dejected, Indra has now bowed down before the majesty of established order and stands disposed of his land (GoWB, 1972, 8).

Indra Lohar's vulnerability did not stem from his status as an unrecorded bargadar alone. Recorded bargadars were routinely victims of landlord violence as well. The case of a tribal bargadar, Ramdhan Tudu from Patna-Bhairabpur village in Hooghly district illustrates the point. Ramdhan's landlord challenged his tenancy rights. In collusion with the Junior Land Reform Officer he got a field enquiry done, in which an upright Revenue Officer relying on local information rejected the landlord's claim. Ramdhan was recorded during the khanapuri (preliminary writing of records for settlement operation) and bujharat (local explanation before the Settlement Officer) in 1975. In spite of that, the landlord prevented

Ramdhan from sowing seeds on the land. When he complained to the police, the police refused to register it, instead the landlord slapped a criminal case against him. Based on a police report Ramdhan was ordered not to enter the field by the Sub-divisional Executive Magistrate, who dismissed his claims as a bargadar. During the harvest in November that year, when Ramdhan approached the land with his wife and a group of tribal women to protest against his removal, they were beaten up by the landlord's men. The police arrested 12 protesters including Ramdhan and six women. He was detained for no less than two months (GoWB, 1978a).

These instances, and nine other cases documented by some junior land officers (kanungos) few months before the Left Front took charge (GoWB, 1977), reveal a distinct method of treating a bargadar by the landlord. An unrecorded bargadar was allowed to cultivate till the beginning of the government's settlement activities. Just on the eve of the settlement, the bargadar was told to quietly relinquish his claims either by pressure or by promise of reinstatement once the settlement was over or by an 'offer' of an alternative land unknowingly vested in the government. If the bargadar refused to give up so easily, he was threatened, if he managed to sow seeds, fresh seeds were sown, if he attempted to harvest, he was prevented. In this, the landlord frequently got help of the local settlement officer, or procured 'stay order' from a lower court, which relied on the police and other officials for reaching a verdict. Such a choreographed mechanism involving the lower bureaucracy, the police and the court gives a clear indication that in absence of any solid political resistance by the vulnerable classes, violence by the dominant classes assumes a governmental proportion by taking full advantage of the existing state institutions at the ground level. The form of government deployed by the left – which is referred to as 'government as practice' – had to counter precisely these instances of everyday violence if it were to emerge as a real alternative.

Violations of law

The landlords broke the existing land reform laws with impunity and, in some cases, with ingenuity. Take the case of Estate Acquisition

Act 1953 (Act 1 of 1954), which the communists were the first to criticize for its 'limitations' and subsequently were its most ardent implementers. Attempting to abolish the intermediary classes, the Act declared individual holding in excess of 25 acres of agricultural and 20 acres of non-agricultural land as illegal. However, by leaving land under tank fisheries, orchards or forests, and land held by religious or charitable institutions as outside the scope of ceiling, the Act gave ample opening to the landlords for hiding property. In a society where land was coterminous with influence and power, the landowners indulged in various kinds of spurious transfer once the bill was passed. The commonest form of illegality was benami transfer, or transferring part of possession to a fictitious name, of an individual or institution, or making pre-dated transfers, setting up religious and charitable trusts or inundating lowland to claim as tanks.[6]

The Act also exempted some religious customary transfers by the landlords within the family such as Denmahar for the Muslims and Nirupanpatra for the Hindus, of which full advantage was taken (GoWB, 1983a). Though a majority of Hindu families followed the Dayabhaga school of inheritance, which was curbed by the Act, they frequently claimed that they belonged to the Mitakshara school, which the law left unaddressed. In 1971, the Congress government brought few amendments to the Land Reform Act of 1955 applying land ceiling on families rather than individuals. An appeal was made for self-declaration of land held in excess as a family, which obviously was ignored despite extending the deadline thrice over a two year period. The landlords distorted family records, changed marriage dates, tampered birth certificates, altered school registration, 'adopted' children and produced fake solemnization documents (GoWB, 1983b).

If concealment was the idiom for above-ceiling property, for land under crop sharing it was deceit. The sharecroppers were usually tied to their landlords with a mutually agreed cost and crop sharing arrangement which, at times, ran for decades. Every new law after independence attempted to enhance the rights of the sharecropper, raising his share of crop while reducing his burden of input or leaving it unaltered. This created a tension in the customary relationship between the sharecropper and landowner. For instance, the West Bengal Bargadar Act of 1950 prohibited eviction of a bargadar except on the grounds of self-cultivation by the landowner or negligence by the sharecroppers, and made illegal eviction a punishable offence. Insisting that share of produce should be split by an agreement between the two parties, in event of any dispute it made a simple prescription: two third of the produce should be equally shared by both, and the remaining third should be split in proportion to the costs shared. The West Bengal Land Reform Act of 1955 amended the law of 1950 by fixing the shares of the bargadar and the landowner as 50:50 (where landowner paid the cost) and 60:40 (where the cost was shared by the bargadar). In 1971, the Congress government introduced some radical amendments, raising the bargadar's share from 60 to 75 per cent and making sharecropping rights hereditary. A slew of other changes were introduced as well that included a compulsory issue of receipt by the landowner on receiving his share, the bargadar determining the place of threshing, and keeping at least 1 hectare even if the landowner regained land under the 'self-cultivation' clause, which too was limited to a maximum of 3 acres. The laws on paper seemed flawless in protecting the sharecroppers, but their implementation, as seen above, was a different story.

Left promises

Two critical demands for radical land reforms were 'abolition of landlordism' and 'land to the tiller'. The CPI(M), at least in rhetoric, had favoured an immediate implementation of both these demands in the later part of 1960s and the greater part of 1970s. A resolution of the party's central committee had stated: 'The breaking of the monopoly of the land enjoyed by the landlord class – both of the old feudal as well as new capitalist type – is in the common interest of the entire peasantry including the agricultural labourers' (CPI[M], 1973, 6).[7] The party, therefore, demanded 'fundamental' (*maulik*) land reforms by abolishing landlordism without any compensation whatsoever (CPI[M], 1973, 3) and treated Congress government's legislation on land ceiling, minimum wages, fair prices, taxation, etc. as 'hollow' and 'pitiful' (CPI[M], 1973, 4). As 'alternative amendments' to Congress legislation the party insisted on total abolition of landlordism to 'ensure land gratis to the landless agricultural labour and the poor peasant' (CPI[M], 1973, 3–5). Prepared to ally with the rich peasants, whose family members participated in agriculture, it considered the non-working landlords as its vital 'class enemies'.

Once the Left Front government came in power, the Krishak Sabha drastically changed its slogans. It now regarded fundamental or maulik land reforms as 'a long term goal'. In the short term, the Left Front government – which was only a provisional and provincial government and not a government of people's democracy – could scarcely take a giant stride in that direction.[8] The Krishak Sabha in its first meeting after the Left Front came in power continued its call for an abolition of landlordism 'immediately and completely' but not without adding a critical rider: 'The Sabha can in no way undertake this alternative policy for implementation within the present state structure. This can be successful…only through the establishment of a people's democratic state' (WBPKS, 1979, 92–93). Nonetheless, the new government came to power with some stock of radical fervour. Benoy Konar, then a young and firebrand Krishak Sabha leader, defending the first budget of the new government announced at the legislative assembly in August 1977:

> Some people could not find any ray of hope in this budget. Some people even tried to find a revolution in it… Please don't take the trouble to look for revolution on the pages of this budget… You will get revolution…in the struggle of the millions of Bengal's workers and peasants who will use this budget as a pretext to escalate their fight against the billionaires and the owners and the landlords, they will intensify class struggle and dig the graveyards for the looters, the billionaires, the jotdars and the landlords of our country; this government will incite them, will tread by (them) with all its limited resources and opportunities (WBLA, 1977, 206).

For the parliamentary left, as we shall see below, Konar's radical prognosis proved a difficult – if not an impossible – benchmark to accomplish.

Political manoeuvring

During the first decade of Left Front rule, when most land reform laws got implemented in West Bengal, the CPI(M) and the Krishak Sabha demonstrated a good deal of tightrope walking on the ideological front. The challenge for the party was to clip its programmatic angularities to gain political acceptance in the field of competitive democracy, for which enlisting support from a large spectrum of rural communities, which constituted around 70 per cent of the state's population, was crucial. 'It is impossible to advance the peasant struggle', the Krishak Sabha argued, 'without the support of all sections of the peasantry including the rich peasants and the democratic people in the countryside' (WBPKS, 1986, 14). The 'unity' of all peasant classes became a buzzword in the literature of the governmental left. Yet 'peasant struggle', another oft-repeated phrase in the literature, presupposed the poor peasant and the agricultural labourer as its principal axis. The question was: while unity was desirable for electoral consolidation, could that be obtained without compromising the interests of the poor peasants, bargadars and agricultural workers?

Inside the peasant organization, opinions differed. One view was that the party should refrain from moving close to the rich and middle peasants who always remained 'unreliable as allies'. Instead, effort should be made to stand exclusively by the poor peasants and agricultural workers as that had always strengthened the party while 'very few rich and middle peasants stayed back with us' once their demands were met. Harkishen Singh Surjeet, a politburo member of the CPI(M) from Punjab, rejected this view. 'What the comrade says', he asserted, 'reflects neither the West Bengal experience nor the experience of the peasant movement in the rest of the country' (AIKS, 1982a, 28–29). Surjeet talked about the need for 'a new orientation' in peasant movement based on the awareness

> that without raising the demands of the peasantry as a whole, including the rich and the middle peasants, and without merging

the different currents into one, we can neither advance towards the agrarian revolution nor will we be able to raise movement to the level of land occupation' (AIKS, 1982a, 29).

The 'new orientation' was perceived as less divisive, more inclusive and, indeed, electorally more promising. 'It is true', the Sabha admitted after the CPI(M)'s second consecutive win, 'but for the support of an influential section of the middle peasants, this victory would have never been possible' (WBPKS, 1982, 122). The necessity of winning elections by shoring up a large constituency of support premised on the unity of various peasant classes now became paramount.

This 'new orientation' received a strategic shape in various Krishak Sabha sessions through the 1980s.[9] It nonetheless had a deeply negative effect on the well-being of the agricultural workers. 'On wage demand', an AIKS document explicitly stated, '[it] may be necessary to settle for a wage which is lower than the basic demand to win over the rich and the middle peasants' (AIKS, 1986, 70). The uneasy truce between 'struggle' and 'unity' became a serious management issue for the Sabha as the local peasant leaders frequently found it unpersuasive at the ground level.[10] The Bolepur Thana Committee of the Pradeshik Krishak Sabha defied the 'new orientation' and decided to campaign exclusively for higher wages, tenancy rights, and land titles (patta) for the landless even at the cost of alienating the middle and rich peasant classes (WBPKS, 1984, 13). The top leadership of the Sabha, instead, emphasized on identifying a 'new class' of capitalist landlords and conducting a campaign to 'marginalize' the class rather than taking any strident class action (WBKPS, 1979, 46–48). In the rapidly changing environment 'abolition of landlordism' or 'struggle for people's democracy' were increasingly seen as mere 'slogan for propaganda' with little practical relevance.

With the Left Front in power, the left leaders claimed, political conditions had 'vastly changed' from the United Front period, so there was no need to press on popular agitation against the landlords anymore which the party had encouraged in the late 1960s (WBPKS, 1979, 46). Earlier the landed classes were very big and isolated from rest of the peasant community, so identifying and targeting them was convenient

(WBPKS, 1989b, 92). Peasants also rose to grab land in those days because popular opinion was morally directed against the big landlords who used various illegal means to conceal large tracts of land from the effects of the Estate Acquisition Act. By contrast, under the present Left Front, the 'land of the big raiyats vested in the government is small in amount' and therefore unlikely to generate similar resentment from the toiling classes (WBPKS, 1979, 46–47). Moreover, it was necessary then, unlike now, to convince the landless that the khas (demesne) land held illegally by the 'oppressive zamindars' could truly be their own, for which the party had to whip up 'popular passion' (WBPKS, 1989b, 91). With these compulsions allegedly absent, the Left Front in its desire for a lasting social peace in the countryside seemed rather keen to erase the rambunctious United Front regime from the memories of rural West Bengal.

The changed emphasis was perhaps nowhere better illustrated than in a speech that Benoy Krishna Chaudhury, the land reforms minister of the Left Front government, made at the legislative assembly in 1989. 'I can tell you even as I stand in the premises of this House', he said, 'that we must act as an agent of a class someday'. This, however, could not be done 'merely by making laws'. At the same time, he warned, 'one has to realise the impossibility of taking struggle too lightly'. The task, therefore, was to 'look into the conditions at the field level' to 'develop a united movement rather than talking too loud'. An escalation of tensions in the countryside, he believed, would cause harm by 'fostering fresh enemies' (WBLA, 1989b, 7–8, emphasis added). In another speech the same year he drew attention to 'other ways to live and grow in a community that cannot be done by confrontation and conflict, it has to be parallel and consistent' (WBLA, 1989a, XX). The question is, what change did these modifications bring on the left's treatment of the tenants/sharecroppers and the agricultural workers 'at the field level'?

Shifting priorities

In its On the Agrarian Question in India in 1949 the CPI had proposed 'land to the tiller' as its preferred policy, which rendered any form of tenancy, fixed or shared, untenable (Herring, 1983, 163). If any government pursued that line of action, all tenants would have got ownership of the land they cultivated. The first communist government in Kerala in 1957 made attempts to implement such a policy and, as a prelude, proclaimed the 'Stay of Eviction Proceedings Ordinance' aimed to protect the tenants and the labourers with huts on landlords' land. As the government was soon toppled, a similar attempt was made again in 1969, with some bit of success. Before the mid-term election in 1969, the communists in West Bengal were also broadly in agreement with their Kerala counterparts ostensibly to gain support of the sharecroppers (Frankel, 1971, 1983). Even in 1973, the CPI(M)'s 'Resolution on Certain Agrarian Issues' maintained that the 'right of the tenant to the ownership of the land he is cultivating is to be guaranteed, except to those who are lease-holders from small owners'. Where the cultivating small landowners were involved 'such land under tenancy [will] be equally divided between the tenants and the smallholder' and the 'tenant will continue to pay a fair rent on the portion of the land he cultivates [as a tenant]' (CPI[M], 1973, 7, parentheses added). So when the Left Front government was formed some years down the line it was reasonably expected that the left's approach to the sharecroppers or bargadars in the state would be in step with their Kerala comrades.

However, the left's governmental line in West Bengal – both in the United Front and the Left Front phases – deviated from the official position of the CPI(M) and the Krishak Sabha. Sharecroppers did not constitute a 'pure class', and if some exceptional cases of reverse tenancy were set aside, peasants who leased in land did so to supplement their income from small holdings or wages. As has been noted, they were traditionally subjected to eviction, extortion, non-payment of dues, denial of hereditary tenancy rights, etc. A majority of those leasing out was in no way big landowners either, they rather belonged to middle or small landholding classes. Absence of a clear divide between sharecroppers and landowners made any drastic policy (such as abolition) difficult.

Calling it a 'very complex issue' that 'cannot be ended by a stroke of pen' Harekrishna Konar, the land minister in the United Front government, stated unambiguously that 'if banned by legislation it will go on covertly and also more crudely' so long as the present social structure was in place. His interest was rather 'to think how this system could be better regulated in the interest of the peasantry' (Konar, 1979, 189). A decade or so later Benoy Krishna Choudhuri also expressed similar views. Unless all tenants were recorded, the octogenarian minister argued, even a casual suggestion to abolish tenancy would trigger a panic among the landowners who would waste no time to evict them (Chowdhury, 1985, 29).

Such similarities notwithstanding, Konar and Chaudhuri differed on the method to be adopted to protect the tenants. Konar believed that the eviction of tenants could be stopped only by an organized resistance of the tenants themselves. Taking part in a debate in the state legislature in 1967 he said: 'You cannot prevent eviction simply by making laws if the sharecroppers do not fight against their own eviction'. To make that possible, he continued, 'We will not allow the police to get there, we shall tell the sharecropper you resist your eviction, you take a stand, if the landowner complains about injustice. I will simply say: we are not prepared to send the police' (WBLA, 1967, 531). The Left Front, on the contrary, was in no mood to allow a section of the peasantry take the law into its own hands. Instead it amended existing laws, as shall be seen shortly, and started recording the sharecroppers at a rapid speed to make eviction both difficult and challengeable in court.

The bottom line is this: The CPI(M) in its central committee resolution demanded a radical abolition of sharecropping by transferring land under tenancy to the actual cultivator (CPI[M], 1973). The CPI(M) in the United Front maintained that share tenancy could not be abolished without changing the 'present social structure', but encouraged independent initiative of the sharecroppers to protect their rights against the landowner. The CPI(M) in the Left Front suspended transfer of tenancy land until all the sharecroppers were recorded which it regarded as a vital security against their constant threat of eviction. This, in a nutshell, illustrated the governmental left's shifting positions through 1960s, 1970s and 1980s vis-à-vis share tenancy in West Bengal.

More than the sharecroppers, the class that the governing left rhetorically claimed its own, but actually kept at bay, was that of the socially and economically marginal agricultural workers. According to Krishak Sabha nearly 75 per cent of its primary members were agricultural workers (WBPKS, 1986, 62). A quick look at the documents of three Krishak Sabha conferences between 1982 and 1989, however, shows that attendance of agricultural workers was less than 9 per cent on average (that of poor peasants less than 24 per cent).[11] The picture was not very different at the all-India level either.[12] An overwhelming majority of participants in these meetings were the middle peasants and non-peasant middle classes who obviously carried the show.

In 1981, a separate organization for the agricultural workers was constituted within the AIKS, whose membership touched 1.5 million (AIKS, 1989, 65). However, the Krishak Sabha was reluctant to form any such organization in West Bengal despite frequent suggestions to 'safeguard the interests of the agricultural workers' and 'wean them away from the bourgeois-landlord parties' (AIKS, 1986, 86; AIKS, 1982a, 30). It seems that the real reason to propose a separate organization for the workers was not so much to secure their interests as to protect the rural middle class from their numerical strength in the Krishak Sabha. At a state level meeting of the Sabha some members opined that the absence of a seperate organization for the khetmjurs and consequently their presence in the Krishak Sabha conferences deterred the middle classes from expressing their views without inhibition (WBPKS, 1986, 31). Similar complaints were made at the all-India level as well (AIKS, 1982b, 22).

Such strategic flip-flop by the governmental left, and the rising gap between its declared intent and actual practice, did not particularly endear it to the agricultural proletariat. In the early 1980s, the CPI(M) admitted that it failed to make the class the 'driving force for the entire peasant movement' (CPI(M), 1981–82, p.16). The source of the failure, in party's own admission, was in its reluctance to 'spread struggle and arouse awareness of the agricultural labourer and the poor peasant' (WBPKS, 1982, 120). No wonder, as seen above, the left was ready to settle for a wage lower than the basic demand to 'win over the middle and rich peasants'

(AIKS, 1986, 70). This was not just ideologically indefensible, but also pragmatically problematic. By suppressing class demands, foregrounding unity and going extra miles to secure the leadership of middle-peasant and non-peasant middle classes, the governmental left did manage to 'broaden' its rural constituency that helped it win elections repeatedly, but at the same time – and due to the same set of reasons – it failed to build a political base that could promote the interests of the economically poor and the socially marginal with a good deal of consistency.

Retrieving land

Within this general frame of political ambiguities the left formulated and implemented its land reform laws. The Left Front government began its journey calling land reform 'the most effective measure for increasing employment… in the labour surplus agrarian economy' and promising 'to recover all lands held in excess of ceiling through various clandestine means and to distribute these vested lands to the landless rural workers' (GoWB, 1979a). Its first task was to ascertain how much land could be recovered as surplus for vesting in the government. Estimates varied widely. For instance, at the start of implementing the Act of 1953 it was expected that some 2 million acres could be recovered, which was reduced later to 1.2 million acres since nobody in the land revenue department seemingly had a clue on 'how these (previous) estimated were arrived at' (Sarkar, 1981, 86). With the introduction of the Act of 1971 that set the ceiling on families rather than on individuals some more land was released for vesting, 83 per cent of which the government claimed as accomplished by the early 1980s (GoWB 1981b:i). Adding up the aggregate quantum of land to be vested from these two legislations the government claimed that the figure stood somewhere between 3 and 3.5 million acres (GoWB, 1981f).

As we know already, the left rightly saw the popular potentials of turning agricultural wage workers into smallholding cultivators and therefore in the first decade and half of coming to power took some long strides to identify and vest surplus land and then distribute it among the landless. Up to 1977, when the Left Front took charge, only 59.8 per cent of land already vested in the government was distributed. By 1990, the proportion of land distributed rose to 71.92 per cent, in all 1.941 million people got 0.46 acres each (GoWB, 1990b). While these numbers are of little relevance in themselves, they help one to get a sense of the change such land promised in a state that had in the 1980s barely 13.6 million acres arable land with per capita availability of 0.34 acres (GoWB, 1989a). Critics were quick to raise doubts about the agricultural 'viability' of these 'small' holdings which, they alleged, the left distributed purely out of 'neo-populist' considerations. In reply those who backed the government observed with a dash of sarcasm: 'how "viable" is a holding when the producers semi-starve: presumably more "viable" than when they are dead' (Patnaik, 1981, 46).

In its effort to control the benami transfers the government brought a new West Bengal Land Reforms (Second Amendment) Bill in September 1980 and sent it to the Select Committee. After overcoming many roadblocks – including the mandatory approval of the President – the Bill was finally enacted in 1986. The Act not only included fisheries, orchards, bazaar or religious trusts etc. for calculating land in excess of ceiling, it was also made binding retrospectively since August 1969 to rectify past violations. In addition it expanded the definition of 'raiyat' to plug possible loopholes that the landlords frequently took advantage of. While 'raiyat' previously meant any person or institution holding land for the purpose of agriculture, now it referred to 'a person or an institution holding land for any purpose whatsoever' to eliminate large holdings maintained for so-called 'non-agricultural' purposes (GoWB, 1989b, 8–9).

Curiously, the expectations generated when the Bill was introduced were allowed to dissipate once the law was enacted. The Krishak Sabha initially claimed in the early 1980s that more than 600,000 acres could be retrieved from the landlords once the Bill was passed (AIKS, 1984, 13). A member of the CPI(M) reiterated in the state legislature that some 520,000 acres would be released once the Centre approved the Bill into a law (WBLA Proceedings [mss.], p. 87/2 [7.4.81]). By February 1986, less than a month before the Bill received the Presidential assent, the party took an about turn: 'Although some concealed land can still be recovered here and there', a Krishak Sabha document stated, it was 'unlikely that the State government would get much land for distribution' (WBPKS, 1986, p.14). Within years after the law was passed a CPI(M) legislator confirmed: 'A few thousand acres or so would be available within a short span of time' (WBLA Proceedings [mss]. p.54/1 [31.3.88]). Since New Delhi was smugly sitting on the Bill for some years, it seems with the advantage of hindsight, that the left's initial claims were way too high to create a political pressure on the Centre, to show how the latter was bent on foiling yet another state initiative with boundless welfare potentials. Or, one wonders, if the drastic reduction in the estimates of surplus land a sign of Krishak Sabha's silent capitulation to powerful interests of the propertied classes.

How far the government remained true to its initial promise of recovering 'all land' in excess of ceiling to distribute among the landless wage cultivators? If one looks at the rate of vesting and distribution, bulk of the work was done in the first five years or so, and then it tapered off. For example, of all land vested between 1977 and 1990, 87.77 per cent was accomplished by 1982. Similarly, of the total land distributed in the same period, some 62.5 per cent was completed by 1985 (Agro-Economic Research Centre, 1986). Benoy Krishna Chaudhuri, however, was unhappy even with the early performance of the government. 'The achievement in matter of distribution of vested land', he complained on 31 March 1982, 'has not been satisfactory though highest priority was assigned to this job' (Sarkar, 1989, 63).

If one compared the Left Front government's performance with that of the preceding United Front, one indeed had reasons for concern. The United Front managed to vest 0.5 million acres (GoWB, 1983c, 8) in its short tenure (1967–69) as against less than 0.3 million acres by the Left Front during the first 13 years in government (GoWB, 1990a, Table 3). Nevertheless, when compared with the rest of the country West Bengal stood out in terms of the quantum of land distributed by the end of the 1980s. With only 3.4 per cent of the country's total cultivated area, 18.7

per cent of the country's distributed land belonged to West Bengal. With just 5 per cent of India's intended beneficiaries, West Bengal's share of actual beneficiaries was as high as 48 per cent. While only 5 per cent of the intended beneficiaries (the landless) were actually given land in the country as a whole, in West Bengal the rate was 40 per cent (Sengupta, 1989, 17).

Where the Left Front government actually stood out in comparison with all preceding governments was in its mode of implementing land laws. Land reforms, as we have seen, used to be a purely bureaucratic exercise conducted in a top-down manner through the line departments, making it difficult – if not impossible – to reach its benefits to the rural poor through the prism of coercive collusion of the lower bureaucracy, the police and the landlords. The left, by contrast, aimed to deploy its peasant unions and, since 1978, the village panchayat members to monitor the administrative procedures of land reform laws and scuttle the influence of the big landed classes. In 1978 about 25 million rural voters elected more than 60,000 members to the three-tier panchayat in the state for the first time ever. This combination of organizational and representational pressure gave the Left Front government's land reform a political charge, which was missing earlier.

Getting the bureaucracy to partner with the panchayat was, of course, not easy. A barrage of complaints was registered in no time against the 'incompetence' of the panchayat members, their 'inadequate understanding of procedural details', or their frequent failures to appreciate the 'urgency and the importance of the programme as a whole' (GoWB, 1980d, 4–5). A more serious charge was brought against the 'Unnnayan o Parikalpana o Bhumi Sanskar Sthayee Samiti' (Standing Committee for Development and Planning and Land Reforms) of the panchayat for its failure to regularize the undelivered pattas from the pre-1977 period (GoWB, 1985a, 33). A possible solution, as suggested, was holding patta camps, where villagers, the local representatives and the officials could interact following which the panchayat members delivered the pattas to the beneficiaries satisfying all 'procedural requirements' (GoWB, 1980d, 4–5). Admitting that it was impossible to implement reform laws without the detailed local knowledge that the panchayat had, the Board of Revenue complained that the joint action was not producing the 'desired effect' because the panchayat allegedly failed to even draw a priority list of potential beneficiaries (GoWB, 1981c, 4).

While it is impossible to judge the veracity of these complaints, that there were obvious teething problems in the panchayat and its interaction with the line departments cannot be denied. It was only to be expected as the panchayat as a form of everyday state embedded to the locality was on a learning curve as far as governmental techniques were concerned; it could not be expected to be an 'expert' in procedural details from the beginning. Leaving criticisms of the panchayat on these lines aside, it seems that there still was a distinct reluctance in these bodies to take up distributive land reforms with all the urgency it deserved. The sharply falling rate of vesting and distribution, the sluggish performance of the Left Front government when compared with the United Front and, above all, Benoy Krishna Chaudhury's expressed unhappiness with what was achieved in West Bengal, indicated that the parliamentary left did not quite keep up to its early promise 'to recover all lands held in excess of ceiling through various clandestine means and to distribute these vested lands to the landless rural workers'.

Recording barga

Next, we move to the Left Front Government's tenancy reforms, codenamed 'Operation Barga', which perhaps was its most widely debated agrarian policy.[13] Integral to the policy was a series of small but effective changes that the left introduced to the Congress-made tenancy laws of 1971 inherited from the previous government. In the event of eviction of a bargadar by the landowner, the earlier law placed the onus of proving one as de facto bargadar on the bargadar himself. This was a deterrent, since bearing the legal expenses was almost always beyond the means of the poor bargadar. The West Bengal Land Reforms Act, 1979, transferred to the landowner the burden of disproving a cultivator's claim for a bargadari status. Moreover, while the Act of 1971 had provisions that made the drawing of receipts by the landowner mandatory on receiving his share, the Act of 1979 made a failure to issue the receipt a criminal offence liable to imprisonment for six years in addition to fines. The Act of 1979 also introduced a residential clause, which made landowners' retrieval of barga land on the plea of 'personal cultivation' difficult. As a cover for poorer landowners of whom, as noted, the left was much concerned, provisions were kept for reclaiming barga land if the landowner could prove that he derived his principal income from that land and promised to cultivate the land himself or with his family members, not by farm servants or hired workers. In every sense, the new law strengthened the position of the bargadar and enhanced his or her security.

Laws alone hardly make much difference; we have witnessed how the rich and the powerful routinely subverted well meaning laws. The Act of 1971 had stipulations for keeping a record of the bargadars with the government, but hardly anything ever moved. The left identified recording as the key for legal recognition of the bargadars and their rights. It, thereby, launched its massive campaign of 'Operation Barga' to get 'all bargadars' recorded as quickly as possible (Bandyopadhyaya, 1981, A42). This could not be achieved by administrative means alone, for it is known that the locally dominant players were deft in scuttling top-down policies without much difficulty. This, therefore, had to be a political campaign, involving the left parties and the peasant organizations to press upon the lower officials to act and impress upon the local power to yield. It also opened rooms to involve 'the party' with matters of administration in a popular and intimate way, and with the participation of the local government institutions it inaugurated a new governmental process for the left, localized and integrated, decentred and connected, embedded and unencumbered by excessive bureaucracy. At the same time it contained the left's revolutionary programme of 'land to the tiller' within a pragmatic limit of what was possible in a constitutional democracy, generating a tense truce between the left's ideology and practice within a field of ambiguity.

Though the attempt was to inspire the bureaucracy and the peasant unions for a common cause, they frequently tended to work at cross-purposes. A government document subtly recognized this when it said that the Operation was working bit like a 'grinding stone', delivering the results desired because both its wheels were hard and moving against each other to crush the pulses (GoWB, 1979b, 3). There was little doubt, however, that the campaign was more political than bureaucratic, law-bound than radical and sustained than sporadic receiving the highest priority in the first five years of left rule in West Bengal. To maintain a critical balance during the campaign, some 'stages' were meticulously planned which illustrated its new logic of government (Ghosh, 1986, 77–121; 1981, A50–A51; GoWB, 1978d; GoWB 1991b).

At the beginning of the Operation, the periodic assessment of landholding (khanapuri-bujharat) was yet to start in 18,000 maujas, while in 24,000 maujas it had already been completed. In the former set, the government intended to record all sharecroppers 'within a year' (30 June 1979), while in the latter recording was 'to be taken up on a selective basis'. The settlement officers and the additional district magistrates assigned to land reforms were instructed to consult the peasant unions for selecting priority areas. The work was done by a composite squad of junior land reform officers and the kanungos, under the leadership of a senior land reform officer sent from the district headquarter. A detailed plan was chalked out for the squads requiring them to hold meetings at a time most convenient for the sharecroppers and wage workers, in the afternoon or evening, for which issuing a public notice well in advance was made mandatory (GoWB, 1978d, 1). A massive administrative mobilization was unleashed. Between October 1978 and June 1982, 1,300 kanungos and 300 junior land reforms officers held 8,000 camps and recorded 675 million bargadars (Ghosh, 1986, 88). These camps were occasionally preceded by 'reorientation camps' to collect information directly from the peasants. Little doubt that Operation changed forever the fabric of governmental practices in rural West Bengal.

Typically, the camps for recording were set up for three days at a public place, such as the premises of a school or the panchayat office (definitely not in the house of the landowner). They were attended by the land officials of various ranks, the panchayat representatives, the local MLAs, as well as the leaders of various peasant unions and political parties. The first day of the camp was meant for group meetings, explanation of the government's intentions and discussion. It often turned into war of words in which bargadars pitted their claims against those of landowners under a close, seemingly encouraging, watch of the officials. At the end of the day a tentative list of bargadars was prepared awaiting field enquiry and verification, which were conducted on the second day when a more complete list was prepared and circulated. On the third day, after hearing the landowners, the final list was drawn, names of the bargadars were recorded and the all important certificates were issued. In its design, the Operation was meant to be transparent, dialogical and egalitarian, making the denial of rights to the bargadars impossible.

Until October 1978, there were only 506,100 recorded bargadars in the state. In the first month of the campaign 18,720 more were recorded (GoWB, 1985b, 26–28). However, the campaign which was due for completion in June 1979 got extended several times. By December 1990, some 1,429,319 bargadars were recorded out of an estimated 2,310,000 (GoWB, 1990b). The monthly rates of recording fell sharply since 1982, the year when the left coalition was elected for the second time in a row. Following the discontinuity of the evening meetings the recording was eventually carried out as part of the normal settlement work under the unified command of the settlement and management wings of the state administration. A survey conducted in several Indian states revealed that West Bengal had the largest share of recorded bargadars (82.8 per cent) as well as tenants willing to get recorded (69.5 per cent) (Iyer, 1990, 34–37).

Despite its mixed results and short lifespan the campaign helped the left put on display its newly acquired organizational muscles in front of the lower officials of land bureaucracy, known to be 'friendly' to the landlords. It also created preliminary conditions for the poor to be accounted for, which earlier was rare in the rural localities. And it exposed the bureaucracy's feigned impartiality by forcing it to set its protocols in tune with the messy demands of popular politics. Moreover, the left had no clue for how long it was to be in power; so, getting as many bargadars recorded as quickly as possible was a way to ensure their participation in any future movement without the fear of eviction.

The priorities began to change once the left consolidated its government. By early 1980s there appeared to emerge a broad consensus in the state that 'under the present socio-economic condition, 25 per cent of the total number of bargadars will remain out of bounds of even the most efficient of recording systems' (Ghosh, 1981b, 18–19). There is no reason to believe that the powerful middle and rich peasant lobbies in the Krishak Sabha would have been happy if the campaign continued for long. Here again, as in the case of land distribution, the demand for a broad electoral alliance of conflicting class interests got precedence over the need to protect all the sharecroppers from the malaise of insecure tenure, as was originally promised.

After reforms

So what impact did the reforms have on the marginal cultivators, especially on the bargadars and the agricultural workers? Was the legal share of 75 per cent ensured for the bargadar, and the social conditions changed in ways that made hounding him or her out of the tenanted land impossible? Several local studies from the 1980s give a sense of what the agrarian policies of the left actually achieved at the field level. A survey found out that two years after the launch of the campaign the recorded bargadars were forced to pay 50 per cent of the crop even when the landlord only 'partially' shared inputs, though legally the landowner had to pay for all major inputs (seed, fertilizer, irrigation etc.) to ensure that share (GoWB, 1981c). If the bargadar was unrecorded, the situation was much worse. The owners, in such cases, shared 50 per cent of the produce without sharing any input at all: 'Though the Bargadar is aware of the legal provisions, the situation did not improve', remarked a report of the statistical cell of the government's Board of Revenue (GoWB, 1981e, 7).

A small sample survey covering 50 sharecroppers almost a decade after the launch of the campaign found that only 22 received the legal share due to their organizational 'weakness' and the prevailing consensus in favour of customary practices (B. Dasgupta, 1987, 15). A larger study covering 323 sharecroppers concluded that the 'exploitative' relations continued unabated in the state: of the bargadars interviewed only 15.2 per cent reported that they received their legal dues (Iyer, 1990, 20, 26). Another study after five years of the Operation found out that though the bargadars' income had risen by more than 30 per cent, the crop sharing rates had either remained the same or only marginally changed in his favour. On the other hand, 'in more than 50 percent of the cases... the sharing of costs...by landlords has gone down' (Agro-Economic Research Centre, 1986, XXVII [Table 6.1], 11). These local studies, therefore, indicated that though the tenancy reforms made eviction of the sharecroppers difficult, the bargaining power of the sharecroppers remained compromised as the left allowed the political influence of the landowners to continue unchallenged.

The point was more convincingly illustrated in the correlation between the nature of sharing (of output and input) and the level of unionization (of landowners and sharecroppers) that prevailed in the mid-1980s. A survey found that the landowner's share uniformly rose for both kharif and boro when he was a more active in the peasant union than the sharecropper. On the other hand, cost sharing did not respond to levels of activism either of the sharecropper or the landowner in any significant manner. However, when the sharecropper indulged in a higher level of activism than the landowner his income increased by 25.9 per cent, he managed to retain a greater share for boro crop and was met more often with the landowner's reluctance for cost sharing arrangements (Agro-Economic Research Centre, 1986, Tables 4.11, 4.12 and 6.5). Even though the landowner felt more comfortable to share cost with the unrecorded sharecropper, it did not prove cost-effective for the latter since access to institutional credit was conditional upon the recorded status of the sharecropper. If one combines the bargaining weakness of the sharecropper throughout the 1980s with the incentives for the landowner to maintain a high degree of political activism, one can probably get a better understanding of why the left peasant unions proved so inviting for middle and rich peasant classes pushing the poor sharecropper further to the margin.

At a macroeconomic level, nonetheless, these structural changes had important consequences including reduction in rural poverty. In 1983, six years into land reform, nine out of 16 major states in the country had less inequality than West Bengal in terms of rural consumption. By 1993–94 that number came down to four and by 1999–2000 to only three.[14] The important question was, whether West Bengal's relative decline in rural inequality accompanied a static or a growing agricultural economy. While making its villages a more equal place for living, as the data presented below would show, the state simultaneously achieved a rapid reduction in rural poverty in the condition of agrarian growth.

In 1973–74, before land reform was adopted, the Headcount Ratio of rural poverty in West Bengal was 73.16 per cent. It steadily declined to 40.8 per cent in 1993–94, 31.85 per cent in 1999–2000, and further to 28.6 per cent in 2004–05. During the first decade of the twenty-first century the decline of rural poverty in West Bengal was fastest among all major Indian states (Government of India, 2010, 95). In 1977, the year the Left Front government was installed, 60.52 per cent of the state's population was in the Below Poverty Line (BPL) category; in 1999–2000 only 27.02 per cent were so (Guruswamy, Sharma and Mohanty, 2005, 2155). It is sometimes claimed that land reform, while good for reducing poverty and inequality, is inimical to raising agricultural productivity.[15]

However, evidences from rural West Bengal tend to counter that claim. Due to factors not confined to land reforms alone, the state recorded an estimated annual growth in foodgrains production by 6.5 per cent during the 1980s (from 1981–82 to 1991–92), the highest among the country's 17 major states. Several studies have corroborated with such an unusually high growth figure which followed decades of impasse.[16] This growth, however, was short-lived. During the period 1991–2006 the rate of growth dipped to merely 2 per cent (Government of India, 2010, 45). Nonetheless, in the early 2000s West Bengal ranked just third from the top in agricultural intensity among all Indian states with almost 77 per cent of its land under cultivation (Guruswamy, Sharma and Mohanty,

2005, 2152, Table 2).[17] This was achieved in a state that was third from bottom in the intensity of irrigation. In volume of foodgrains produced, West Bengal ranked third after a much bigger state Uttar Pradesh and an exemplar of Green Revolution, Punjab.[18]

This chapter critiques the left's celebrated land reforms in West Bengal through a close reading of official documents prepared by the CPI(M), the Krishak Sabha and various departments of the state government to reveal the fundamental deficiencies internal to the process. The left launched land reforms to plug the loopholes in, and extend the scope of, the existing land laws introducing significant changes in the mode of their implementation. Earlier the reform laws were driven almost exclusively by the state officials who treated the potential beneficiaries as passive recipients. This allowed the locally dominant classes, who stood to lose from these measures, to subvert the laws by colluding with the lower rung of the bureaucracy and the police. The left within a year of coming to power introduced an alternative system of deploying the laws that required government officials to engage with potential beneficiaries, panchayat representatives, leaders of the peasant unions and of the political parties in village-based 'camps'. It helped create an entirely new atmosphere of deliberation and dialogue, and generated some elements of accountability and transparency in the administration through 'counter-democratic' mechanisms of vigilence, denunciation and evaluation. [19]

By implementing land reform laws in this manner, the left could earn a good deal of trust especially of the poorer sections of the peasant population and the wage workers, producing a sense of ethical government for the majority. It helped the left link its radical rhetoric with the everyday tactic of political conduct, its 'revolutionary' programme found a way to justify its pragmatic compulsions within the established 'system'. Bridged by the interface of the left parties and peasant unions, and hosted in the so-called 'camps' that opened up a social space for a new kind of dialogue in matters of administrative action, conditions were ripe for the production of what is referred to as 'government as practice'. This gave the rural popular sphere a new sense of purpose, and the left parties managed to orchestrate a temporary truce between classes with conflicting interests. Thus a broad constituency of support was born for the left, whose lingering effects were more durable than the actual run of the land reform programmes.

Within few years the constituency, which greatly helped the left's stay in power through periodic elections, developed a logic of its own: the left was determined to preserve the constituency at all cost. This led to two related consequences. On the one hand, driven by its pragmatic calculus of maintaining 'unity' between different classes, the left attempted to homogenize the rural public sphere in violation of its own stated ideology of sharpening class struggle. On the other hand, the land reforms measures were left incomplete and eventually discontinued; no urgent steps were taken to meet the emerging complications. As a result, despite the left's claims to the contrary, the interests of the poor peasants, sharecroppers and agricultural workers rapidly got overshadowed by those of the landed rich and middle classes. In an ambience of massive illiteracy and deep inequalities, the poor and the marginal population groups could not but rely on cultural and political capital of these classes for representation in the party, the panchayat, and the peasant unions.

Shortly, such dependence weakened the representation of the poor as a new breed of political elite took these bodies in their firm control replacing the previous leadership of the big landlords and jotedars. As a force deft in mediating conflicting interests, the new leaders gave the left's political constituency some predictability and stability, electoral success and 'social peace'. However, in view of the continuing social exclusion and economic deprivation of the rural poor, the 'basic classes', the left's principal political constituency remained an outwardly robust yet internally fragile electoral asset indicating a devaluation, if not debasement, of its ideological premises. In the context of such political paradoxes, we now turn to the principal agents of the democratic left in rural West Bengal - the village school teachers - as they travel from the heights of popular trust to the depths of social aversion.

Endnotes

1. The Estates Acquisition Acts of 1953, as we shall discuss in some detail, imposed no restriction on tank fisheries and orchards and so, just like religious trusts, the number of so-called orchards and fisheries by inundation grew at an amazing pace following its enactment to enable the landlords evade the ceiling.

2. These studies include two reports (Bhaduri, 1973a; Bhaduri, 1973b, 11–15) on 26 villages of Birbhum, Nadia and Murshidabad, a chapter (Frankel, 1971, 157–90) on the High Yielding Variety cropping district of Bardhaman and several essays (Rudra, 1975b, A58–A63; Rudra, 1975a, 1049–53; B. Chattopadhyay, 1986, 126–31) on a study of 89 villages in 14 districts (except Jalpaiguri and Howrah) of West Bengal and Santhal Parganas of erstwhile Bihar.

3. For a detailed account of Salihan see GoWB 1971b and for a summary of this and the following case studies mentioned in the section see Bhattacharya, 1993, 46–51.

4. A catalogue of such flaws were included (a) obsession with maintenance of law and order at the expenses of implementing land reform laws; (b) traditional concern to protect the sanctity of private property and intolerance towards any perceived threat to it; (c) responsibilities of the Magistrate and the Collector discharged by the same official, with the role of the Magistrate almost always eclipsing that of the Collector; and (d) emphasis on criminal law over other laws in the event of conflict between rural segments. The Report also states in unambiguous terms: 'the preventive sections of the Cr. P.C. are being very widely used by the designing landowners to evict their bargadars from their lands. By getting an order restraining the other parties from entering upon the land they are very effectively throwing out bargadars totally bypassing the provisions regarding the eviction of bargadars'. (GoWB, 1971b, 9).

5. The Board of Revenue Circular No. 22563(15)GE dated 14 October 1969 and reiterated by the Board of Revenue Circular No. 25003(15)GE dated 10 November 1970 as quoted in GoWB, 1971b, 9–10.

6. For various modalities of concealing land above ceiling see Bandyopadhyay, 2007, chapter 7, 201–36.

7. This statement, at least programmatically, nullifies an observation that Atul Kohli made that, 'It indeed makes a funny type of communism which treats pre-commercial, 'feudal' landlords as enemies but not those involved in the capitalist mode of production.' See Kohli, 1987, 100.

8. The 'people's democratic revolution' was conceived by the CPI(M) as an intermediate revolutionary phase positioned between the existing 'big bourgeois-landlord state' and the socialist state of the future. This was to be achieved by a progressive coalition of the working class, peasantry, petty bourgeois intelligentsia and national bourgeoisie under the predominant leadership of the working class.

9. The Cooch Behar session of the Pradeshik Krishak Sabha held in 1986 introduced a concept 'dialectical unity' and defined it as one that 'tightly held' the middle peasants, invited the rich peasants 'by transforming their demands into movements' and opposed any compromise on 'the struggle for wages in order to advance peasant unity' (WBPKS, 1986, 56, 76).

10. In my fieldwork in the early 1990s, I observed that almost every wage negotiation between the agricultural workers and the landowners in Amrakuchi, a village in erstwhile Medinipur district, was routinely preceded by a strike. The labourers usually stuck to a rate supplied by the CPI(M), which regarded such strikes as manifestations of 'class struggle' against the landowners; the landowners usually agreed at the end of the negotiation to raise the wage up to a rate lower than the official rate with the full consent of the party; the workers withdrew their strike in response and got back to work with a sense of gratitude to the party. Such a sequence of a rather ritualistic strike action usually kept both parties satisfied. It helped the party retain its 'militant' image among the wage earners and its 'managerial' image among the landowners. For details see Bhattacharyya, 1999.

11. The percentage participation of agricultural labourers and poor peasants was 8.48 and 21.46 : 6.58 and 16.12 and 7.46 and 23.38 respectively in the 26th (1982), 27th (1986) and 28th (1989) sessions of the Krishak Sabha. See WBPKS (1982, 6; 1986, 5; 1989a, 4).

12. At the 26th Conference (1989) of the AIKS the proportion of attending agricultural labourer was merely 4.85 per cent and that of the poor peasants 24.28 per cent (AIKS, 1989, 105).

13. For contemporary debate on Operation Barga see B. Dasgupta 1984, A85–A96; K. Dutt 1981, A58–A60; R. Ghosh 1981, A49–A55; Khasnabis, 1981, A43–A48; Rudra, 1981, A61–A68; for a summary of the debate and related issues see Bhattacharyya, 1993, 11–16.

14. The extent of inequality can be measured by representing rural income or consumption as Gini coefficient, a number between values 0 and 1, where 0 denotes complete equality of income or consumption and 1 denotes all income or consumption usurped by a single entity. Gini coefficient of rural consumption in West Bengal declined from 0.286 (1983) to 0.250 (1993–94) to 0.224 (1999–2000), Government of India, 2002, 148 (Table 2.3). 16 major states compared here are Andhra Pradesh, Assam, Bihar, Gujarat, Haryana, Himachal Pradesh, Karnataka, Kerala, Madhya Pradesh, Maharashtra, Orissa, Punjab, Rajasthan, Tamil Nadu, Uttar Pradesh and West Bengal.

15. For counter arguments and a recent discussion on farm size and productivity see Lipton 2009 (especially chapter 2). It is spurious to pose land reform as a substitute for Green Revolution or high growth strategy in agriculture because in absence of institutional reforms such strategy is found to be inadequate for a sustainable

initiative against poverty and hunger. Lipton shows how land reform has unleashed entrepreneurial potential for growth in many East Asian countries.

16. The figure quoted in Chattopadhyay (2005, 5601–02) from Centre for Monitoring Indian Economy (CMIE) 1993. Corroborating studies referred to in Chattopadhyay (2005) are Saha and Swaminathan (1994, A-2 to A-11); Bhalla and Singh (2001). For an analysis of positive effects of tenancy reforms on agricultural productivity see Banerjee, Gertler and Ghatak (2002, 239–80).

17. West Bengal has the third highest average yield in India (2,424 kg per hectare). It was substantially higher than the national average (1,739 kg per hectare).

18. The growth of crop production in West Bengal was largely due to the rise in Boro (winter) cultivation aided mainly by small-scale private investment in irrigation (diesel-run shallow tube-well and submersible pumps). This was facilitated by tenancy reforms and mini kit distribution by local government. See Bardhan, Mookherjee and Kumar (2012a, 222–35). Also Moitra and Das (2004).

19. For an unconventional history of democracy's journey with a focus on public oversight ('vigilence', 'denunciation', and 'evaluation') that incessantly from the ancient times to the modern attempted to make different regimes of power accountable to popular scrutiny see Pierre Rosanvallon, Counter-Democracy: Politics in an Age of Distrust, (Translated by Arthur Goldhammer).

3

AGENCY: SCHOOL TEACHERS

It is widely expected of a leftwing government to place priority on universal school education, which can greatly improve the material conditions of the poor and marginal sections of the population. A quick look at some of the key indicators reflecting more than three decades of left rule, however, tell us a different story. As a Planning Commission document noted in 2010, West Bengal in creating infrastructure for primary education ranked third from the bottom, only above Jharkhand and Bihar, among 16 major states in the country. In literacy, West Bengal ranked sixth, which did not change during the long rule of the left. More critically, Scheduled Castes (SC), Scheduled Tribes (ST) and the Muslims had lower literacy rates than the state's overall average, indicating the continuity of a systemic inequality and exclusion.[1] The question is, why after three and half decades of left government West Bengal cut such a sorry figure in elementary education, and, more importantly, what does it say about the character of the government?[2]

Teachers as leaders

West Bengal's poor, and exclusionary, record in elementary education is certainly not due to any lack of activism on the part of the state's large body of primary school teachers. In 2006–07, almost 78 per cent of the state's 155,000 primary teachers were members of the pro-CPI(M) All

Bengal Primary Teachers' Association (ABPTA) (Sarkar and Rana, 2010, 4), a good number of whom were for quite some time 'natural' leaders of the left (Pratichi, 2002, 5). Primary teachers maintained a level of civic activism for decades, as one can trace ABPTA's lineage to the Nikhil Banga Prathamik Shikshak Samiti (henceforth, Samiti) founded in 1935. In its conference resolutions and petitions sent to the colonial government, the Samiti however placed more stress on the need for education as an abstract public good; there was scarcely any demand for raising the paltry salary that the primary teachers received,[3] or any sharp criticism of the government on political grounds. The Samiti was also silent on issues of social exclusion, there was no strong demand to educate women or Muslim students, though access to education was severely constrained for both these groups (Nikhilbongo Prathamik Sikshak Samiti, 2007; Poshchimbongo Prathamik Sikshak Samiti, 2009; Sarkar and Rana, 2010, 5–13).

After the partition of Bengal in 1947, the Samiti was rechristened as Poshchimbanga Prathamik Sikshak Samiti (West Bengal Primary Teachers' Association), which split in the late 1960s when the dominant group of left-leaning teachers formed a rival organization adopting the old name, the ABPTA. Now, unlike the past, the teachers began raising political and social demands for extension of education among the poor and the minorities, for larger representation of teachers in state educational boards, for distribution of free textbooks, uniform and midday meal etc. It was also recognized that schools cannot be insular from the surrounding communities and, therefore, demands were made for inclusion of educated locals in the governing bodies of the primary schools. A clear need to modernize curricula and train teachers for the purpose was emphasized. Despite such widened perspective, the organized primary teachers still remained silent on issues of social disadvantages, of identity-related backwardness, which contributed to the perpetuation of lower literacy rates among the Adivasis, Dalits and Muslims.

Curiously, while it was suggested that educated locals be inducted into school boards, there was no insistence for a larger involvement of the parents – rich and poor, educated and uneducated. Also there was no demand for education as a right, and no comprehensive plan was drawn to link children's education with arguably the world's largest child-related programme, the government-run Integrated Child Development Services (ICDS). Slowly, but steadily, devoid of a holistic approach to child education and any critical intent to make the government accountable, the primary teachers' organization effectively got absorbed into the administrative infrastructure of the state. Since the late 1960s, when the United Front was in power, a high degree of correspondence developed between the ABPTA and the state administration, so much so that even after the United Front government was unseated from power, the association could maintain its influence over the passage of the Primary Education Act in 1973 and the constitution of the new syllabus committee in 1974. With its increasingly 'governmental' accent, therefore, the ABPTA was content to keep its public action limited to selective and strategic bureaucratic interventions, rather than taking a politically strident step for bringing popular pressure upon the government to recognize education as a matter of fundamental right and social justice.[4]

One cannot help but recognize that in preparing the groundwork for subsequent Left Front decades such an overtly administrative character of the organized body of primary teachers came handy to the left. Chapter 2 has shown how the left broke the stranglehold of agricultural landownership in excess of legal limits and how specific political and governmental measures were brought to bear the distribution of such land and the registration of sharecroppers to infuse a sense of security and justice for a vast majority of West Bengal's rural poor. Born in the course of movements of small peasants and landless agricultural workers, these measures were slowly appropriated by the middle peasants, and 'struggle' eventually turned into a rhetorical coinage bereft of its past radical charge under the pressure of the government and the party machinery bent on maintaining social peace above everything else. The twin imperatives of land reforms and representative local government produced a new mode of government for the left in West Bengal's specific historical and social conditions, a mechanism that has been referred to as 'government as practice'. The rural schoolteachers, especially those who were in the primary schools, played a key role in making this new mode of government work. A majority of these teachers were rural in origin, mostly from middle peasant families, and members of the left-affiliated ABPTA. Being educated in an ambience of vast illiteracy and equipped with some basic knowledge about the norms of official transactions, they now emerged as veritable political leaders of the left, and agents to mediate with myriad governmental agencies for the local population. In the panchayat elections that followed, a sizeable number of primary teachers were sent as village representatives. In short, primary school teachers were the prime agents of the left's government as practice in rural West Bengal.

Organization above education

The expectation was that once in government the left would take a consorted initiative for public education, especially elementary education for the poor and the lower castes. With a majority of the primary school teachers within the fold of the left, it was also logistically possible for the new regime to coordinate such actions with requisite political will despite the government's limited infrastructural and financial resources. In addition, the extended grid of the left's party organization and decentralized local government institutions could offer the much needed platform for launching a popular movement for universal education. However, what followed once the Left Front took charge was quite different. The organized might of the school teachers and their proximity with the left helped them enhance their own position within the rural society rather than that of the left's basic constituency – the rural poor. Idealism of some left school teachers got jettisoned over the years by routine unionism of the ABPTA.

This discrepancy between the expected and the actual was captured in a report on the condition of education in West Bengal submitted by the Ashok Mitra Commission appointed by the state government in 1991 (GoWB, 1992). The report noted some significant improvements in primary education during a decade or so of left rule. The number of primary schools, for instance, increased by more than 10,000 between 1976–77 and 1991–92, with student intake rising by 81 per cent. The state had a rise in literacy, from 45.78 per cent in 1981 (India 41.42 per cent) to 57.72 per cent (India 52.11 per cent) in 1991. The share of education in state budget also went up from 12.89 per cent in 1976–77 to 26.04 per cent in 1990–91 with the national average being 19.94 per cent. Per capita investment in education also increased during the Left Front years reaching ₹ 250.39, behind only those of Punjab (₹ 268.87), Gujarat (₹ 253.92) and Kerala (₹ 252.11). An important question was who were the greatest beneficiaries of the rising expenditure on education?

A closer look at the report of the commission and other commentaries reveals an uneven allocation of resources for education. The state government spent more on higher education than primary education which was no different from the trend in the rest of the country.[5] However, reflecting on Mitra's report Tapas Majumdar observed that the share of higher education in West Bengal's education budget was 'much higher than the share of higher education in Assam, Gujarat, Maharashtra and Tamil Nadu among the better performing states' (Majumdar, 1993, 920). Of the money spent on education, a large proportion went to meet the teachers' salary, leaving little for infrastructure and other facilities for students.[6] The minimum pay of the primary teachers increased five-fold from ₹ 60 to ₹ 300 per month in less than four years of the Left Front in power, and that of a teacher with postgraduate degrees in the secondary schools from ₹ 220 to ₹ 550 in the same period.[7] Also, the share of the salary part was larger in primary and secondary sectors in comparison with that in higher education.[8] Such pay rise was happening at a time when West Bengal took no special initiative for spreading literacy. Observing that the state preferred to toe the central policies on literacy with none of its own, Mitra called it a 'demure camp follower of the centre'. He offered several concrete proposals that ranged from raising fees for higher education and holding the teachers accountable, to banning private tuition during school hours etc.

So the picture of managing education, elementary education in particular, did not show the organized body of leftwing school teachers in a very positive light, nor did it suggest that the left government had its priorities right. Rather than linking its avowed politics of class with a demand for universal education so that those systematically excluded due to economic backwardness or social marginality could be equipped to attend schools, both the left government and the ABPTA seemed more inclined to improve the teachers' emoluments and employment conditions within the status quo. True, as seen, teachers were severely underpaid in the pre-Left Front days, and it was only legitimate to respond to their demands. But equally, if not more, important was to take genuine steps to reduce (if not remove) the structural hindrances internal to society by building a popular movement for education. Addressing the teacher's concern without the society's, as shall be seen in a while, had serious implications not just for the teachers who began to feel a disconnect with the local communities, but also for the left's entire political project in West Bengal.

Though the Left Front cannot be credited for initiating a large-scale mobilization for basic education, it nonetheless adopted a series of popular measures within few years of coming to power. It set up thousands of new schools, gave financial aid to schools established by local communities, streamlined bureaucracy to implement the Act of 1973, launched local campaigns for literacy, dropped English at the primary level to break the language barrier, made education up to class 12 free of cost, gave free textbooks and uniform to primary students, and changed the curricula to reflect the social and cultural world of the under-classes. The central government took some concrete steps in the 1990s to decentralize education across the country in sync with the 73rd Amendment of the Constitution. A District Primary Education Programme was launched to look after the district-specific needs, and every village council (sansad) got a Village Education Committee (VEC) to ensure community involvement in primary education.[9]

West Bengal conformed to these administrative changes in 1997–98, allegedly with some reluctance and under a tight control of the ruling party (Roy and Banerjee, 2012). In 1998 the state government set up

Shishu Shiksha Kendras (SSKs, literally, Children Education Centres), small learning huts for infants in neighbourhoods where there were no primary schools.[10] Since 2001–02 the Sarva Shiksha Abhiyan (SSA, literally Journey for Universal Education) was carried out as part of a national initiative to build physical infrastructure for primary and secondary education.[11] All these initiatives were exclusively bureaucratic in character, frequently sponsored by New Delhi with strict financial implications, and none originated as an independent political move of the ruling left. As a result the impact of these measures was limited. Kanti Biwas, the state's education minister, admitted in 2003 that despite the SSA, over 700,000 children in the state had never gone to school. 'Add to this another 24 hundred thousand students who drop out between class V and VIII and we have a serious problem on our hand' (*Times of India*, 9 September 2003).

Political dependence

That the ABPTA lost its grip over the ground level reality was quite evident from its flip-flop over a number of key policies. In 1995, the central government launched a National Programme of Nutritional Support to Primary Education, popularly known as 'midday meal scheme' in few blocks and within two years decided to extend it across the country (Government of India, 2006, 1–2). The Left Front government, on its part, decided to allot a monthly quota of foodgrain to every child instead of daily cooked midday meal though the latter is widely valued for ensuring a minimum nutrition and enhancing school attendance. A voice of criticism should have come from the ABPTA, but 'surprisingly' it remained silent though mid-day meal had been featuring in its charter of demands since 1962 (Sarkar and Rana, 2010, 25). However, when the state government finally opted for cooked meal in schools, the ABPTA lent its support and took an active part to break 'an undercurrent of resistance among many … teachers' (Pratichi, 2010, 26).

That the ABPTA turned itself into the government's tail with little independence was proven once more in its flip-flop on English at the primary level. In 1983 the state government discontinued English literature and grammar in the primary schools and introduced what it called 'functional and communicative' aspects of English. The government insisted that English literature and grammar, alien to those from lower socioeconomic background, discouraged learning and widened the social gap between the privileged and the rest. The Ashok Mitra Commission also endorsed the view, though two of its members dissented. Sunanda Sanyal, for one, believed that the suggested method was 'highly teacher-dependent' requiring 'an army of teachers' that the state lacked (Mitra, 2002). Expectedly, the ABPTA stood firmly behind the government. In absence of a good number of quality teachers the policy was counterproductive. Children from privileged backgrounds opted for private schools and mushrooming coaching centres imparting lessons in English. The underprivileged crowded the government system where English continued to be poorly taught.[12]

At the beginning of the new millennium, as India's engagement with the global market deepened, a demand for re-introducing English grew even within the left. Under pressure, the government set up a one-man commission (chaired by Pabitra Sarkar) (Bhattacharya, 2003). Initially, the ABPTA stuck to its earlier stance in opposition to English. Surprisingly (or rather routinely), 'when, following the Commission's recommendation, the Government re-inducted English at the primary level the ABPTA chose to close the issue...without registering any protest' (Sarkar and Rana, 2010, 25–26). On both issues of mid-day meal and of English the ABPTA stood exposed with its lack of autonomy in relation to either the government or the dominant political party. This lack of independence, coupled with the social disconnect, severely compromised the authority of the local agents of the left parties: the school teachers.

Grassroots transformation

In 1997–98 a prolonged fieldwork was done in Purulia and Bardhaman districts of West Bengal to understand the political salience of the rural school teachers and their changing importance in the public sphere of the villages. Purulia, located in a semi-arid part of West Bengal, is one of the poorest districts in the state with a low rate of literacy, no industry and low human development indices. Bardhaman, on the other hand, is among the most prosperous regions, considered the rice-bowl of West Bengal, with vast stretches of fertile land feeding a robust commercial economy supported by a powerful centre of industry. The class-caste dynamics in the two districts are also very different. While Purulia has a high ST, SC and Other Backward Caste (OBC) population groups,[13] Bardhaman – a beneficiary of the Green Revolution – has a dominant peasant caste at the epicentre of its social and political world. While the villages studied in Purulia were more or less of similar demographic and economic character, in Bardhaman there were considerable variations between villages. The fieldwork, therefore, focused more on individual teachers in Purulia, while in Bardhaman the village became an important unit of analysis. Both Purulia and Bardhaman were 'red districts' at the time of this fieldwork. Both had the Zilla Parishad (District Panchayat) under the control of the left, and barring a village in Bardhaman, which had elected TMC representatives, in all other locations studied the CPI(M) was the dominant player. This section focuses upon only those aspects of the fieldwork which help us understand the changes in the conditions of the rural primary teachers halfway through the Left Front rule. The rest of the findings can be obtained elsewhere (Bhattacharyya, 2004a).

We have already noted that the teachers were key mediators in the local society's interaction with the agencies of the government. That the teachers were more educated and better equipped to handle legal and regulatory protocols of officialdom was not the only reason for them being able to function as local agents and interlocutors with the government. As a precondition, they also had to earn credibility in the local society, prove themselves as trusted members of the community whose knowledge was not just useful, but also accessible. Lambodar Mahato, a Purulia teacher who was also the Assistant Secretary of the district Krishak Sabha (the CPI[M]'s peasant organization), told:

I always wanted to do something 'good' for the poor. I had no idea about how to bring big changes in their lives. I joined others in running a night school. We collected books for their children, kept a close vigil on health and diet of these kids. On the days of major examinations, we made early morning rounds in the village calling them out by name to wake them up in time.

Paltu Mahato of Kumarsol village narrated a similar experience:

We have set up a free homeopathy clinic in the village where a few doctors visit regularly. If everyone joins in to repair the village road, we also lend our hands. Villagers love to be entertained, so we arrange cultural programmes and bring artistes from the city. I am also a member of Vivekananda Sports Club. The point is to remain involved in all kinds of public activities…

Another teacher, Birendrakrishna Mahato of the same village noted: 'It is not difficult to understand why people are fond of us. A mother who sends her child to us cannot afford to be indifferent'. 'Nobody else in the village commands the aastha (confidence) that we do', declared Anil Mahato, a primary school teacher in Amakocha village. This mutual acceptance and accessibility made the teacher a source of information about the world for the village, and also turned her – as she literally doubled as a collector of decennial census data – into a vehicle of information about the village for the world at large.

In Purulia a good number of elderly school teachers affiliated to the left in the 1990s had earlier been members of a Gandhian organization, the Lok Sebak Sangha (LSS). When in 1972 the LSS decided not to contest the state election and distance itself from the 'politics of power', many teachers felt disappointed and left the party. For most of these Bengali-speaking teachers joining the Congress was not an option at that time because the party's ambivalence on Purulia's cessation from Bihar to merge with West Bengal was still fresh in their memory. Moreover, driven more by a communitarian egalitarian outlook than by strictures of non-violence, they found in the CPI(M) a 'natural ally' devoted to a 'classless society'. As a veteran member of the LSS put his ideals in a pithy verse: *'nei ko raja, nei ko praja, nei ko koumi dwesh / gorbo mora shob shomaner desh*' ('No king, no subject, no communal enmity / We'll build a land of equality for all'). This in some way gelled with the claims made by Nakul Mahato, then the secretary of CPI(M)'s Purulia District Committee: 'The days of jotedar domination and mahajani (moneylender) extraction are gone… now the village is politically polarised in the favour of the reds'.

It will be simplistic to assume that the public profile of the school teacher – built over years of multilevel engagement with the local society – invariably prepared the ground for her to emerge as a political leader in every village. In the three villages I studied in Bardhaman district it was evident that the political importance of the schoolteachers was proportionate to the economic and social backwardness of the village. Thus, Mobarakpur village, which was highly literate and had more than 60 per cent population from the upper caste Hindus, had several leading members able to both represent the village in the panchayat and work as local leaders of major political parties. Thus the village headmaster Sushanta Chaktaborty, although highly respected, did not take the mantle of any political party. 'A teacher in politics is not accepted and trusted by many despite his qualifications because his political identity prevails over that of a teacher', he believed. Not a single teacher in his Mobarakpur Vivekananda Primary School had any partisan profile 'though they are free to have their political preference in their private lives…' he told me.

The situation in two other Bardhaman villages – Salarpur and Mohespur – as well as in all villages in Purulia, was clearly different. Unlike in Mobarakpur, in these places the scheduled categories and Muslims made up more than 50 per cent of the population. Also, these localities had higher levels of poverty, landlessness and illiteracy. Their schools also bore more prominent marks of impoverishment compared to Mobarakpur where private funding supplemented meagre government resources. The poorer and more backward the village, the higher the chances of a teacher with superior cultural capital to stand above the rest, and the larger the dependence of the local population on the mediation of the educated teacher. The teacher in these settings chose not to confine herself to teaching alone, and got increasingly sucked into the world of

99

politics as a much needed representative of the village population. The representational function, paradoxically, depended on the extent to which the teacher, despite being perceived as culturally superior, could minimize her social distance with the local population: the closer the bonding, the higher the popularity, and the greater the acceptance of the teacher as one who stands for the village as a whole.

We have already seen that the ABPTA had inducted a vast majority of these teachers into its fold. They became the veritable foot-soldiers of the left as an elaborate grid of governmental practices and reformist policies were being laid out during the early Left Front years. In much of rural West Bengal the teachers with their capacity to mediate, negotiate, convince and control occupied the interstitial space between the organized domain of the party and the activated sphere of the society, cementing the two in a crucial way that contributed to the solidity of the regime. At a time when the ruling Left Front was implementing land reforms and installing local government, the lower rung of the peasantry got mobilized and many rural teachers found a concrete opportunity to express their egalitarian ideals, their intent to 'build a land of equality for all'. This was coeval to what we would call the 'hegemonic moment' of party society in chapter 4. The situation, however, was short-lived, as at least three currents of change surged forward in a dynamic politico-economic landscape.

First, as has been discussed in detail in chapters 1 and 2, the agrarian reforms initiated by the Left Front in the late 1970s ran out of steam within a decade or so and its governmental practices focused increasingly on maintaining the social status quo. Comfortably ensconced in power, the object of left politics now veered towards sustaining a 'machine' for the coalition's electoral renewal. In the shifting scenario, the role of the rural school teachers also changed from one of a leader of the village community to that of a manager of the party society, from an agent of political change to a monitor of social peace, and from a practitioner of idealistic traditions to a schematic executor of quotidian manoeuvring. Second, as mentioned before, the primary school teachers in West Bengal, with the help of the ABPTA, succeeded in getting the Left Front to agree to a much needed raise in their salary. As previous governments were reluctant to respond to the teachers' longstanding economic demands, the pay hike was rather substantial and dramatic. While it brought the 'friendly' constituency of school teachers even closer to the left, it also had an unintended consequence especially in rural West Bengal: it turned the teachers into a 'privileged class', enhancing their distance with rest of the village, thereby weakening their representative functions. Ironically, the audacious signs of teachers' prosperity, their changing lifestyle, were more palpable in poorer villages that – for reasons we have discussed before – kept maximum *aastha* on the local school teacher. As Ajoy Mohan Ganguly of Purulia Municipality Managed School remarked, 'Yes indeed, we now form an elite distinctly wealthier than rest of the community'. Even a walk down a backward village road could tell you in the 1990s that the panchayat and the school buildings apart, the only other brick house visible in the landscape was that of the school teacher. Even the left parties had little doubts now that reliance on school teachers as their local nodal agents was fast running its course.

Another change was also apparent in the rural political economy with far reaching consequences. As noted in chapters 1 and 2, the left did not take its land reform measures to their logical conclusion and, therefore, after a spurt of agricultural growth in the 1980s, West Bengal's agrarian economy entered a long phase of stagnancy. With rising input costs, growing demographic pressure on land and not so promising price of agricultural produce, cultivation ceased to be a sustainable occupation for many. Those with very little education now struggled to acquire some skills and aspired to migrate to the city as informal workers, to take up jobs in construction, service or manufacturing units. In absence of enough employment in industry or in government services those with some skills and education moved into petty commercial economies as small-scale traders, transporters, labour contractors, ration shop dealers, middlemen for land and real estate transactions, construction material suppliers, government contractors, Ponzi scheme agents, etc. They eventually emerged as local entrepreneurs of a sort rivalling the school teacher both in prosperity as well as connectivity. In the burgeoning non-agricultural economy of West Bengal's new rural, school teachers were not just faced with a depletion of trust they once elicited, their status of an invaluable conduit between the village and the world was also eroding.

In the new climate the left parties, the CPI(M) in particular, quickly revised their approach to school teachers. Officially, the left now claimed that by involving themselves in politics and by standing as representatives in the local government the school teachers were neglecting their primary responsibility of teaching. Since the early 1990s the opinion within the CPI(M) that no school teacher should be fielded as a candidate for the party in panchayat election gained ground. In 1993, the Left Front government issued an executive order to district headquarters carrying an instruction that teachers who wanted to serve at block or district levels of the panchayat were required to take an 'extraordinary leave' from their respective institutions. Another circular in 1997 made participation of school teachers in local elected bodies considerably difficult. Clearly, for the left in West Bengal the school teachers were rapidly losing their political salience.

Instead, the left started relying more on the rising segment of petty entrepreneurs to exercise micro political control. In turn, these new players in the local economy involving risky manoeuvrings and physical prowess badly needed the support of the party in power. The emerging relationship between the two – the party and its new agents – was very different from that was there between the party and the school teacher. The new players were driven almost exclusively by their instincts for survival. They affiliated to the left parties not because they found its ideology or idealism attractive, but because their instrumental reasoning guided them to support the party in power, any party in power. This brought big changes in the left's government as practice at the ground level: the balance between pragmatic and programmatic got disturbed as quotidian, everyday and contingent interests of a powerful section now began to overwhelm its long-term agenda for transformation. No sooner than the regime's moral credentials were severely challenged bringing it on the brink of a defeat after a record run (more on this in chapter 5) these local agents of the left, the key levers of its mammoth 'machinery', swiftly changed sides offering a ready network to the opposition TMC for rapidly expanding the latter's operations.

Hierarchy and social distance

Now let us take the discussion in a somewhat different direction. Both the estrangement of the school teacher from the local rural communities and the left's failure to improve West Bengal's national ranking in literacy during 34 years of its uninterrupted rule, I argue, had a common set of reasons. In a class divided society reeling under centuries of social exclusion and gender discrimination universal education cannot be realized if left only to the goodwill of salaried teachers and the institutional intent of schools. There has either to be an 'explosion of demand' for education as a result of new economic opportunities in which education is a prerequisite, or there must be a political impetus to carry out a systematic campaign from below in the form of a social movement for inclusion and enfranchisement. During the long rule of the left new economic opportunities remained inadequate, and the political will to treat education as a vehicle for social inclusion of the marginal communities continued to be painfully weak.

Instead, the left attempted its educational enterprise by administrative fiats from the top or by financial support alone that catered primarily to wellbeing of the school teachers, its political constituency. This proved counterproductive not just because the teacher got estranged and her ability to politically represent the local society diminished. More important constraints, in fact, emerged inside the classroom. In the absence of any (ascending) social mobilization for inclusion in the public sphere, a teacher continued to treat students from the under classes differently and, thereby, reinforced the extant social distance. Such treatment – as we will see when we take up the testimonies of the school teachers later in this chapter – was not necessarily conspiratorial, nor did it reflect condescending attitude of individual teachers who could be trained to behave differently. Rather, such interaction was structural, and worked its way by inflicting what Pierre Bourdieu calls 'symbolic violence'. When social distance operates as a homology for differential class interests, however much a teacher may try on the contrary, educating pupils from poor and marginal groups remains an incomplete and unachievable project. The political debasement of West Bengal's left, among other factors, was linked to its inability to appreciate this basic dynamic.

The left, in other words, failed to understand that the problem with primary education in West Bengal was not just of poor infrastructure or inadequate schools, lack of teachers or the burden of poverty, low literacy rates or high drop-outs. More critically the problem was rooted in the left's lack of political initiative to break the limiting equations that bound access to education with the structured social hierarchy. Poromesh Acharya, based on his empirical survey of four villages in 1978, was among the earliest to point this out. He found 'a very close correlation between educational achievements in terms of literacy and enrolment and agrarian class structure'. In fact, the frequency distribution of families to agrarian class, caste and income level in his survey indicated 'a close relation if not perfect correlation between them' (Acharya, 1985, 1785). In the villages he surveyed, more than 84 per cent of the total enrolled students at the primary schools came from *jotedar* class, made up of rich and middle peasant families, which had a combined population in these villages of merely 52 per cent. Such overrepresentation of the upper class-upper caste combine could not be more emphatic: while 100 per cent of the children in the age group 6–11 from the *jotedar* families were enrolled, the figure from their counterparts from the agricultural workers' families was merely 6 per cent.

One doubts, Acharya pointed out, 'whether the expansion of educational facilities [by successive state governments] was meant for educating children or for providing jobs as teachers to educated unemployed young men from the upper and middle strata of society' (Acharya, 1985, 1786). In fact, these teachers played 'a rather negative role in regard to the education of the children from lower strata'. There was a distinct feeling among the lower strata in the rural society 'that these teachers, leaders of village institutions and government officials are either against or reticent' about their education. In these circumstances larger investment by the government for education could actually reproduce the same discrepancies. An expansion of educational facilities with distribution of free textbook, school uniform or mid-day meal may well help the privileged 'capture' the benefits and 'in fact ...sharpen the differentiation in rural society rather than reduce it' (Acharya, 1985, 1786). Universal education, he pointed out, was predicated on policy initiatives to alter the distribution of social power between communities.

Another survey conducted three decades later on primary schools in the remote interiors of rural West Bengal found that only 18 per cent students came from 'general' castes in these schools, while 61 per cent teachers were from that category. Moreover, only 12 per cent teachers were Muslims, though the share of Muslims among students was 45 per cent (Pratichi, 2009, 60). Such disparity in the social composition of the teachers and the students had a telling effect. When taken together with the teachers' economic and cultural distances with the rest of the rural society, the students and the teachers appeared as belonging to two different worlds. The question is what happens to the school, to the practice of teaching, to the interactions between the teachers and the students, and above all, to the teachers' capacity to establish a social leadership in the midst of such incongruities? More bluntly, does school as an educational institution by itself reinforce the existing social gaps in a class divided society or bridge them?

Bourdieu's diagnosis

In a very different political and social context, the French sociologist Pierre Bourdieu dealt with a problem that was not, in its essentials, very different from our own. He sought to explain the unequal scholastic achievements of children from different social classes by relating their academic success to the distribution of what he called 'cultural capital' between the classes and fractions of the classes. This eventually led him to develop a set of theoretical hypotheses on different forms of capital – both material and symbolic – in their specific yet interdependent manifestations in the economic, social, cultural and political fields of power. It will be interesting to see how Bourdieu's conceptual horizon looks from the distant world of a postcolonial polity, and how some of his ideas can be used as heuristic tools to deal with the problem at hand. We make a brief digression through the conceptual matrix of Bourdieu's diverse and often inconsistent sociological repository, before re-entering the villages in West Bengal for a detailed ethnographic and textual reading of the teachers' predicaments.

In *Homo Academicus*, after examining 154 files containing progress reports of individual pupils from a girls' *première supérieure* in Paris, Bourdieu concluded that these documents, established in the 1960s, offer a remarkable insight into a pattern of evaluation of the students by their professors. Students who were from bourgeois and Parisian backgrounds ended up getting more unqualified appreciations than those who came from petty-bourgeois families of provincial character. The words used in the remarks are subtle, often euphemistic, and could only be understood in their real essence as integral to the whole – their combination and placement within a sentence. More strikingly, the remarks were sharpest and less euphemistic when two pupils from divergent social backgrounds got the same marks (Bourdieu, 1988, 199). These remarks frequently covered criteria external to what the 'technical definition of performance demanded'. They targeted the handwriting of individual pupils, and for oral work their accent, elocution, diction, and 'finally and above all the bodily "hexis", manners and behaviour, which are often designated, very directly, in the remarks' (Bourdieu, 1988, 200). Bourdieu points out that such a convergence of social classification and academic evaluation was simultaneously relayed yet screened, accomplished yet unacknowledged. While being implicit, however, it was precisely such dominant taxonomy that marked out the superior from the mediocre, the expansive from the clumsy, the refined from the vulgar, and the sincere from the conscientious.

> Working as an ideology in a state of practice, producing logical effects which are inseparable from political effects, the academic taxonomy entails an implicit definition of excellence which, by constituting as excellent the qualities possessed by those who are socially dominant,

consecrates their manner of being and their lifestyle (Bourdieu, 1988, 204).

In sum, what Bourdieu suggests here is this: the homology that is found between educational system and the evaluative taxonomy deployed by the teachers both reflects and affirms – in an instrumental mechanism of 'symbolic aggression' – the hierarchical social order behind a mask of academic neutrality. So what the teacher critiques is the 'mere academic' character of a dissertation, or 'barely acceptable' quality of a term paper, never its 'petty-bourgeois' grossness or lack of 'culture'. As a result, 'in all good faith and genuine belief', the academia works overtime as a machine to 'transform social classifications into academic classifications' since 'academic taxonomies classify according to the logic of the structures whose products they are' (Bourdieu, 1988, 206–07). The teachers who are given to exercise such classifications can actually undertake a social classification because it is done in the guise of an operation of academic classification. They are not conspirators in such elaborate act of mystification; rather they are 'mystified mystifiers': 'because they are actually doing something different from what they believe they are doing; and because they believe in what they believe they are doing' (Bourdieu, 1988, 207). A teacher's judgment cannot be purchased with money, and a teacher always judges the intellectual personage of her pupil. This gives the judgment a philosophical righteousness, and masks any possibility of evaluating the pupil on the basis of her social personage (such as provincial, working class, poor). Yet, academic verdict matters for the student, pushes her to opt for a vocation in preference to another; in other words it constitutes the persona of the student. Therefore,

> the transmutation of social truth into academic truth (from 'you are a petty bourgeois' to 'you work hard but lack brilliance') is not a simple game of writing of no consequence but an operation of social alchemy which confers on words their symbolic efficiency, their power to have a lasting effect on practice (Bourdieu, 1988, 207–08).

Bourdieu, however, is not suggesting here that the social position of the students in some way determines the reactions they obtain from the teachers. To say that would be to indulge either in reductionism –

that takes social distance between the two as essential markers in the transactions of education – or in a conspiracy theory – assuming that the teachers consciously victimize students despite the latter's personal competence owing to their cultural difference (backwardness). While reductionism offers a structuralist or objectivist treatment of social facts associated with the common readings of Durkheim or Marx, the difference angle tends to produce a subjectivist or constructivist understanding of the social universe employed by various schools of cultural relativism or representational theories. For Bourdieu, the 'scientific' position is somewhere in between, where objective facts and subjective concepts are in a 'dialectical' dialogue with one another.[14] 'If I had to characterize my work in two words', he once announced while speaking to his American audience, '… I would speak of constructivist structuralism or structuralist constructivism…' (Bourdieu, 1989, 14). To understand what he intends to imply here, one can refer back to the 'alchemy' of objective and subjective elements in marking the students. While being driven by a genuine demand for excellence, what 'academic' neutrality conceals within it is a field of symbolic power. It is by mobilizing the resources for such power, and by simultaneously disavowing them, that the space between the teachers and students is both constituted and condensed.

In order to characterize the dual tendencies of symbolic power Bourdieu provocatively uses the term 'symbolic capital'. Symbolic capital is understood as the 'other' of economic capital, as distinct and different in principle. Yet by incorporating the characters of capital, it is not taken as entirely detached from the deeper structure of the economy. While economic capital is driven, in principle, by the intent of maximizing self-interest, symbolic capital avowedly gets its inspiration from a neutral, disinterested quest for intrinsic value. Bourdieu shows that such claim to autonomy is both necessary and unsustainable. It is necessary for the reproduction of symbolic capital in its embodied as well as institutional forms. It is impossible since symbolic capital is homologous to economic capital; the two are entangled in a generative (if not a deterministic) relationship. However, all forms of symbolic capital – cultural, linguistic, scientific, artistic, social etc. – tend to deny their instrumentality (or attachment to the economic) by projecting some innate, neutral standards as their principles of being. Thus the object of scientific capital is presented as the discovery of 'truth', that of social capital altruistic bonding with the community, of cultural capital aesthetic taste, of linguistic capital the preservation of legitimate language and so on.

By denying that it is nothing but a 'transubstantiated' type of economic capital, symbolic capital commits 'misrecognition' or 'symbolic violence' (Bourdieu, 2004, 16).[15] Such violence is perpetrated routinely by attaching distinction to the 'noble' against the 'vulgar', much like the ritualistic split between 'sacred' and 'profane' in Durkheim. Two aspects of symbolic or cultural capital demand attention in this respect. First, while being homologous to the material or economic, the principles of cultural capital cannot be reduced to those of the economy. Economic capital can be transferred instantly, such as by the fortuitous turn of the roulette, cultural capital preciously needs time to transfer. Economic capital can be inherited as an externality; cultural capital can only be embodied: it evolves and dies with the person. To acquire cultural capital one has to 'work on oneself… with all the privation, renunciation, and sacrifice that it may entail' (Bourdieu, 2004, 18). Economic capital cannot be translated to cultural capital: money can buy cultural artefacts, but not the capacity to appropriate them in the 'right' manner. Universal schooling creates the possibility for a fairer distribution of cultural capital, but not a sufficient condition, as the economists championing human capital insist. Inequality persists because 'the scholastic yield from educational action depends on the cultural capital previously invested by the family', and on the previously existing, and unevenly distributed, social capital (Bourdieu, 2004, 17).

Second, the logic of cultural capital – its identification of 'taste' – is internally arbitrary and externally homologous to social division of power. The standards that culture set as 'noble' (as opposed to 'vulgar') cannot have an independent point of verification; its determination is based on internal classifications that reinforce taste as 'structured structure'. Those who are uninitiated, the misfit, those who misuse cultural artefacts due to a deficit in cultural capital, embrace their conditions and 'misrecognise' the arbitrary as essential. 'It is a virtue made of necessity which continuously transforms necessity into virtue by inducing 'choices' which correspond to the condition of which it is the product'. In contrast to the 'vulgar', an agent of taste 'has what he likes because he likes what he has, that is, the properties actually given… and legitimately assigned to him in the classifications' (Bourdieu, 1984, 175). Moreover, traits of cultural capital, while they appear as personal attributes, are in effect socially structured qualities betraying, however unwittingly, the predispositions of a field of power, of habitus. What the petit-bourgeois (uncultivated) touches turns into 'middle-brow' not because the 'nature' of the class so demands, but because of

> 'the very position of the petit-bourgeois in the social space, the social nature of the petit-bourgeois, which is constantly impressed on the petit-bourgeois himself… It is quite simply, the fact that legitimate culture is not made for him (and is often made against him), so that he is not made for it, and it ceases to be what it is as soon as he appropriates it… (Bourdieu, 1984, 327).

Furthermore, cultural capital is also embedded in social hierarchy as it requires 'cultivation' for acquisition, which is proportionate to the 'free time' that family of a given individual 'can provide him', 'i.e., time free from economic necessity, which is the precondition for the initial accumulation' (Bourdieu, 2004, 19). So the impoverished life of an agricultural worker, whose time is essentially aligned to subsistence labour, is unlikely to imbibe any cultural capital of distinction.

Bourdieu, in short, gives meaning to the distance between those with symbolic capital and those without. He substitutes the simplistic bipolarity between the dominant and the subaltern in social relations with a multi-polar and uneven field of power in which different forms of capital – economic, cultural, social, political – constitute specific enclaves of reciprocity between those with 'distinction' and those without. While these different fields of power stand in disjunction with each other (i.e., a group highest in cultural capital can well be an economically dominated faction of a dominant group), together they operate within a hegemonic order, that produces a set of arbitrary and artificial modes of classification which every strand of symbolic capital seeks to conceal (He expands this argument further in Bourdieu, [1992] 1996). Such concealment happens to be the precondition for the perpetuity of the hegemonic field of power. Thus sacral value of cultural capital is 'taste', while its impious interest lies in perpetuating an aesthetic endogamy.[16] Social capital claims its object as altruism and equality, while it thrives on a network of mutual recognition and benefits. Likewise, political capital remains hegemonic as long as it can obscure its material goal of exercising control behind the symbolic screen of justice and community. Social transformation happens when the profane bit of symbolic capital stands exposed, when the standards of distinction fall apart, the carefully construed schemes of classification collapses. Until such catastrophes, the distance between those with higher symbolic capital and those without is bridged only euphemistically, which effectively reinforces the distance. As Bourdieu argues:

> I have in mind what I call strategies of condescension, those strategies by which agents who occupy a higher position in one of the hierarchies of objective space symbolically deny the social distance between themselves and others, a distance which does not thereby cease to exist, thus reaping the profits of the recognition granted to a purely symbolic denegation of distance ('she is unaffected', 'he is not highbrow' or 'standoffish' etc.) which implies a recognition of distances. (The expressions I just quoted always have an implicit rider: 'she is unaffected, for a duchess', 'he is not so highbrow, for a university professor', and so on) (Bourdieu, 2004, 16).

Applying Bourdieu's conceptual matrix, especially his layered understanding of symbolic capital and its homology with social and economic hierarchies that prevailed in Paris of 1960s and 1970s to vastly different rural schools in West Bengal would be a pointless exercise unless sieved through sufficient criticality. For instance, the primary schoolteacher here is at once culturally distant and physically integral to the village society, rendering futile any pretence of students' evaluation from a standpoint of 'academic neutrality'. Here the social personage of the student – her caste, class, ethnicity, parent's education level etc. – weighs heavily and explicitly (with little 'euphemism') on the teacher's attitudes and prejudices. What is at stake here is not the problematic interaction between the Parisian elite and the provincial petit-bourgeoisie where the education system caters to popular 'strategies for converting economic capital into cultural capital' (Bourdieu, 2004, 21). Instead it is an encounter between the 'cultured' and the 'vulgar' where acculturation is more often perceived in terms of benefaction by the elite than of strategic demand of the vulgar. Due to the long history of French university's struggle for autonomy a 'very large proportion of professors' in Bourdieu's study 'refused to classify themselves in political terms' (Bourdieu, 1988, 37, 39). By contrast, in West Bengal the political preference or union affiliation of individual teachers was often a matter of public discourse.

What one can derive from Bourdieu, nonetheless, is the vital observation that in a class divided society schools – as an institution for imparting cultural capital – are designed as instruments for reproduction of social exclusion and economic hierarchy. Teachers are effectively agents for maintaining a skewed distribution of cultural capital, a form of symbolic capital, euphemized as 'academic excellence'. Bourdieu shows the difficulties that provincial petit-bourgeoisie faced in adopting 'strategies for converting economic capital into cultural capital' (Bourdieu, 2004, 21). The difficulties remained despite a 'schooling explosion' in the aftermath of large-scale industrial and urban expansion in the nineteenth century and early twentieth century France. In conditions of poverty and economic stagnation, such that prevailed in rural West Bengal, a teacher's relationship with majority under-class students was far more fraught with an 'unbridgeable' cultural hiatus, even when the teacher's intentions were 'noble'. This could only be overcome not so much by initiatives from above, but if a consorted movement by the poor and the socially excluded found success in challenging the institutional direction of the school, if a radical pressure from the margins could generate popular strategies for converting political capital into a new cultural capital, if the left could introduce a transformative social politics capable of exposing the profaneness of symbolic capital.

Instead, the left effectively reinforced the institutional design of the school, its 'symbolic aggression', as its government spent generously to meet the demands of the teaching unions, as the routine activism of a good number of teachers got the better of their commitment to the school, as in their lifestyle and income the teachers ended up marking a social distance with the rest of the village, especially in backward regions where dependence on the school teacher was maximum. It has been noted earlier how all this strained the leadership of the school teacher in the village, and how an emerging segment of petty entrepreneurs managed first to replace the teacher and thereafter to debase the left. Now it may be argued that this social distance in a rural setting did not just make the teacher ineffective as a leftwing political agent, more critically it rendered her vulnerable in the face of a growing popular wrath. To illustrate this let us listen to what the teachers themselves were saying.

Teachers' testimonies

Pratichi Trust in India, an organization that studies various indicators related to human development organized 10 workshops for the primary schoolteachers in West Bengal between March and July 2011. In these workshops the rural teachers were invited to speak among other things on the problems they face in school and in classroom, and how they try to overcome them. After sharing their experience with colleagues, Pratichi Trust invited to record their thoughts as concise written pieces. Many of these essays were later published in an edited volume titled *Kalamchari* (The Pen Drivers) (Rana, 2012, all unnamed references in parentheses drawn from this volume). 'Our questions (for the teachers) were comprehensive: what are they thinking in the recent times and how? Rather than restricting them to some narrow queries our aim was to allow them to express on issues that they considered important' (14; all translations have been done by the author).

A large number of teachers enthusiastically participated in these workshops. They wrote extensive essays, at times valuable also for their literary merit. Many were passionate, making genuine attempts to engage with serious pedagogic issues. Others were pretentious, projecting the teacher's self in rather idealistic terms. Nonetheless, 'when... they

113

began to write', what struck the editors of *Kalamchari*, was 'their deep concentration... each of them continued to write for about two hours in a meditative, contemplative mood'. When asked what he liked about the act of writing, a teacher replied: 'We never imagined that we could write our thoughts this way... it's a big opportunity for us, it allows us not just to write what we want, but also gives us a chance to evaluate ourselves' (Rana, 2012, 15).

These essays were not overtly political. Instead they tended to focus on pedagogic issues, narrated mostly through classroom events, especially the difficulties one faced in conditions not particularly conducive to teaching. The principal purpose for many was to get some recognition for the work they did in remote villages, outside the gaze of the urban public sphere. The point was to make their individual devotion, sacrifice and originality visible, to obtain the respect they deserved but often were denied. Frequently, the aim was to portray themselves in 'ideal' terms, highlighting the behaviour that they reckoned a teacher ought to have for endearing students (akin to what Bourdieu calls 'strategies of condescension'). This constitution of a moral self, however, could not be without its own politics in its broader sense of reshaping relations of power. It saw the principal goal of rural teachers as one of connecting with the students who – in a teacher's words – 'appear to come from another planet' (Ibid, 2012, 111).

In these 89 handwritten essays in Bengali, the teachers mainly talked about three or four basic constraints for reaching out to their pupils. For instance, they frequently wrote about their disliking for the 'cultural' orientation of their students, their use of 'filthy' language, their 'inappropriate' manners, or their general recalcitrance (an illustration of reinforcing the 'structured structure' as Bourdieu saw it).

A Madrasa teacher (Shrabani Saha of No. 39 Lalgola High Madrasa) from Murshidabad writes:

> Teachers try their best to raise the moral standards of the students. I am optimistic. But students stay in school only for few hours. After that, what? Where do they go? They use filthy language after the school hours, engage in gambling for which their parents are reluctant to take action. Almost every Class 4 student gambles. When

we complained to the parents, they were annoyed with us. 'But our kids don't do that during school hours', they retorted. Rather, the parents were not happy with the school as their girls spend too much time there: 'when will she get the time to roll up the bidis (country cigars)?' they ask.

Poverty routinely dragged children away from the school. The most sensitive of teachers found this as an insurmountable problem. When demand for subsistence gets the better of that for education, a teacher can only be a helpless bystander. Another Murshidabad teacher (Subimal Ghosh of Talibpur Uchcha Prathamik Bidyalay) visited the house of a Muslim brother and sister, two bright kids studying in class 4, after they stopped coming to school. He assured the parents that the school would bear the cost of their children's education as both were exceptionally bright. This made the kids go to school for a week or so, after which they stopped again. The teacher writes:

'Several weeks later, on my way to the school, I had a chance meeting with Naiim. He asked if I could send him the English textbook for Class 5. 'But what for?' I asked. 'Sir, I'd try to study at home', he answered. 'Why, then, did you stop coming to school'? Naiim replied, 'Sir, I have to get my elder sister married and also make sure that my younger brother can continue in school. I've started to earn by helping a mason. Once I learn the work I'd travel to Kerala. Where's the time for school, Sir'? I kept quiet, had no answer.

Students from different linguistic groups, speaking marginal tribal languages or dialects of Hindi in the regions bordering Jharkhand, posed another set of problems for the teachers. Some teachers tried learning the local language to communicate in the class. Thus Mohammed Jinnat Hossein who taught in a Malda school took lessons in *Santhali* from his friend, Dharma Hembram (257–58). In the same district, Sadikul Islam picked up 'the Khotta language' to 'scale the Wall of China standing between the students and myself in the class' (Ibid, 2012, 121). Most teachers, however, preferred imposing Bengali as the 'agreed' medium of instruction (a clear act of 'symbolic violence'). Some even urged the parents to 'encourage their kids to forget their mother tongue' and pick up the 'common language'. For example, Susanta Sarkar, who taught in another school in Malda district, wrote:

> Three out of four villages surrounding our school belong to the Oraon and the Mahato communities. When I first joined the school I faced real difficulties (in communicating) especially with the students in Class 1. The Oraon kids in particular couldn't follow what I said. They used to stare at me with a blank face … After a consultation with the headmaster I told the Oraon parents to meet me at the school. When they came I told them that they needed to speak with their kids in Bangla at home, just as they were doing with me. The parents were convinced that this would help their kids and promised they'd follow what I said. The language problem in our school was solved accordingly (Ibid, 2012, 139).

The teachers also wrote on the problem of tackling religious differences, particularly the difficulties that the Hindu teachers (who, as a survey has shown, were disproportionately greater in number than Muslim teachers) faced in their interaction with Muslim students. The Muslim teachers, however, maintained silence on this. Some Hindu teachers wrote that what needed to break the ice was a constant, almost a daily interaction with the Muslim parents. This ordinarily did not happen, but when it did the results were spectacular. A Muslim teacher (Muhammad Hefzur Reheman) who taught in an intensely Muslim neighbourhood recounted an occasion few days after he joined the school when a hugely popular headmaster, a Hindu, retired:

> A meeting was called on the day Mr. Abhay Mitra, the headmaster, retired. I could not believe what I saw. Parents and ordinary villagers in a backward Muslim region formed a chain and stood along a kilometre on both sides of the road. Their eyes full with tears. Why was there so much love and affection showered on Mr. Mitra? The headmaster, I was told, used to enter the village from one end calling out each child by name as he went past their houses, and after the school he met the parents whose children were absent on that day. This was a daily routine. So he developed a bonding (ekatmota) with every parent. I concluded that Abhaybabu was 100 percent successful in his work (Ibid, 2012, 116).

While these individual initiatives to sort out difficulties between different ethnic, linguistic or religious groups or to enquire about students' absenteeism were indeed laudable, one wonders what the role of the VEC was, which was meant to formally look after these things. These committees as well as the Governing Boards of the schools were now filled up by the new village notables, the rising petty entrepreneurs. Talking about his problem of choosing a medium of instruction a teacher wrote:

> The VEC hardly pays any attention to language problem of the students. Their main interest is in the money sanctioned for construction works in the school. The Secretary of my school has set up a kindergarten in his own house. Many people have told me that he insists that primary schools are worthless and that the parents should send their kids to his kindergarten. If a VEC President or a panchayat functionary makes such comments one can imagine its impact on the villagers. He incites the locals by pointing at us as 'government's party workers'!(Ibid, 2012, 192).

In spite of little institutional backing and dismal infrastructure, and an overall atmosphere of reluctance if not despair, some teachers did try to respond to their 'patriotic call' of building 'future citizens' for the country. A lady teacher (Sutapa Das) from South 24 Parganas compared her job to that of an idol-maker, who turns mounds of clay into the body of a Goddess.

> The primary teacher begins her work with a mound of soft clay... The country it seems has given its command: we have placed before you a mound of clay, now make an idol, we want a good citizen. Those of us who have got so much from our motherland cannot afford to fail in our responsibility' (Ibid, 2012, 131).

Such a sense of duty notwithstanding, the teachers clearly felt that their authority was increasingly being questioned, not just in the society at large, but more painfully inside the school. For many of them the public debate on banning corporeal punishment in schools appeared as society's lack of confidence in their ability to be good to the kids. 'If we love them, do we not have the right to discipline them'? 'Such lenience may work in cities, but can one teach in a rural school without strictly dealing with the rowdies'? In their essays they raised these questions repeatedly. Thus the same lady teacher who treated children as a 'mound of clay' wrote:

'Don't you think that even a mound of clay needs to be broken in order to bring it to shape? Only then you can create an image after your imagination, and make it presentable. We are now told not even to scold a child. But how can you make a child understand the difference between home and the school if you don't discipline her? Thanks to radio, television and newspapers, we are forbidden even to touch her.'

Then she went on to describe how teachers got even beaten up by parents on the alleged ground of 'misbehaving' with the kids:

If the parents bring charges against the teachers, verbally abuse them in unspeakable language, beat them up after the school hours in front of other villagers, how can the teachers be expected to return to the school and take classes next day? Teachers are not mechanical robots; they also have a sense of dignity… Our ancient texts tell us that students are like our children. Then why cannot we discipline our students? (Ibid, 2012, 132–33).

Another lady teacher (Shrabani Saha) lamented:

The law and the media portray the teachers almost as butchers… Psychologists allege that teachers beat up students either out of vengeance or due to their disturbed mindset. I ask these experts, are we the only mentally disturbed people around? Today if we give a boy even a light punishment, he gets back to us and warns 'I will make you rot in jail'. Who is responsible for the teacher's disgrace? …Alas, we are expected to keep our mouth shut (Ibid, 2012, 117–18).

These essays also reveal how reluctant the teachers were to manage the government's mid-day meal programme for the children in school. A major complaint was that it took a good chunk of time away from the classes, and causes distraction. However, the teachers felt obliged to continue as 'it is absolutely necessary so that the poorer kids get some nutrition and their parents find a good reason to send them to school'. Still, one cannot help getting struck by the sense of humiliation that a teacher felt as she became a target of suspicion for allegedly siphoning off money from the programme. A headmaster (Uttam Kumar Majhi, Fosco Prathamik Bidyalaya) wrote:

I think the biggest problem for a headmaster is managing the midday meal programme. People, in general, have a misconception that one can earn a lot of money from it. The teachers are routinely heckled. Any villager can threaten a teacher by falsely claiming that the students are not getting enough to eat. Or that fish or meat is not regularly served. Some allege that the primary teachers have a double earning these days, they steal from the midday meal scheme on the top of their usual salary' (Ibid, 2012, 214).

The school teacher has travelled far and wide in rural West Bengal from the early days of the Left Front to the present. From a local leader, a role model, an idealist foot soldier of the left political parties in the vast stretches of the countryside to a tormentor of children, a pilferer, a 'government's party worker'. Clearly, the teacher's 'symbolic capital' is put to severe questioning, its 'profane' character stands revealed, the carefully crafted 'standards of distinction' have collapsed, and the 'hegemonic field of power' disintegrated. Of course, the changes are exaggerated, but there is no denying that a general drift is overtly palpable across the board, turning the village school teacher into an object of ridicule and wrath, defiance and violence. Between 2007 and 2010, 23 primary school teachers were brutally killed by the 'Maoist-TMC united front' – some inside the class while they were teaching – for allegedly acting as 'police informers' in the Junglemahal region of West Bengal (*The Telegraph*, 24 September 2010). All those killed were partisans, either members or sympathizers of the left parties, principally the CPI(M). While incidents like these deserve condemnation and should warn us about the character of the new dispensation that in 2011 managed to defeat the left government, they should equally reveal the vacuity in the politics of the governmental left, which reaped huge benefits by exploiting the teachers, their idealism and social trust, with the promise of undertaking a project of social transformation (including universal education) but delivering little more than piecemeal reforms focused narrowly on winning elections.

It is impossible for the left leadership to deny anymore that the gaping hole between their promise and actual policies, between rhetoric and ground level realities, had in effect exposed those acting internuncially between the party, the government and the popular society, made them critically vulnerable and imperilled. The dramatic slide of the teacher was, therefore, but a metaphor for a tectonic shift in West Bengal's political landscape, where a groundswell of opposition stunned the left's 'machinery' and threw it into a paralytic slumber. Before analyzing the momentous collapse we now turn to the nuts and bolts of that machinery.

Endnotes

1. In 2001, West Bengal's overall literacy rate was 68.6 per cent, while it was 59 per cent among SCs, 43.4 per cent among STs, and 57.5 per cent among Muslims (Rana, 2010, 2).

2. A recent report of the National University of Educational Planning and Administration points out that of the major 16 Indian states, West Bengal ranked 10th in a composite educational development index that included all primary schools, government and private (NUEPA, 2011, 47).

3. An illustration of the severity of primary schoolteachers' poverty in the period is cited in Sarkar and Rana, 2010, 7 (footnote 16): Sarat Bose, the eminent political leader of the period, commented at the second conference of the ABPTA in 1937: 'The wages received by the primary teachers in Bengal is too small even to meet the expense of food for a dog or a cat'.

4. If one sifts through the pages of the organizational history of the ABPTA (Nikhilbongo Prathamik Sikshak Samiti 2007; Poshchimbongo Prathamik Sikshak Samiti, 2009) one cannot but be struck by the steady de-radicalization of some of its demands. For example, in 1953 the organization demanded that a minimum of 25 per cent of West Bengal's total revenue should be spent on education with at least 50 per cent of that for primary education and the union government should spend 15 per cent of its revenue on education of which 40 per cent should be for primary education. By the late 1970s, however, the organization demanded only 10 per cent of central outlay and 30 per cent of state outlay for education, without any specific demand for primary education.

5. It must be said that this bias against elementary education is an all-India phenomenon. As Mehrotra points out that despite achieving 90 per cent literacy and complete enrolment in primary education by 1900, the countries of North America, Australia, New Zealand and Europe were allocating 90 per cent of their education budget to elementary and secondary levels. 'In India the share of education spending allocated to higher education over the first 40 years since

independence was much higher (between 25 and 30 per cent) and even in the last 10 years has continued to be higher than that in industrialized countries around 1900.' (Mehrotra, 2006b, 269).

6. The proportion of teachers' salary in the expenditure of elementary education was estimated as 97 per cent in India as a whole. While it was higher than that in Indonesia (82 per cent), Malaysia (73 per cent), and Philippines (87.5 per cent), it seems to be a phenomenon not typical of any one country (Mehrotra, 2006, 31).

7. I could not find a more authentic source to verify the exact magnitude of the raise as was given in a newspaper report (*The Telegraph*, 24 September 2010). However, that the salary of school teachers increased manifold after the Left Front government came to power was corroborated by my numerous interviews with rural school teachers, some of which I include later in the chapter.

8. 'What makes the situation less than satisfactory is that in the case of both primary and secondary education, as much as 95 per cent of the total outlay goes to pay the emoluments as against 80 per cent in respect of higher education' (Singh, 1993, 1504).

9. In the 1990s, central spending on elementary education increased mainly because 'the central government finally agreed at the end of 1990s to borrow externally for elementary education. A number of Externally Aided Projects (EAPs) initiated mainly during the 1990s, with small beginnings made in the mid-1980s, focused attention of different aspects of the primary sub-sector of elementary education'. (See Mehrotra, 2006, 31)

10. Between 2001 and 2006 the number of such SSKs doubled in the state, from less than 8,000 to more than 16,000. (See Government of India, 2010, 134).

11. Government of West Bengal, Economic Review, 2007, shows that 1801 new school building and 42640 additional classrooms, and 500 Circle Resource Centres in the district sub-divisions were constructed as part of SSA. This apart, almost 10,000 units each of drinking water and toilet facilities were provided in schools. Initially, the central government funded 75 per cent of SSA, but the central share was reduced over the years and the share of the state government was increased.

12. As an evidence of the departure of privileged students from the government-run system one can refer to a survey that found disproportionate enrolment of Dalit, Adivasi and Muslim students compared to the upper caste Hindu students in government schools. The enrolment coefficient (enrolment of particular community divided by its share to the total population multiplied by 100) of the Dalit, Adivasi, Muslim and upper caste Hindu students were found as 123.9, 129.1, 119.8 and 73.8. (See Rana, 2010).

13. In the 1931 Census the Kurmis (17.8 per cent) were registered as the principal middle castes followed by Kumhars (3.1 per cent) and Telis (2.68 per cent). Among

the 'depressed classes' the most important section were the Bauris (6.69 per cent). This apart the region was home to a large tribal population such as Santals (15.5 per cent) and Bhumij (5.7 per cent). It is evident, therefore, that more than half of the region's population belonged to backward and scheduled categories. The 2001 census showed that the SC and the ST population constituted about 18 per cent each of the Purulia's population. The district had very little urban population as the share of rural population was 89.93 per cent. In 2011, the average rural literacy was 62.73 per cent – for males the literacy rate was 76.83 per cent and for females the rate was a meagre 48.06 per cent.

14. See Bourdieu, 1977 (1972), especially 'From the mechanics of the model to the dialectics of strategies', 3–9. Also Bourdieu, 1990 (1980) where he says: 'Asserting the universality and eternity of logical categories that govern the 'unconscious activity of the mind'' amounts to ignore 'the dialectic of social structures and structured, structuring dispositions through which the schemes of thought are formed and transformed' (41). Then he talks about the need to analyse the dialectic of objective structure and the structures incorporated in every practical action without which the critiques of subjectivism fall into the trap of crude structuralism, of fetishizing 'social laws'.

15. 'As I have noted', observed a commentator on Bourdieu, 'a concern with symbolic violence runs throughout Bourdieu's oeuvre. But, it is nowhere more prevalent and important to his arguments than in his works on education'. (See Schubert, 2008, 187).

16. 'Aesthetic intolerance can be terribly violent … . This means that the games of artists and aesthetes and their struggles for the monopoly of artistic legitimacy are less innocent than they seem. At stake in every struggle over art there is also the imposition of an art of living, that is, the transmutation of an arbitrary way of living into the legitimate way of life which casts every other way of living into arbitrariness. The artist's life-style is always a challenge thrown at the bourgeois life-style, which it seeks to condemn as unreal and even absurd…' (Bourdieu, 1984, 56–57).

4

MACHINERY: PARTY SOCIETY

In the last chapter we saw how in the rural public sphere the relationship between the local society and the leadership of the left changed over the years, how the school teachers – who in the early days of the Left Front were the principal agents of popular engagement at the grassroot level – eventually turned into socially distant entities, even 'enemies' of the poor and marginal groups. This transformation took place within a larger geography of power, a populated space made of intricate relationship between social classes and institutions in the countryside with its own unique characters evolving through decades of a mutative government as practice. Much of the parliamentary left's ground level politics in rural West Bengal derived its meaning and consistency from the rationale of this networked grid which may be called by the name 'party society'. Here we trace its roots, follow the genesis of its instrumentality and its eventual crisis before changing hands from the ruling left to its fiercest rivals. Born in the midst of pro-poor promises we explain below how party society metamorphosed into a dangerous outfit for reproducing social marginality and political exclusion.

The idea

Analysing the CPI(M)'s repeated electoral renewals in the light of its rhetoric of 'development', Partha Chatterjee had highlighted the mediatory nature of its politics. The left's rural developmental records were not exceptional, nor did it patronize a solid block of electorate as its client on a durable basis. Then how could it retain such a long and unprecedented electoral dominance, especially in the rural areas?

> The point is rather that a field of political transactions has been opened which is within the reach of most villagers and where matters of local interest can be negotiated and sorted out on a day-to-day basis. It is in that field that the CPI(M), with its permanently mobilized corps of workers, enjoys an advantage in the matter of the daily renewal of the legitimacy of power (Chatterjee, 1997, 160–61).

The 'field' got a theoretical expression in what Chatterjee later called 'political society' (Chatterjee, 2004). The political society consisted of the poor and the marginal population groups, which constantly strived to protect or enlarge their livelihood needs and entitlements. These groups were historically excluded from civil society due to lack of access to education, wealth and associated social and cultural capital. They were denied the basic rights of the citizen in any substantive sense. To protect their livelihood, in absence of those rights, these groups formed solidarities along the lines of kinship communities to negotiate their entitlements with the state and civil society. Such solidarities were forged to meet contingent and strategic interests of the population groups in response to specific governmental policies. A range of political manoeuvrings in India's postcolonial democracy involves management and representation of political society on a daily basis. In a state like West Bengal the CPI(M) with the help of its well-orchestrated, locally embedded and vertically connected party-machinery performed this function better than others. For most part of its long political tenure, therefore, the party remained the undisputed leader of political society in the state. 'The real story of political society', Chatterjee, expected 'must come from rural West Bengal' (Chatterjee, 2004, 64).

In a later essay, Chatterjee expanded his ideas of mediation and welfare more specifically in India's peasant society that was experiencing a rapid economic transformation (Chatterjee, 2008). He argued that though capitalist transformation dislocated the small holding peasants from their means of livelihood, the latter were not turned into a class of 'proletariat' as happened in advanced industrial countries, nor could they be absorbed into the new production economy. Advanced labour-saving technologies and restrictive immigration laws did not allow a swift induction of the workers into factories or their migration to a new world. At the same time, the Indian state could not afford to ignore this vast population group because the conditions of democracy demanded that the impact of their loss be met with some provisions for alternative livelihood means. Thus, in the economic sphere small-scale private property or 'non-corporate' capital was allowed to survive alongside large-scale 'corporate capital' with the support of a number of welfare policies (such as employment guarantee or food security schemes). The distinction between corporate and non-corporate capital largely coincided with that between civil society and political society respectively, while the former was competitive and accumulative, the latter could not survive without sharing and cooperating with as many agencies as possible. Government's welfare policies were instruments to integrate the two in the hope of a wide consensus for capitalist transformation. 'It is striking', Chatterjee observed, 'that even the CPI(M) in West Bengal, and slightly more ambiguously in Kerala, have, in practice if not in theory, joined the consensus' (Chatterjee, 2008, 57).

'Political society', as a conceptual tool, has many advantages for understanding popular politics in India's democracy. It opens ways of reading popular politics outside of legal-juridical and institutional domains of liberal government. Moreover, by focusing on the population on the society's margins, where the need for subsistence is indistinguishable from the need for popular bonding, it helps us to think beyond the binary of economy and polity, and offers a space to imagine a new, non-reductive, political economy. Crucially, political society fuses a Foucauldian notion of bio-politics – a proliferation of instruments to connect government and population – with a principal concern of postcolonial democracy: strategic use of welfare to include the excluded. However, Chatterjee drew almost all his concrete empirical cases of political society from the urban or semi-urban milieus: pavement hawkers, shanty-town dwellers, book-binders, or devotees believing in the reincarnation of their spiritual leader. Rural West Bengal – where he said the 'real story of political society must come from' – remained largely unattended in his formulation.

I think that although largely explanatory, formations of political society do not help us to adequately understand the changes underway in rural West Bengal. The social and political conditions obtained here were somewhat different from what was found in the urban settings. Firstly, political parties dominated the socio-political sphere of rural West Bengal to the extent that other channels of public transactions were either weak or non-existent. As a result it was difficult for the rural population to draw assistance from any agency other than these parties. Secondly, there had been a clear distinction between the elements of local society and their pattern of representation by political parties in rural West Bengal. While the society had deep lines of division along caste, religion or ethnicity, the political parties tended not to highlight these differences. Thirdly, while the CPI(M) or any of its coalition partners dominated a vast majority of rural localities in most of the Left Front years, they were constantly challenged by rival parties, however small in presence. Partisan contestation on almost every political issue had not only been frequent, more critically, all types of opposition (familial, social or cultural) rapidly assumed partisan forms. Fourthly, political parties – at least until recently – acted as accepted moral guardians in the public life of society and the private lives of families. It was not rare to solicit intervention of the parties even in the most intimate and private affairs. Finally, even government institutions – such as the panchayat – were intertwined with the political parties. We have seen in chapter 1 how frequent incursions by the political parties into the institutional norms of these bodies eroded their capacity to take independent decisions (Veron et al., 2003).

Given the ubiquitous presence and prominence of political parties and their supreme mediatory role in rural West Bengal a specific kind of sociability – which I call 'party society' – emerged in the state. Party society is the modular form of political society in West Bengal's countryside. A deeper look into the operations of party society, however, reveals some areas of stark contrast with the principles of political society.

While population groups in political society tend to strategically congeal around shared interests in the shape of a community, in the conditions of party society they try to bond into a political group in opposition to other groups, thereby splitting settled communities on partisan lines. In political society, parties compete to offer their managerial skills, connections and networks as a day-to-day affair to protect the livelihood demands of the population. Since they function within a larger matrix of other available agencies of civil society and the state, there is a limit to which the political parties can make electoral calculations their exclusive or even primary consideration for action. In party society, on the other hand, the overriding goal is to protect the constituency of a party's support-base and expand it periodically from election to election. So elections are central to party society. Moreover, political society operates through modes that are contingent and flexible, and uses power strategically with considerably large institutional options on offer. By contrast, though schools, cooperatives, clubs etc are important sites for party society, its principal institutional format is the panchayat. This can have very different political implications.

Political change

If party society truly offers us a more appropriate conceptual tool to understand West Bengal's rural politics, we are faced with a series of specific queries. How does party society consolidate itself? What are its modes of persuasion and coercion? What relationship does it share with West Bengal's left politics? Is it autonomous of class, caste, religious or ethnic divisions? What are the major challenges it faces today? This section, will address some of these questions on the basis, primarily, of three field-based studies of political change in six villages that Rajarshi Dasgupta, Manabi Majumdar and myself conducted in 2005–06, immediately before a series of rural protests shook the state and unsettled the ruling coalition (Dasgupta, 2009; Majumdar, 2009; Bhattacharyya, 2009a). These six villages were Sitai (Cooch Behar), Uttar Harishchandrapur (Malda), Jagatpur (South 24 Parganas), Chatma (Purulia), Galsi

(Bardhaman) and Adhata (North 24 Parganas). My purpose in this chapter is very different from what these studies originally intended. I will draw empirical instances from them as illustrations to feed into my conceptual framework and, simultaneously, use my framework to tease out different meanings for some of these instances.

How did party society evolve? Party society had its roots in the violent class-based movements of the poor peasants as they fought against the domination of the landlords. We recorded in chapter 1 how the left parties facilitated these movements for food, land, security of tenure, and freedom from excessive rent and high rates of interests, to create new opportunities for 'the intrusion of the excluded'. The peasants rose against the foundations of an agrarian society based on structurally unequal and economically exploitative relations of power. The movements combined the issues of material deprivations and symbolic representation as the rural poor, belonging mainly to Dalit, tribal or minority communities were mobilized for social justice against indignity, humiliation and segregation. The left parties, under the circumstances, offered them a more disciplined, equal and democratic alternative. So the story of party-society is inseparable from the story of peasant movements in the state, from the communists' organizational support to such movements, and the key role that the left activists played in them.

The Communist Party's ascendancy in the rural society was made possible by sacrifice and dedication of a group of left leaders who almost always came to the village from outside and mobilized the peasants on some local issues of economic exploitation or social exclusion. These young and educated 'comrades' who gave up the comforts of an urban life and career in their commitment to take up 'the cause' were both a source of inspiration as well as transformation.[1] In Adhata, for instance, Hemanta Ghosal and Ashok Bose who were leaders of the tebhaga movement came and stayed when the CPI launched a campaign against the nagade system of labour-hiring in the late 1950s (Bhattacharyya, 2009a, 65). In Sitai, Bijay Ray, the Forward Bloc leader of the 'food movement' (1959–60) played a vital role in the left's gaining popularity in the region (Dasgupta, 2009, 73). In Kalipur village of Hooghly district, Pakhi Murmu, an elderly tribal leader was quoted as recounting: 'Those days were different when we established the party here by shedding our blood. We were tortured severely by the Congress, the zamindars, and the police. The leaders were also made of different stuff then'. By contrast, for Murmu, politics in the recent times had turned into 'a kind of entertainment' (Roy, 2009, 120). Ruud's village study in Bardhaman also showed how the left leaders expanded their popular base by deploying 'symbolic capital' mobilized not in the spirit of accumulation, but of personal sacrifice to establish cultural elements of power with a lasting effect (Ruud, 2003, 162).

Once elected to power in 1977, as shown in chapter 2, the left parties started implementing legal reforms – land reforms and decentralization – that created scope for better social condition for the poor. These initiatives – undoubtedly ahead of what was happening in most other Indian states in the late 1970s – would soon have faltered if these parties did not act on the strength of a strong organization and a determined ideology as genuine custodians of the legal rights of the beneficiaries. While both land reforms and panchayat were critical legislative steps, they also clearly demonstrated the limits of how far one could deliver simply by relying on law (Bhattacharyya, 1994). It soon became evident that reform laws do not work unless backed by a robust political will (by 'lathi, guns and flags' as an old landless labourer mentioned) at the ground level. The local chieftains, lower bureaucracy and the landed classes violently opposed these moves. A strong and ideologically coherent organization of the left parties was necessary to counter the ferocity of their resistance. The need was to present the differentially articulated 'democratic demands' of a spectrum of rural classes as a common opposition inscribed on an 'equivalential' political chain that Ernesto Laclau, in his study on the logic of populism, calls universalistic 'popular demands' (Laclau, 2005, 83-93). As the CPI(M) had the most cogent organizational 'machinery' among the left parties, a strict political discipline, and a dedicated bunch of workers who placed idealism above crass individual interests, it could push democratic demands in a large variety of fronts.

With a reform-oriented political force beginning to mediate between rural classes and communities in such a big way, the character of social and political interaction in the village changed substantially. Now political parties, assuming centrality in the rural public life, started to foreshadow other actors – such as caste and religious organizations, sports and social welfare clubs, as well as the collectives of the landed classes – who for long could exercise effective control over local societies on account of their easy access to cash and their ability to influence the police and the bureaucracy. The 'party' began to play a steering role in almost every sphere of social life ranging from the panchayat to the school, from the sports clubs to the family. This party-driven governmentalization of the local in absence of localization of the government, as already discussed at length in chapter 1, indeed affected the autonomy of the social. Few, however, complained as the left acted as vital facilitators for a vast majority of the poor to gain their first entry into the portals of powerful administrative bodies. The underprivileged and illiterate rural population also found in these parties an instrument to deal with the complex web of regulations and laws. Most importantly, they needed these parties to protect their newly won rights and entitlements achieved with sweat and blood, if not legally then by the deployment of the force of number. Not surprisingly, the rural poor perceived such consolidation of party society as a favourable change of regime.

That party society marked a new political phase in the life of the peasants became apparent in the course of our interviews with particularly the elderly people in the villages. The Dalits in Galsi frequently drew a clear line of distinction between 'the past' and 'the time since' the Left Front was formed. It is not that 'the past' was dark, and the 'time since' uniformly good, a phase of all-round prosperity and protection of all basic rights. It was far from that. People recounted instances of betrayal which at times made the left's pro-poor rhetoric sound either hollow, not backed by enough action on the ground, or ritualistic, in which actions – such as the strikes of the landless for higher wages – were a matter of routine performance merely to appear credible. The 'time since', nevertheless, made an unmistakable sense of difference. Deenabandhu Majhi, a sharecropper in his mid 50s who also doubled up as a gharami (builder of mud houses), and an elected member of the Galsi panchayat told us how he worked as a munish (agricultural worker) for the upper caste babus for 12 hours a day for a meagre ₹ 12 and a sher of rice or often less. 'I was offered my khoraki (meal) in broken utensils that the members of the babu's family wouldn't even touch'. Though beaten up under any pretext, people like him were 'grateful' to the babus for the short-term dadan (advances) they offered – the going monthly interest rates were often as high as 100 per cent. He believed that his conditions had doubtless improved once a 'garib-dorodi-dal' (literally, a party sympathetic to the poor) came to power. Deenabandhu's tale was typical of a generation of agricultural workers and poor sharecroppers who were at least in their 20s in the 1970s. Three decades later, however, his needs had changed: 'The party should pay more attention to the education of our kids', he asserted, 'that's the only way we can climb the steps of society' (Bhattacharyya, 2009a, 63).

Such changes in the status of the poor, and the growing sense of dignity, were associated with the rise of the party in Adhata as well. Here a repressive system of labour contract – nagade – demanded almost a complete submission of the agricultural worker to his landlord with little possibility for a wage hike or mobility. Resembling bonded labour in agriculture, the nagade worker was typically either a poor namasudra or a landless Muslim peasant, and the employer an upper caste Hindu or a Muslim landlord frequently aligned to the Congress party. Though it was unclear exactly when the system ceased, or may be because no such clear dateline existed, the elderly poor in the village associated the system and its lack of freedom with the 'previous regime'. The 'new regime', by contrast, was one of better wages, of moderate improvement in the living standards and, most importantly, of the replacement of the landlord's power by the institutional authority of the panchayat. Majumdar has observed that the change in the villages she studied was perceived as 'the eclipse of the erstwhile feudal ethos of power, yielding place to institutional politics with a broader social base' (Majumdar, 2009, 89). In Galsi, a member of an upper caste landed family, which had lost its pre-eminence after the left reforms, vented his anger rather crisply: 'Democracy has turned things upside down: the lower classes are now the rulers and the middle classes their agents!' ('nichu sreni raja hoechhe, modhyobittwa hoechhe dalaal') (Bhattacharyya, 2009a, 61).

Interestingly, in the village interviews, this change in regime – or what I call the making of party society – was narrated through the prism of a troubled relationship between the locally dominant families. We recorded a number of such intriguing stories of conspiracy, falsity and injustice. What we found fascinating was how these stories, their stray pieces and disjointed imageries, captured a more profound and systematic change underway in the institutional domain of rural politics, how by way of narrating particular relationships between some families in the village they ended up projecting a larger picture of partisan disputes and political differences. Earlier, the dominant families indeed supported rival political parties. However, their social standing rather than their partisan identity was the decisive factor in the way they were treated by the state and its institutions, the police or the local bureaucracy. In the new regime, on the contrary, the partisan identity of a family critically tended to override the correlates of status and social position of a family or a group in the village society.

Take the case of the Duttas, a powerful landowning family in Galsi, who wielded enormous influence by combining coercion (falsely implicating rivals, subjecting them to police torture) and benevolence (spending for community welfare, offering loans, or repairing the local temple). The Congress party put such influence to good use: the Duttas helped the party with men and money before every election. The principal rival of the Duttas was the Ganguly family. Some 50 years ago (mid-1960s), when Anupam Ganguly was just 17 he formed a dal (group) with Srijib and Debdas – the sons of the local priest Dayaram Mishra – to oppose the 'highhandedness' of the Dattas. The Dattas, in turn, slapped a case of robbery against the three and tried to get them arrested by the police. The case fell because nobody could be convinced – not even the police – that Dayaram's sons, widely reckoned as 'nice fellows', could have any criminal association. On another occasion, in 1972, some people were caught while stealing fish from Ganguly's pond. Anupam and some of his friends beat them up, and handed them over to the police. When one of them – a man in his 20s – later died of his injuries, some Congress supporters brought a case of murder against Anupam and his friends. The local police, however, helped the latter escape as they had a 'good' social standing in the village. On both occasions, all those involved belonged to locally influential families and the police action was more in tune with the 'general opinion' of the village, rendering partisan affiliations of little consequence (Bhattacharyya, 2009a, 62).

When Gangulys replaced the Duttas as the most influential family in the locality, it was symptomatic of a deeper structural change in the mode of social power in rural West Bengal. Unlike the Duttas, who were only moderately educated and, therefore, almost entirely dependent on their income from land, some male members of the Ganguly family had college and university degrees, some were even employed in government services. So the Left Front's land ceiling laws hit the Duttas more acutely than the Gangulys. Active in the CPI(M)'s students' or employees' unions, some young members of the Ganguly family were well-versed in organizational politics, and were equipped to set up the party in the village. In the new scenario, their political network proved vital; local influence was no more an obvious outcome of large landed estates. Although caste and economic hierarchy remained entrenched in the local society, power now was also an effect of organization and popular endorsement. Leadership now shifted to a new group of elite less dependent on extractions from land and more oriented to educational and cultural capital – typified in the figure of the rural schoolteacher – who claimed to represent the under-classes. Agricultural workers or various Dalit groups could not stake claims to leadership positions within the village, yet they experienced a change in their location within the matrix of power. With the village beginning to get bounded in a web of local governmental formalities, education and the resultant ability to work with administrative regulations, as seen in chapter 3, became a new marker of distinction.

Thus, party society was born at the conjuncture of popular movements and governmental reforms, at the moment of reconciling differential struggles of peasant classes with the equivalential claims – social, economic and political – of the rural poor and of adopting a number of concrete administrative measures to respond to these claims. In addition to political benefits that the left accrued from the moment, it also opened an opportunity for social exchange between the CPI(M) and bulk of its popular constituency: the sharecroppers and the agricultural workers, a majority of whom were Dalits and Muslims. In three out of five general elections between 2001 and 2011, around 55 per cent SC votes on an average went in favour of the left parties (See Appendix 1). At the same time, however, as shown in chapter 1, the higher one moved on the ladder of elected governmental functionaries, the lower had been the representation of the scheduled classes, the proportion of higher castes rising exponentially. We explained this sustained support for the left parties by the lower castes despite insufficient representation in the governmental bodies as an outcome of the left's ability to deliver material benefits to these segments while strategically avoiding a serious engagement with the inner structures of social hierarchy. Caste, in the left's scheme, stood for class, deserving no special treatment or affirmative measures other than a 'war against poverty'. This, as we saw, helped the left spread out fast establishing a chain of linkages between various segments in the rural society but also spread out thin as its overtly political face held out only a limited social appeal for the under-classes. In chapter 3 we have seen how the initial moment of intimacy between the rural society and the local leadership of the left – epitomized in the popular figure of the rural school teacher – eventually ended in an unbridgeable social distance, marked by a rising conflict of interests over both material and symbolic capital overshadowing the collective spirit of the community.

Initially, therefore, even when the Dalits felt estranged by the top leadership of the left parties, which was overwhelmingly upper caste, they never publicly reckoned this as a hindrance for achieving larger social equality. In both Adhata and Galsi, the bulk of the namasudra, bagdi, or kaibarta peasants were with the CPI(M), although the party's local leadership had few prominent Dalits.[2] The party, in turn, infused with the radical rhetoric of 'class struggle', saw society as a potential subject of distributive reform to 'objectively' resolve the issues of social hierarchy. As late as in the parliamentary elections of 2004, a large sample survey conducted in the state showed that the left parties received Dalit (57 per cent), Other Backward Classes or OBC (55 per cent) and Muslim (45 per cent) votes far above their political rivals. In fact, such massive support at least from the OBCs carried an element of surprise, as West Bengal was among the last state governments to recognize the OBC as an official category (Bhattacharyya, 2009b, 331). As a reformist force though the left could not transcend any community identity (such as caste-based, ethnic or religious), it rendered it largely 'invisible' – at least for three long decades – in the organized domain of state politics.

Crucial to the making of party society, therefore, was something akin to the hegemonic moment of the reformist party in the Gramscian sense, where consent was deployed over coercion, persuasive politics over regulatory idioms of power, and moral force of the community over the might of the sovereign state.[3] In effect, it helped convert a volatile people into a systematized, manageable population, extending and deepening the technological hold of government over society. The hegemonic moment, as elaborated in chapter 1, was coeval to the making of government as practice and, just like the latter, had a limited lifespan. As maintaining social peace in the countryside became the overriding agenda for the left, the earlier conjunction of movement and reform gave way to a more accommodative approach to ongoing social and economic injustice. The earlier balance between idealism and pragmatism now made room for various strategic compromises, reducing the hegemonic party society (that largely succeeded in representing the particular interests of the rural poor as an impossible whole, which Laclau calls an 'empty signifier') to a mere instrument to cogulate the flow of differential class interests, a device for enforcing a reconciliation of the irreconcilable. Striking a popular middle ground now became a perennial anxiety of the left. Despite such changes, the moral resources of party society lasted enough to produce succeeding electoral renewals for several years. The 'permanent incumbency' of the left became another unique mark of West Bengal's party society withstanding for decades Indian democracy's iron law of periodic regime change.

The crisis

What caused instability in party society and how did it recast the political? Party society, under the conditions in which it was born, was destined to die young. Once established, it faced a classic dilemma. On the one hand, it was unable to reproduce its initial conditions of being; it could not regain the spirit of movement as governing the population on institutional lines became its primary objective. On the other hand, this inability steadily, but surely, pushed the organized domain of politics away from the social mode of power and closer to the structural logic of state power. While the former was based on a popular solidarity for establishing rights and entitlements over material and non-material objects, the latter was highly formalized, with a set of established legal-rational norms, and driven by the force of law rather than consent. This steadily undermined the hegemonic appeal of the party, which now converged with the statist logic in the moment of passive revolution of capital seeking to appropriate in the name of accommodation, integrate in the name of inclusion, homogenize in the name of normalization, target policies in the name of identification. Its energy to counter the slide, to stop the alienation of the party from the society, to resist its increasing étatisation, sapped. The parliamentary left strove to tide it over by clutching on to its populist rhetoric (whose linkages with the left's early ideological priorities was getting increasingly weak), hoisting it as a screen before the masses. Such a screen, however, also had a short life span.

Various factors worked together to dissolve the screen. Detached from a movement and comfortable with the munificence of administrative power, a section of the party's leadership acquired bureaucratic habits of conducting itself, keeping restricted to strict limits of the permissible without any initiative to push boundaries of the possible. Various corrupt and accumulative tendencies thrived, and the reformist party's organic linkage with the everyday lives of the masses and communities snapped. Over the years, governmental institutions (such as the panchayat), which once helped the party to innovatively respond to popular demands, despite several attempts of administrative reforms, became dated and ineffective. They not only failed to handle new aspirations and demands of the population; what is worse, for maintaining order and peace and enforcing its control, the party became non-participatory and secretive, often acting in contravention to the welfare of the population.

In the realm of praxis, the reformist party faced an acute crisis: its interventions became increasingly indefensible from its professed ideology. In the short run, the gap was filled by vacuous rhetoric; in the medium run, by pragmatism; in the long run, by a complete lack of imagination. Such deficiencies became starkly visible in the most dynamic social sphere: the economy. Especially in the context of the strengthening of market-forces in local society (commercialization of the peasant economy), and their spread across the national economy (to shrink the state and the public sector), the imprudence of the reformist party was glaring. In the post land reforms local economy it failed to build any mechanism for monitoring the unregulated cash-nexus; in the market-driven global economy it virtually turned itself into an apologist for corporate capital. All these, in conjunction, left the carefully crafted discursive screen of the old reformist party in tatters.

As people started to see through the screen, the organic link between the reformist party and the local society began to disappear, triggering off a series of processes over which the party had little control. The social groups realized that the party had lost the moral authority to represent them. They now found the proximity of the party to be intrusive, totalizing, and threatening for their newly sensitized autonomy. Once the party began to suffer from a deficit of legitimacy, the social groups started their search for substitutes, to enable them continue their transactions with the governmental processes in the organized realm of politics. Such substitutes could be alternative political parties, or caste and religious associations, or a combination of both.[4] In response, the reformist party attempted either to retain a sense of purpose by drawing from the moral resources of the past and inducing the promise of 'development' for the future – or deployed a politics of sheer force in the form of arrogance, violence and suppression, putting the state machinery on an overdrive to 'manage' an increasingly defiant population. Such responses, however, instead of bridging the gulf between the population groups and the government, widened it further. Particularly critical was the policy that involved large-scale displacement or dispossession of the peasant population, as we shall see in chapter 5. With the party's ability to negotiate taking a back seat, its politics of force made headway, pushing the party further into the spiral of a legitimacy crisis. A party of hegemony eventually transformed into a party of violation.

Violations and violence

In our village studies, conducted before the major protests against the government's acquisition of peasants' land in the state, we came across several instances that can suitably be interpreted as multiple symptoms of such violations. To understand the transformation of the villages, I will mention here a few instances from three different institutional spheres of rural society – the public sphere of the school, the administrative sphere of the panchayat, and the productive sphere of agricultural land. All three stories indicated a troubled relationship between the organized domain of politics, which we identify through the idiom of 'the party' in post-1977 West Bengal, and the institutional domain of the rural localities.

It is widely argued that schools are not just socio-cultural institutions, but also political instruments and the school teachers, as seen in the previous chapter, are key political actors in rural West Bengal. We have mentioned already how the reformist left found popular trust in teachers useful during the initial years of its spread, and how such a pillar of authority over the years became unstable. Once the teachers were found making profit from their political capital, it took little time before the notional autonomy of the school crumbled and particular schools were singled out for partisan treatment. In Rishi Bankim village a schoolteacher complained that a building grant of ₹140,000 was denied to the local secondary school, just because the School Board had majority members from the opposition parties. He went on to list other discriminations, including denial of contributions from MPLAD (MP Local Area Development) and MLALAD (MLA Local Area Development) funds, keeping teachers' positions vacant for years despite repeated appeals, and the Block Development Officer's lack of initiative to provide drinking water for 900 odd students (Majumdar, 2009, 84–85). In Adhata, we got some details from a local TMC leader the extent to which the political parties interfered into the affairs of the school. According to him, a local committee member of the CPI(M) was known in the locality for finding suitable 'duplicates' to sit for the Board examinations, a practice that nobody dared to stop. In the School Committee elections, a candidate for the Secretary's position was invariably a nominee from a political party, and since the parents were the voters, the parties competed to enrol children from their 'trusted' families. In some villages the finger of accusation for these violations pointed at the left parties, in some other villages at the TMC. 'Party' mattered, its affiliation notwithstanding.

Without the panchayat, as discussed in chapters 1 and 2, several provisions of the land reform laws could not have been implemented. The institution, because it organized the village into a geography of representation, had tremendous potential for creating a space for engaging and participatory debates over the complex and everyday issues of welfare and development. Instead, something very different happened. Participation was reduced to staged-attendance, debates to commands, and committees to facets of partisan directives. Instead of enacting self-government, the panchayat was eventually turned into an extension of bureaucracy under partisan control. We have several examples to draw from our village studies. In Galsi, we witnessed a crucial Gram Sansad meeting in which the Village Development Council (VDC) was constituted. The meeting, attended by about 45 people, was presided over by the pradhan in presence of the elected member from the booth. Though the villagers were expected to propose names for the VDC, they did not. The pradhan read out names from a piece of paper, and those present simply raised their hands to ratify the list. Of the 20 members chosen, 10 were very close to the CPI(M). In Harishchandrapur, Tajkera Begum was elected as the pradhan because the seat was reserved for women; it was her husband who clearly acted as the de facto pradhan, directing each of her steps. In the same village we were told that political parties prefer not to offer important panchayat positions to competent women functionaries, lest they refuse to listen to their male leaders. Thus, women like Muslima Bibi and Dilera Bibi, who were known in the locality for being articulate and upright, were eternally left out (Dasgupta, 2009, 80). During another survey in rural West Bengal the author came across a curious coinage, the 'pradhan chalak', literally one who drives the pradhan (Centre for Studies in Social Sciences, 2006, 129). The 'driver' was invariably the local leader of a 'party'.

Land had always been a politically contested issue. As shown in chapter 2, land reforms discontinued the process of widespread de-peasantization, which had been a result of gross violation of ceiling and tenancy laws by landlords during the pre-left Congress regime. To jog our memory, while the reforms enlarged the scope of small peasant holding and enhanced crop intensity with massive escalation in ground water irrigation generating an agrarian growth in the early 1990s, eventually the rising input costs, receding fertility, declining land-man ratio and a depressed market ate into the income from land as agriculture entered a long period of impasse. Simultaneously, in many places of southern West Bengal, land turned into an attractive commodity for trade frequently for non-agricultural and speculative purposes. In the villages we studied, land was being bought and sold at a high volume through murky dealings, especially in places that were close to urban settlements or highways. Let me give a somewhat detailed account of a tussle between two CPI(M) factions over a fraught piece of barga (sharecropped) land in Adhata, a clear illustration of how the left's orientation was changing in the face of a rapidly transforming economy at the ground level.

The dispute was over Ashok Krishna Dutta's land (about 20 bighas or 6.6 acres) next to National Highway 34. Ashok Krishna, an influential Congress leader, stayed elsewhere, and Haladhar Karmakar, his employee, supervised the property. Haladhar rented it out to 11 sharecroppers (5 tribal, 3 Dalit and 3 Muslim) all of whom were recorded by the government. A section of CPI(M) 'workers' (whom another section called 'mere voting supporters') contacted Ashok Krishna and persuaded him to sell the land to a Barasat-based real estate promoter, Satya Sen, who agreed to buy it for ₹ 16 lakhs and made a prompt advance payment of ₹ 30,000. The promoter tried to negotiate directly with the tenants. When the latter refused to even talk, Satya contacted Prashanta Biswas, the CPI(M) pradhan of the village panchayat, who had considerable influence over the bargadars. Prashanta also refused to mediate, calling the deal 'illegal'. After repeated appeals from Satya, Prashanta agreed to reconsider only if a factory was built on the plot and jobs assured to all the sharecroppers. In addition, he demanded that the promoter paid a sum of ₹ 32 lakhs to the tenants, as the market price of the plot was estimated to be more than ₹ 60 lakhs.

Satya Sen allegedly had very different plans. He wanted to split the land into small plots for housing. While claiming that a factory was being planned he took other initiatives. He received the power of attorney for the property and slapped a case against the share tenants before the Block Land Revenue Office (BLRO) for alleged non-payment of dues (case no. 19/2002). If the case could be proved, the sharecroppers would have lost their tenancy rights. The BLR officer made an enquiry (on 26 December 2002) to which the tenants claimed that they made regular payment to Haladhar. Though Haladhar denied the officer saw through the design and instead of taking action against the sharecroppers decided to re-record them. The number of registered sharecroppers on the disputed land went up from 11 to 13.

When the legal attempts failed, Satya used other means. He started to allure the tribal sharecroppers promising ₹ 30,000 for every bigha (a tenth of the market-rate). Eventually seven of them succumbed and 'sold' their land, three accepted a part payment while three other refused. When Prashanta learnt about it, he persuaded those who had accepted partial payment to return the money. As a ruse, Satya Sen visited the village with some officials of a biscuit manufacturing company as 'potential investors', but Prashanta declined to meet them. The promoter subsequently took control of the land he 'purchased' from seven bargadars and made a makeshift shade on it. When Prashanta with some of his followers went to pull down the structure, Satya sent a large number of armed goons. At the time of fieldwork, a stalemate continued with possibilities of a violent clash imminent. We were told that a faction of the CPI(M)'s district leadership

(Amitabha Bose and Amitabha Nandi) was backing Prashanta, while Satya Sen received support from a rival faction (Subhas Chakraborty).

Superseding control

From these field accounts, it was possible to discern a change taking place in the character of party society in West Bengal. From a unified, hegemonic and reformist force, it was sliding into a coercive, managerial and factional mechanism devoted primarily to maintain a stable constituency of support in periodic elections. Another change was also apparent: the left was losing its grip over party society as the oppositional forces were slowly gaining ground. Much of this I will discuss in the next chapter. Here, I pick up an incident that took place in a period of in-between limbo, when a regime was dying while a new one was yet to take its place within the lingering mode of rural politics.

A massive popular unrest broke out against the corrupt ration shop owners (known as 'dealers') between July and September, 2007. Kumar Rana and I visited many of the villages that had experienced peaceful as well as violent protests against the dealers.[5] Many ration dealers routinely sold part of the subsidized wheat they procured from the government in the open market. The part that was sold this way was meant for the relatively well-off section of the villagers, known as Above Poverty Line or APL in government parlance, who seldom collected wheat from the ration shops, preferring to purchase better quality grain from the market. With a sudden rise in the price of wheat that year, these people decided to buy their quota from the ration shops. They demanded not just their current entitlement, but also their dues for the previous eleven months. When the dealers failed to deliver, these locally powerful men mobilized a sizeable support, marched to the ration dealers' house, insisted on getting the outstanding amount, imposed a steep fine and, in some cases, turned violent, assaulted the dealers, ransacked their property and even torched it. In some places the police retaliated, fired at the crowd causing injuries, even death. The agitators forced the dealers to sign on stamped court papers agreeing to pay a high monetary compensation, they sent complaint letters to district and block officials, boycotted party leaders who sought to protect the ration dealers, and compelled the police to register cases against them. Signs were clear that the left's ability to control party society and maintain social calm was put under a severe stress.

In July, rumours spread in Khiruli village of Birbhum district that in a neighbouring village, a ration dealer was forced by the local people to sell wheat at a reduced price as penalty for denying the APL population their dues. It was also reported that the dealer was forced to pay a hefty compensation in cash to all village households. The TMC, the Socialist Unity Centre of India (Communist) or SUCI(C) and the Jamiyat-e-Ulema-e-Hind in Khiruli wanted similar compensation from the local dealer. The dealer went to the CPI(M) for protection. The CPI(M) insisted that no cash should be distributed but asked the dealer to pay back by selling wheat to the villagers at a reduced price. After releasing some additional grain for two months the dealer stopped paying any compensation. The locals were seething in anger, though when we visited the village the initial drive for collective action had largely waned.

A similar pattern was witnessed in Jadabpur village of the same district. Rumours spread from other villages, the villagers here demanded compensation both in cash as well as in kind at a reduced price. The CPI(M) attempted reconciliation by opposing any demand for compensation by cash. Unlike in Khirluli, in Jadabpur a good number of APL families had been regularly procuring wheat from the ration shop, this took the steam out of the demand for compensation. A 'peace committee' was set up in the village where the younger members insisted on taking a 'drastic action' against the dealer while two elderly gentlemen in the committee tried a 'balanced' approach. Finally, the dealer was forced to compensate by selling wheat at a reduced price. In his interview with us the dealer said that 'only the CPI(M) families' in the village stayed away from purchasing wheat at a concessional rate.

In Abinashpur, a Birbhum village with a high proportion of Muslim and SC inhabitants, the dealer lived in a large house, and was notorious for mistreating the local poor. The locality was a TMC stronghold though the panchayat was still under the control of the CPI(M). In September

143

2007, emboldened by similar rumours from neighbouring villages, people here also forced the local dealer to sign on a stamped court paper carrying a promise of ₹250 as compensation to every ration card holder in addition to wheat at a reduced price. When the dealer refused to pay the cash, the locals gheraoed (encircled) his house and smashed his windowpanes. The dealer collected the district food controller and the head of the local police station who tried to pacify the agitators insisting that any compensation by cash was illegal. Still, the crowd, in presence of the officials, got him to sign another such stamp paper, 'agreeing' to pay ₹150 instead. Before any payment could be made the dealer fell seriously ill and got his dealership cancelled.

What happened in Radhamohanpur village in Bankura district was somewhat different. Here the protest took a turn directly against the CPI(M). On a Sunday (16 September 2007) morning a group of agitated villagers started shouting slogans against the 'corrupt' local dealer. On the same day, the CPI(M) was having its 'local committee' meeting on the playground of a higher secondary school, where district leaders were also present. Suddenly, the crowd marched to the school and demanded that the pradhan of the village panchayat, who was also attending the meeting, talked to them. People believed that the dealer could not have carried his corrupt practices without the complicity of the pradhan. When the pradhan refused to have any discussion with the agitators, the latter turned violent. They ransacked the venue of the meeting before the party workers chased them away. When the police arrived to clear the area, people started pelting stones. The police allegedly shot at the crowd, injuring two, one of them a student, an onlooker. The incident enraged the locals, who were on the boil even during our visit a couple of weeks later. What surprised many was that the poor villagers could actually muster the courage to take on the mighty CPI(M), which got both its pradhan and the MLA elected from the constituency. Though it appeared as a spontaneous outburst of the local protesters, it was driven mainly by a longstanding belief that the party was in league with corruption and was indifferent to the burning issues of price rise or irregular supplies in the public distribution system.

These incidents, I repeat, were indicative of a transitory period when an occupant in party society was losing its grip and another was yet to consolidate. They displayed all signs of confusion, anxiety and uncertainty, characteristics of a period of transmutation. First, the left's organized and disciplined channels of communication, which were known for carrying vital and useful information to the population groups in the high noon of its government as practice, now stood in a wreck. People tended to rely more on rumours – as a supplement for public information – which invariably propelled them to protest. Rumours, as Anjan Ghosh put it, 'are anonymously generated, unverifiable speeches which flourish in situations where there is a lack of information' (Ghosh, 2007, 2). With their typical ambivalence rumours represent a discourse of the subaltern meant to confound the dominant power. Ranajit Guha in his study of peasant insurgency in colonial India treated rumours as 'insurgent communication', simultaneously a subversive and a parallel discourse to power. People in the villages we visited got into action in response to some verbal and non-verifiable news that filtered in from other villages where the dealers allegedly were compelled into paying up compensation. They were driven by something akin to the 'force of the example' that George Rudé has so graphically shown to be sequentially present in the Corn Riots of 1775 in the Paris region (Rudé, 1964, 29). The swiftness with which such rumours spread and the agility with which the villagers reacted, confounded the district and block officials as well as the workers of the major political parties.

Second, the protest against corruption in the public distribution system cannot be treated in isolation from other agitations underway in Bhangar, Singur and Nandigram. In all these cases people rose, among other things, against indifference of the state administration that the party in power refused to address. Consequently, the state acted in a thoroughly bureaucratic and highhanded manner disregarding all local democratic impulses. The events signified a reversal of what the left had introduced with the launching of three-tier panchayat system. Such resurrection of bureaucratic apparatuses in implementing government policies had a regrettable influence on the functioning of all major political parties, most acutely of the parliamentary left. In these protests against the dealers, as we saw, people themselves took the initiative, the political parties were forced to follow people's mood.

Third, although the APL population led the popular unrest, some poor also belonged to the group due to 'inclusion error' (according to an estimate as many as 30 per cent in the APL list should have been considered as BPL). In fact, the sharp rise in the price of wheat and corresponding non-availability from 'fair price shops' hit the poor the hardest. Though most of them had been collecting their quota, they joined the movement partly in anticipation of monetary gains (cash compensation), but more crucially since they considered themselves regular victims of the ration dealers' corruption. The dealers 'misbehaved' with the poor, 'cheated' them, and refused to share critical information on availability and supplies. For many poor villagers, therefore, the anti-dealer movement was also one of reinstating their dignity. The left's most 'treasured' electoral constituency was now taking part in a mobilization that the left parties had no intention to be part of.

Fourth, though the ration-movement was not restricted to the rural elite, the elite nonetheless sought to monopolize it. In the villages we visited, nowhere did we come across any instance where the APL agreed to share even a small part of the cash they received with the BPL. Initially, the leaders saw the participation of the BPL as a welcome trend to enhance their 'number' and they tended to keep the details of compensation vague. The poor were given to understand that they also stood to gain monetarily if the dealer could be adequately fined for all his alleged misdeeds. At the time of final negotiation, however, the BPL section was shut out. Everywhere, the dealers agreed to pay back in cash or kind only to the APL section, and the BPL was told that its demands would be addressed later (*pore dekha jabe*). Despite the ongoing churnings in a coercive party society, the dominance of the middle and relatively well-off segments within the format remained unchallenged.

Finally, unlike left-led peasant movements in the past, the stir against the dealers had no clear structure or goal. It evolved contingently in response to emerging contexts and changed in shape on a daily basis.

Since it was principally critical of the government, it took little time to turn against the CPI(M) wherever possible. Even some CPI(M) supporters and ground-level workers were up against the dealers, defying the line of the party and of the left government. However, no major political party, either the ruling or the opposition, attempted to turn the spontaneous popular surge into a populist protest against corruption inherent in the public distribution system. No serious debate or discussion took place in the affected villages, no move was made to root out the basic malaise. In response to the sporadic character of the agitation, the left's governmental response was also thoroughly bureaucratic if not highly unimaginative. It ordered to form shop level committees comprising a member of the local panchayat, the inspector/sub-inspector of food and supplies, 'one respectable gentleman of the locality' and a woman representative of a BPL family.[6] Prototype committees were recommended also at the block and subdivision levels. It was clear from the beginning that these top-down committees were simply a prop to pacify the agitated villagers with scarcely any will to take on the core issues of corruption, mistreatment or irregular supplies.[7]

By the summer of 2007 it was getting clearer that the left parties, particularly the CPI(M), were losing their safe occupancy over the political habitat in rural West Bengal. Party society, which the left had built from scratch, was proving less efficacious after having worked relentlessly for the preceding three decades, reproducing the Left Front's win in every village, state and parliamentary election. We have seen how over the last two decades or so the machinery had lost its hegemonic sheen, which was achieved in the early years of government as practice when the left was able to deftly marry its spirit of ideology-based movements from below with pragmatic reforms from the top. For the last several years its reproduction was driven more by the logic of domination, which helped maintaining a cold social peace in the countryside manoeuvred by the locally powerful players such as the traders, the promoters, the government contractors, the moneylenders, the ration-dealers – sometimes the same individuals wearing multiple hats at once. In short, all those who were competent enough to use their superior money and muscle power to profit from various commercial entrepreneurships – from investments in 'non-corporate capital' – took control of the left's party society. With the depletion of popular support for the left, as was evident in these incidents, the ongoing structure needed a rebranding, a new political clothing to sustain itself. Siding with the TMC's slogan for 'change' was unavoidable for these players only to perpetuate the existing structure of domination in the rural localities.

The aftermath

The collapse of the left did not entail a collapse of its coercive party-society in rural West Bengal; it was merely handed over from the left to the TMC. Paradoxically, the new dispensation, which gained control over the apparatus did not inherit a coherent and disciplined 'party' which the left characteristically possessed. The TMC leadership was made of disgruntled Congress workers who left the party in the late 1990s led by a determined and volatile Mamata Banerjee to unconditionally fight the CPI(M), which the dynastic leadership in New Delhi 'failed' to inspire. Since its inception, the TMC depended almost entirely on Banerjee's personal charisma and control, leaving the institutional processes within the party highly deficient and weak (Bhattacharyya, 2004b). Three years into power, the TMC government was yet to evolve an impersonal organizational structure with a clear hierarchy. Consequently, the party was plagued with incessant factional fights, gang rivalries and inconsistent priorities. While the left had earned social consent for implementing some pro-poor reforms in the initial years of its government, the current popularity of the TMC appeared less an outcome of any such policy initiative; the party banked primarily on the negative impulses that a vast segment of the state's electorate retained for the preceding, and seemingly unending, regime of the left.

To make for its lack of an 'institutional' party, the TMC struck alliances with the local clubs and community leaders and made them beneficiaries of government funding. Simultaneously, in line with the overall logic of party society, it attempted to make sure that the rural localities were 'cleansed' of all oppositional groups. While the left during much of its coercive dominance deployed its party – in the form of various committees and peasant unions – to accomplish the 'cleansing' job with some efficiency and sophistication (with an emphasis on maintaining 'social peace'), the TMC rather bluntly drove the opposition activists out of their villages, maimed or killed them at an alarming rate, made formal demands to socially ostracize their families, and insidiously used rape or threat of rape as a common weapon for retribution. A combination of promise for 'change', generous government funding, physical assault and verbal vilification had become an operative method for the new ruling party in a decadent party society. For instance, a video footage surfaced recently showing a TMC MP threatening the CPI(M) supporters of rape at a public meeting in Choumaha village in Nadia district.[8] Alarmingly, party society as a machinery now posed an unrestrained threat to the autonomy of the local society, the samaj, especially if the latter dared to show any recalcitrance. Let me conclude with a horrifying incident, one among many, that hit the headlines in the recent times.

In January 2014, newspapers reported that a santhal tribal court (*majhihadam boisi*) in a village in Birbhum punished a woman with a hefty fine for willing to marry a Muslim man who was already married. When the woman's family, excruciatingly poor, stated its inability to pay the fine, the council gave a chilling verdict: the woman was ordered to undergo gang rape by the local youth. The punishment reportedly was meted out on a covered stage set up at the centre of the village. As the news spread, many interpreted it as another case of 'savage' justice that kangaroo courts routinely dispensed in remote villages. The media compared it with the brutality of *khap* (or caste) panchayat in northern India.[9] The police arrested a dozen men, and acting amid the growing outcry the Supreme Court ordered a judicial inquiry sending a judge to the village.

A group of santhal intellectuals disputed the allegation that a tribal court, a mnajhihadam boisi, was responsible for the ghastly incident (Hembram, Munni, 2014; Baske, 2014; Hembram, Nityananda, 2014). They pointed out that the meeting from which such an atrocious verdict was pronounced was attended by a host of non-tribal men, including the local leader of the TMC. A genuine tribal council or mnajhi pargana, the santhal writers claimed, cannot issue summary justice, it can only facilitate a dialogue between all men and women in a village, and that the proceedings may continue for days. Also, instead of punishing the guilty its judgement usually apportions blame between both the accused and the accuser. Their practice in self-governance had been 'democratic, humane and disciplined', they claimed, always keeping the option of appealing to higher authorities open. Cases like monetary compensation or rape were 'unthinkable'. Such verdicts bore signs of what they called 'diku-ayan' or hybridization of the community as young santhal men, economically exploited and culturally footloose, fell prey to mimicking the worst of the outside world (Baske, 2014).

Despite their robust defence of customary santhal practices, the intellectuals were also critical of some tendencies internal to the community. They admitted that santhal women, though 'more liberated than women in mainstream society', were often considered as jinis kanaku drobyo (an 'object' or a 'thing'). Also, the practice of declaring a widow bitlaha (ostracized) to deny her legitimate property rights was acknowledged as 'not rare'. However, they were unanimous in their protest against the incursion of political parties in matters relating to the 'inner domain' of their community as much as they were resistant to formal governmental institutions overriding age old santhal practices. They aired suspicion about the modern institutions of power as such. 'We have learnt from experience that laws, courts or police are for the powerful, they work more as devourers than protectors of the poor and the helpless... Our samaj alone is capable of dealing with these challenges at multiple levels' (Hembram, Munni, 2014). Early on, party society worked as the left's vehicle for 'governmentalization of the local' (chapter 1). As conditions for generating consent degenerated into a mighty apparatus for extracting compliance, the local society evidently lost its faith in the formal institutions of governance.

This chapter, therefore, travels from Deenabandhu Majhi, to whom the left regime was a 'garib-dorodi-dal' to Munni Hembram who lost her faith in 'the laws, courts or police' and in 'the powerful'. We saw how the hegemonic expansion of party society in rural West Bengal slid over the decades into an incursive force of domination and violence. The rural poor, of course, did not accept the transformation passively. They expressed their displeasure in myriad forms, from non-participation in local government institutions to violent protests against, say, profiteering by the ration dealers. These streams of discontent eventually congealed into a massive popular strife against the left, debasing the Left Front government from power.

We noted that the early party society helped to mobilize a plurality of demands of the rural poor against large landowners and moneylenders. It generated a conducive atmosphere for raising a series of particular demands (for tenurial security or land distribution) which assumed the shape of a totality representing, however fleetingly, a popular alliance for justice and fairness. It also carved out an 'internal frontier' pitting the poor 'us' against the propertied 'them' as the fight for rights with 'lathi, guns, and flags' bound the toiling cultivators in an 'equivalential chain of unsatisfied demands' (Laclau, 2005, 74). These demands were cemented by the 'sacrifice' of the left leaders, the 'idealism' of the schoolteacher/ organizer who prioritized cultural/moral capital over material wealth, helping the 'party' – typically the CPI(M) – sublimate its popular identity. Such hegemonic moment of party society grossly corresponded with government as practice. A disciplined political agent capable of linking 'elevated' policies with 'embedded' everyday politics creatively deployed the tensions between its ideological promises and pragmatic possibilities (chapter 1).

The hegemonic party society, we also noted, lasted until the impulses of peasant movements ran out of steam and the land reform laws lost their beneficial effects in the productive economy of rural West Bengal. As the movements petered out and the left government failed to introduce any meaningful post-reform policies, the relationship between party and society changed. In the face of a middle-class ascendancy, the differential elements now overtook the equivalential logic of unity pushing poor peasants and agricultural workers to the margins. The 'internal frontier' on popular lines dissolved into a partisan frontier for selective patronage which excluded a large segment of the poor, especially those not affiliated to the left parties, from their rights and entitlements. With depleting idealism and rising material calculus, the regime became a magnet for self-seeking political entrepreneurs who commanded little 'respect' as leaders and demanded subordination of the population in exchange of favour and/or fear. Their proximity now posed a threat to the local society; their controlling instincts – in absence of consent – were widely seen as a blow to its autonomy. The party society turned principally into a coercive machinery, corresponding the collapse of government as practice. Conditions were rife for another bout of populist upsurge, for numerous discontents – sporadic, isolated and spontaneous – to galvanize into a nominal unity against the left in power. We now turn to the course of events that paved the way for the implosion of the Left Front government.

Endnotes

1. Middle-class urban leadership was also a characteristic of the Tebhaga peasant mobilization in Bengal. An activist-historian of the movement wrote: 'As the movement spread to distant villages it became physically impossible for the few middle-class leaders to keep track of it, and they relied invariably on kisan cadres'. See Sen, 1972. See also Cooper, 1988. Majumdar (1993, 103) makes note of two kinds of urban leaders – those who stayed in the village and those who coordinated from towns and cities.

2. Namasudra, bagdi and kaibarta are all SC communities. Namasudras consist mainly of the self-cultivating peasants and some fishing communities (especially in southern Bengal). They have been the principal beneficiaries of positive discrimination and have experienced considerable social mobility. Bagdis are the worst off, a majority of them landless agricultural workers or poor peasants. Kaibartas are overwhelmingly a fishing community; some are also agricultural workers and small peasants.

3. 'Hegemony' is used here in a restricted sense. As is well known, for Gramsci hegemony was equivalent to the exercise of 'leadership' by a social group before winning 'governmental power'. (Gramsci, 1971, 57 [footnote 6]). Such use of hegemony was distinctive, even among the Marxists. As Anne Showstack Sassoon pointed out: 'It is intriguing how Gramsci uses 'hegemony' to indicate consent, when its usual meaning in international relations, and indeed its use by fellow

marxists like Lenin or Mao, was so different – as domination over a system of alliances.' (Sassoon, 2000, 5). A hegemonic leadership, being alert and responsive to the opposition that seeks to threaten its dominance, has the courage and ability to uphold the 'universal' over its corporatist interests. (Mouffe, 1979, 180). In a more complete sense, as Gwyn Williams indicated in his important article on Gramsci: 'By 'hegemony' Gramsci seems to mean a socio-political situation, in his terminology, a 'moment', in which the philosophy and practice of a society fuse or are in equilibrium...' (Williams, 1960, 587).

4. In the recent panchayat and Lok Sabha elections in West Bengal, the caste groups, especially those of the Dalits and the OBCs, played a far more active role than in the recent past. So have the minority religious bodies. It seems that, in the near future, these groups and organizations could play a more emphatic partisan role in the state's politics and the established political parties will have to address them in order to enlist support on the basis of identity mobilizations.

5. This section follows, more or less, the argument developed jointly by us in Bhattacharyya and Rana, 2008.

6. Government of West Bengal, Food and Supplies Department, Memorandum No 1303/FS:FS/SeECTT/SC-9/96 dated 25 September 2007.

7. Though the dealer was invariably the immediate target of public wrath in these incidents, most of them were susceptible to corruption due to many reasons, including the small margin of profit that they were expected to operate with. Moreover, they being just cogs in a larger wheel of numerous pilferages they were compelled to conform to certain internal norms of transaction. In a letter written to the Chief Justice of the Calcutta High Court a dealer claimed that the average monthly loss incurred by a dealer amounted to ₹ 7000. If one added monthly family expenses of around ₹ 10000 to that how could a dealer be expected to earn without taking recourse to corruption? (*Sambad*, Vol 4, No 184, 12 Kartik 1414 [30 October 2007], Edit page). The dealers' union sympathized with the plight of individual dealers. On 21 August major left party leaders addressed ration dealers from all over the country in a rally organized by the All India Fair Price Dealers' Federation at the Ram Lila ground in New Delhi. The leaders asserted that an attack on the dealer is tantamount to an attack on the public distribution system (PDS) itself.

8. 'If any CPM man is present here, listen to me. If you ever touch any Trinamool Congress worker or their families, you have to pay for this ... . If any rival touches any Trinamool woman, father or child, then I will ruin their generations. I will let loose my boys, they will commit rape. Yes, they will commit rape,' the MP warned. See 'India outrage over MP Tapas Pal's rape threat' on http://www.bbc.com/news/world-asia-india-28103245, accessed on 26 August 2014, 12.40 PM.

9. See *The Hindu*, 24 January 2014, 'Outrage in West Bengal over gang rape at the bidding of kangaroo court', *The Independent*, 23 January 2014, 'Village elders order gang – rape of young woman as punishment for relationship with outsider', *Hindustan Times*, 23 January 2014, '12 gang – rape tribal woman on kangaroo court order in Bengal's Birbhum district'.

5

IMPLOSION: SINGUR, NANDIGRAM

On a sultry August day in 2005, Buddhadeb Bhattacharjee left for Jakarta with a 22 member trade team to sign a Memorandum of Understanding (MoU) with Indonesia's biggest industrial house, the Salim Group of Companies. This was certainly not the first foreign trip by a Marxist chief minister to invite foreign direct investments, Jyoti Basu – West Bengal's previous and the country's longest serving chief minister – made several such trips to Europe and the US. This was, however, Buddhadeb's first major trip outside the country, and the investment proposed – to the tune of ₹ 50,000 crores – was extraordinarily high for the state's dwindling economy. A debate triggered off within the left over whether the government should invite a foreign multinational, if the Salim group – which allegedly had an anti-communist past – should be allowed to invest in the state. On both counts, Buddhadeb got the state committee and the politburo of the CPI(M) to come round his way. At a press conference on the eve of his departure the chief minister said that there was no other alternative, but the government was committed to protect the interests of the state's workers and the peasants. Three days later, on 25 August, the West Bengal Industrial Development Corporation (WBIDC) signed a MoU with the Salim Group to promote an industrial park in the form of a special economic zone (SEZ) in West Bengal. The final agreement was to be inked later, after the company submitted a detailed project report to the government.

This marked the beginning of a long saga in West Bengal's present politics. The left government was copiously doing what an investment-friendly state government does in India's competitive federalism. Major states try to outbid each other to woo private investment for setting up industries and infrastructure as state funding for such projects – which was the case in the pre-liberalized dirigiste economy – got dried up. However, a left state government had to answer a few difficult questions: Should it invite multilateral capital of foreign origin, which had been a target of its ideological opposition for decades? Should it accept proposals for SEZ, whose internal workings – including discriminatory labour law and questionable land-use – had already invited several criticisms from the left parties? Can a state government adequately compensate the cultivators to be displaced by such projects and protect the informal and unorganized workforce? While the leadership of the Left Front government promised a fair deal on all these counts, there was confusion, if not scepticism, even among sections of the left constituents, including within the CPI(M). In sum, it now became clear that the state government had set off on a difficult and untested path that would call for a careful balancing between its ideological and pragmatic calculus, on the one hand, and between conflicting interests of capital and the left's 'basic classes', on the other. In other words, these initiatives posed a serious challenge to the left's decade-old structure of 'government as practice'.

Nobody perhaps could have imagined that the Left Front was winning its last election in West Bengal when in May 2006 it got a landslide for the seventh time in a row. Immediately thereafter, the state government decided to acquire 997 acres for a small car factory in a place called Singur in Hooghly district, some 45 kilometres west of Kolkata on a newly built six-lane Durgapur Expressway. Officials of the Tata Motors, which was to set up the factory, were shown different sites for the project, but they insisted on this fertile stretch of farmland. Apart from the expressway, which connected the place to the metropolis in less than an hour, the location was surrounded by three railway stations – Singur, Kamarkundu, and Madhusudanpur. The land sought by the company was from six maujas – Gopalnagar, Beraberi, Bajemelia, Khaserbheri, Singherberi, and

Joymalyarbheri. The state government in its Gazette notification (19–24 July, 2006) declared that the land was to be acquired under section 4(1) of the Land Acquisition Act of 1894 by the government or its undertaking 'at public expense for a public purpose' such as 'employment generation and socio-economic development of the area by setting up a Tata Small Car Project'.[1]

Almost immediately after the government was sworn in, the chief minister faced the journalists with Ratan Tata sitting to his left. Tata announced two projects – a factory for the world's cheapest car and one for the production of pay-loaders. He said that his dream car would cost just about ₹ 100,000 (about US$ 2,000 at the current rate) and it would roll out from Singur by 2008. For this he would require 700 acres, an additional 300 acres would be needed to set up ancillary industries. 'We scanned the country and looked at various locations before deciding to locate this rather revolutionary project which will give India's truly people's car here in Bengal'. The company, he said, had come to believe that West Bengal was 'the most investor friendly state in the country' and that someone had to turn that belief into reality. 'People's car from a Marxist-ruled state sounds nice, possibly appropriate too', wrote an English newspaper in Kolkata, 'symbolizing the Left's journey from land reforms to what is stands for today'. The chief minister told the journalists present, 'You can all buy one'. A dream was set on the roll.[2]

Troubled beginning

The fact that the announcement made at the top had a serious disconnect with the bottom was revealed within days. On 25 May as the Tata Motors officials visited Singur, they were met with angry protesters, a large number of whom were women armed with broomsticks, shouting slogans against the proposed factory, a clear sign that the company was unwelcome in their neighbourhood. Clearly, the CPI(M) did not expect this, especially at the beginning of a long journey. Jyoti Basu, the octogenarian leader, did not hide his displeasure, as he told the press that he demanded explanation from the chief minister for the government's unpreparedness. How the incident could occur, he wondered, when the Krishak Sabha members were asked to be present en masse. 'Someone told me that the local leader of the party was enjoying his afternoon siesta', he assailed. While Biman Bose, the secretary of the Left Front, blamed the media for 'making a mountain of a molehill', Buddhadeb defended his government, claiming that the locals indeed were consulted before the visit. However, Abdur Rezzak Mollah, the rustic firebrand leader of the Krishak Sabha and the land minister in the government prophetically said: 'kiliye kanthal pakano jai na' (you can't ripen a jackfruit by just hammering it). Nirupam Sen, the suave and coolheaded industry minister retorted: 'The jackfruit will be ripened the way it is meant to be done'.[3]

As disquiet was on the rise in Singur, Beni Santoso, the chairman of the Salim Group, arrived in Kolkata in the middle of June 2006. He visited Nandigram in East Medinipur where the company was planning to acquire 27 thousand acres of which 15 thousand were to be acquired in Nandigram and 12 thousand in Haldia. Of this around 10 thousand acres were claimed for a chemical hub, another 10 thousand acres for an SEZ, and 5–7 thousand acres for a township with schools, colleges and hospitals.[4] Santoso met the local CPI(M) MP Lakshman Seth who assured him that, unlike Singur, 'the atmosphere here is conducive to industrial development'. Seth also assured Santoso that the project will get land from Daudpur, Sonachura and Char Kendemari areas of Nandigram. Santoso could not be taken to Nandigram,[5] reportedly because he was in hurry, but took a bird's eye view of the area from the eleventh floor of Jawahar Tower in Haldia. Next day, after a meeting with the chief minister and the industry minister at the Writers' Buildings, West Bengal's administrative headquarter, he announced that his company was in touch with the Indian Oil Corporation to jointly build the proposed chemical hub. Mamata Banerjee, the TMC supremo, told the press that she had no objection to industry as long as the government did not acquire any farmland. 'Why is the state hiding 'Beni' from us? Is he a burglar or a robber?' she asked bitingly.

The third week of July 2006 inaugurated a flurry of activities in Singur. With the government's gazette notification of the acquisition, Rezzak

Mollah received a letter from the Tata Motors to acquire land. The acquisition was flagged off within two days. Mollah promised that the pace of acquisition in Singur would set 'an all-India record'. He had earlier promised that the 'process' would be completed within 3 to 6 months. As soon as the announcement was made, a group of local protesters blocked the expressway, throwing the traffic to a spin along the busy route. They demanded relocation of the project and immediate stoppage of the land acquisition process

For Nandigram, the state government signed a contract with the WBIDC and the Salim Group rather ceremoniously on 31 July. The project was named 'New Kolkata International Development' (NKID) involving 38,650 acres of farmland and a proposed investment to the scale of ₹ 40,000 crore in East Medinipur and South 24 Parganas districts. West Bengal never received any investment of this magnitude, which the chief minister described as a 'historic'. Both the CPI(M) and the Krishak Sabha fell in line with the government leaving a large space open for potential detractors.

By July-August 2006 several mass organizations spawned with the backing of various opposition parties. They criticized the state government's initiatives on the ground that policies were made without any consultation with those who stood to get affected, who would lose lands and other productive assets to accommodate a mega corporate expansion. Krishak Uchchhed Birodhhi O Janaswartha Raksha Committee (Committee against Peasants' Eviction and for Protection of People's Interests) was set up by the SUCI. Krishi Jomi Raksha Committee (Committee for the Protection of Agricultural Land or KJRC) was set up in Nandigram and Khejuri with the state-wide initiative of the TMC. Gana Unnayan O Jana Adhikar Sangram Samiti (Association for the Struggle of People's Development and Rights) was formed jointly by Jamait Ulema-i-Hind and the Communist Party of India (Marxist-Leninist Santosh Rana faction). The signs were clear. The peasants were concerned because the panchayat or the grassroots party workers knew almost nothing about what the government was up to. All they saw was that the corporate bosses were accorded a reception by the left that people in West Bengal never witnessed before. Such change in government's approach, its disregard for a dialogue, and the looming prospect of losing livelihood combined to instil a dark fear of dispossession into a large peasant population in southern West Bengal.

Two arguments

As pressure was building over industrialization and land acquisition in West Bengal economist Amit Bhaduri wrote two essays criticizing the model of development adopted by the Indian state in the post-liberalization period on which both the right and the parliamentary left, he alleged, had converged. (Bhaduri, 2007a, 2007b). The model assumed that a high rate of economic growth would eventually produce a trickle-down effect bringing economic benefits for the country's entire population: the rich and the poor, the urban and the rural. By assigning the leading role to private corporations, the new scheme expected the state to facilitate acquisition of large tracts of land on which capital-intensive industries and SEZs could be set up, and to coerce any popular resistance against these projects into submission. The model was fully on display not just in Nandigram and Singur, but also in other places like Dadri in Uttar Pradesh, Kalinganagar in Orissa, and Raigad in Maharashtra. Although claimed as good for the country, the policy in fact was to transfer 'more and more resources to the so-called high productivity sector producing for the rich in the name of comparative sectoral advantage'. The poor, at the other end, were denied resources 'because they have no purchasing power'. In this method of 'internal colonialism' that drove tribal people out of their mineral rich land, destroyed the livelihood of peasants and those dependent on agriculture, and threw boatmen and fishing communities out of business, the real aim was to dispossess the majority poor for catering to the insatiable greed of a minority rich.

In Bhaduri's anticipation two possible political consequences could follow from this model of development. It could either generate a crisis of parliamentary legitimacy – no regime that propagated an urban centric development in contemporary India was returned by the electorate either in the states or at the centre. 'There is no reason to believe that this corporate-led growth ideology will not be rejected again by our democratic polity either in West Bengal or elsewhere' (Bhaduri, 2007a, 553). Or it could create possible crisis for parliamentary democracy itself as illustrated by the Maoist upsurge in the tribal areas where government had habitually treated dispossession simply as a case of 'collateral damage' in the country's historic progress. Calling the new economic policy 'terroristic', Bhaduri offered three concrete suggestions for the left's consideration. They should adopt a selective approach to globalization with a focus on the internal market, demand full employment 'by making agriculture and the rural economy the centre of economic dynamism', and fight to scrap the Fiscal Responsibility and the Budget Management Act (2003) which – as desired by the International Monetary Fund (IMF), the World Bank and the multinational corporations – had curtailed public expenditure on health, education and other welfare needs of the poor.

Instead of strengthening popular movements along these lines, Bhaduri lamented,

> what we are witnessing is deliberate connivance on the part of the conventional Left in West Bengal with the interests of large corporations against the poor, perhaps in the hope that the corporations will bring about a miraculous transformation of the state, which they are incapable of doing with state power (Bhaduri, 2007a, 553).

Those 'who not long ago ridiculed the slogan 'China's path is our path', seem to have turned the full circle in admiration of the Chinese way of corporate-led development'. Claiming that a programme for 'decentralised, employment intensive, rural industrialisation through participatory democracy at local level is no utopia', Bhaduri signed off with a high hope that the existing corporate-led industrialization is unsustainable and was bound to collapse.

In contrast, West Bengal chief minister Buddhadeb Bhattacharjee presented the governmental left perspective in a gathering of the CPI(M) unit leaders on 9 February 2007. (Bhattacharjee, 2007). His speech was one of the earliest and perhaps also clearest expositions of his position that attempted to balance the two hats he wore – that of a politburo member of a communist party and of an administrative head of a regional government in competition with other states to attract private investments for industries, infrastructure, SEZ etc. It declared that there was no 'model' of development for his government to adopt, it was on an 'untraveled path' in an economic system not amenable to his party's ideology. 'We do not say that the Chinese model is our model'. West Bengal maintained a steady agricultural growth of 4 per cent per annum against the country's 2 per cent, though many sceptics had doubts about the viability of small-holding cultivation post-land reforms. In addition, the state ranked first in the country in the production of fish and vegetables and attained self-reliance for the first time in the production of paddy. This brought a good amount of disposable cash for rural West Bengal turning it into a huge market for consumer goods. 'Our kisans', Bhattacharjee asserted, 'possess the highest purchasing power of industrial goods in the whole of the country today in the retail sector, be it cement, radio, cycle, motorcycle, or apparel'.

Arguing that 'the transition from agriculture to industry is an inevitable phenomenon both in capitalism and in socialism' and 'we cannot agree with the postulate that agriculture is the last and final stage of development', the chief minister highlighted the crisis that West Bengal would face if the government failed in its responsibility to modernize agriculture and create opportunities for those waiting to move out. With the rising demographic pressure agricultural land was getting fragmented. Agriculture's share in the state's population was 65 per cent, while its share in the economy was a measly 26 per cent. Moreover, the rising input costs made agriculture less remunerative: 'it is becoming difficult for farmers to get minimum procurement prices for their products'. Also, the younger generation was not keen to stay in agriculture. 'They are not willing to go back to the fields after passing out from schools and colleges'. With little investment in infrastructure – refrigerated shades, transport, and food processing etc. – huge amount of perishable produce was routinely getting wasted. 'Because of lack of viable marketing mechanism many vegetables produced are left to rot in the fields'. Some critics of his government, he claimed, wanted him, 'not proceed any further and stay in place… and enjoy the success we have achieved', a sure recipe to 'stagnate and drift backwards'.

Industrialization, from the standpoint of the government, was not a matter of choice. Two main challenges had to be overcome: the paucity of capital and of land. While there was nothing unusual in the state's demand for capital, West Bengal with a high density of population had a serious problem with land availability. Since the early 2000s due to some strategic reasons to be discussed shortly, the state started getting investment proposals especially in iron and steel, chemicals, petrochemicals, information technology etc. The question was how should a state government respond? 'Should we dissuade them?' the chief minister asked. Indeed, the government found it difficult to offer suitable locations for most of these proposals. The state had only 1 per cent of its land as fallow (against 17 per cent in the country), 13 per cent under forest cover, 23 per cent under urban and industrial settlement, and a vast 63 per cent under intense cultivation. To set up industry, Bhattacharjee pointed out, acquisition of agricultural land was unavoidable.

Land acquisition, however, had already become a contentious issue across the country. 'Under capitalism, in India, the expropriation of the land of the peasantry is taking place in a brutal manner' the chief minister observed. 'In our drive for industrialisation in West Bengal', he assured, 'we will not proceed this way'. Recounting left-led peasant struggles in the 1960s and 1970s which brought 83 per cent of the state's agricultural land under the possession of poor and marginal peasants, he said, West Bengal was different from other states where 'the zamindars own the land and the lathi–wielding pehelwans run the panchayat'. Barely five weeks before his police would open fire on the protesting peasants in Nandigram, the chief minister promised: 'We are committed to protect the interest of the farmers. If land needs to be taken, it will be done by providing those owning and dependent on land a fair deal, without coercion'.

Critics had claimed that the Left Front government doled out undue concessions to the Tata Group in Singur for setting up a car factory, and attempted to force its way into Nandigram for building a SEZ by keeping the peasants completely in the dark. The chief minister admitted that concessions indeed were given because the state had no modern automobile plant and unless the right incentives were offered the state had no chance of getting the industry here. 'Tata Group almost decided to set up the motor car factory project at Uttarakhand'. The factory in Singur, he claimed, would create far more jobs than it displace, even the 'work of setting up the boundary wall for the factory itself has created jobs for 3000 people'. In Nandigram

> there was a mistake on the part of the local authority, for it initiated steps without informing the local people … . We have decided not to proceed further here … . Let the debate over SEZ come to a conclusion and then we can look at the project again (Bhattacharjee, 2007).

Replying to those who believed that in the new economy 'the foreign capitalists are rushing in on their own to exploit us', the chief minister reminded that 'the actual picture is different'. In fact, he argued, 'there is tough competition all around, we cannot discourage investment… the idea is that we do need private capital, with limits set, and not everywhere'. Admitting that land 'is a very sensitive issue', the chief minister said: 'The Left always looks after the interests of the poor. The effort should also be on to develop industries. We feel we are at a crucial phase of development. With agriculture as our basis, we shall build industry'.

Common fallacies

Here we have two contrasting approaches, both claimed to be leftwing, both stood by the 'poor' and both considered corporate interests as the driving force of India's economy today. Yet, the two differed radically on their conceptions of 'development' and what the left ought to do to achieve that. Bhaduri proposed an economic alternative based on decentred rural industrialization, full employment, internal market, larger public spending for welfare and dismantling the legal regime of 'fiscal discipline'. He attacked the conventional left for converging with the political right, calling them 'foolish to expect that … corporate-led growth can create sufficient employments to transfer sufficient labour from agriculture to industry and services in the foreseeable future'. He was cynical about the sustainability of the bipolar world created by the present model of economic growth and remained firm in his belief that it 'will collapse'.

Bhattacharjee, on the other hand, standing far removed from such an apocalyptic vision argued that West Bengal under the Left Front stood at a turning point of history. Over the last three decades the state had achieved a degree of success in agriculture, which now reached a point of no return. To realize the state's economic potential and arrest industrial slide, the government had to invite corporate investments and create jobs for a rapidly expanding young and aspiring workforce. Armed with an 'undisputable' pro-poor credential of the left government, Bhattacharjee believed that he could convince the peasants that acquisition of land was for their own good. 'The opposition accuses us of having agreed to capitalist development. Is it possible to talk of socialist development in one state of our country?' he asked.

Both these standpoints, we can argue, suffered from critical blind spots.

Bhaduri was right when he said that the present model of growth as development was not going to accommodate the displaced labour in modern industries, and it was an illusion that enough jobs would be created. He was also right that the model had to have a strong bipolar effect on the society creating a wedge between the rich and the poor. He was, however, unrealistic to assume that a rupture was inevitable. Such ruptures – in the form of war or revolution – were indeed the nodal points in the history of European capitalism, but the Indian case was clearly different. Conditions of universal suffrage, a liberal constitutional regime and the need to conform to a global standard of human rights made it not just necessary but also possible to politically manage such ruptures in the interest of capital's reproduction. He was also unrealistic to expect that the mainstream left running a provincial government, by no means wielding 'the state power', could actually adopt an alternative political and economic strategy undermining corporate capital.

On his part, Bhattacharjee seemed right in arguing that his government could not transcend capitalism. He was also right that West Bengal's industrialization had to rely on private capital, as there was no alternative source of finance within the present economic arrangements. He was, however, wrong in assuming that industry was to radically displace agriculture as the 'future'.[6] Development of capitalism in postcolonial India, unlike in most of Europe, followed rather than preceded conditions of popular democracy thereby annulling expropriation of the peasantry or of the informal workforce that constituted the country's overwhelming majority as a politically permissible project. Instead of considering himself as a facilitator for West Bengal's 'fortuitous' though rather late industrial transition, a left chief minister's firm emphasis should have been on representing the multitude outside the circle of corporate capital to maximize its benefits. That the left completely failed to understand this political responsibility was revealed even when the chief minister admitted that 'there was a mistake (in Nandigram) on the part of the local authority, for it initiated steps without informing the local people'. If in its governmental mentality the left was genuinely inclined to stand by 'the local people', the lapse could not have been perceived as one of information alone, but more critically of its failure to generate popular demands for industrialization by consultation, dialogue, and continuous deliberations at the lowest level to take the most marginal interests on board.

It is important to note that their differences apart both Bhaduri and Bhattacharjee shared a common ground. While one opposed capitalism as a radical left critic, the other facilitated capitalism as a modernizing chief minister, but both held a universal conception of capital essentially derived from its European history. In this understanding, capital is universally capable of subsuming all pre-capitalist economic forms, for better or for worse, and of creating a reserve army of proletariat for its expanded production. That, as we shall see below, is not what transpires in the economic conditions of postcolonial democracy. Here populist compulsions ensure that forces which subsume pre-capitalist economic forms, such as peasant production or small scale manufacturing, are simultaneously retaliated by state policies to enable subsistence economy continue in the vast informal sector. If one keeps this paradoxical situation in mind, then the peasant unrest in Nandigram and Singur does not appear either as a resistance to 'developmental terrorism' (Bhaduri), or a 'flawed anti-industrialism' (Bhattacharjee). Rather, it represents a strong disapproval of the top-down partisan and administrative fiat in complete violation of a consultative governmental process. Quintessentially, it indicated the constitution of the political in India's economic transformation. To conceptualize postcolonial economic and popular protest within this uncharted yet unavoidable exchange between capital and its frontiers it is crucial to return to what Marx had called the 'so-called primitive accumulation' from India's own historical standpoint.

Primitive accumulation

For Marx primitive accumulation was a coercive act of capital in the phase of its making. His was a critical departure from the story of capital's rise that classical political economy (especially of Adam Smith) had made widely popular. In that story primitive accumulation represented a stage in history in which income from honest labour saved through frugality was turned into capital for investment. In contrast, Marx's analysis recorded a bloody history of cutting labour from the means of production to enable its coercive absorption into capitalist process of production. In the new economy, labour owned no property and could expect only wages after deduction of surplus created as value for exploitation by capital. Only after establishing itself in charge, coercion gave way to an appearance of consent as capital introduced its own logic of reproduction with little further need for crude (extra-economic) coercion characteristic of the phase of primitive accumulation. Now, as Marx confirmed, 'the silent compulsion of economic relations sets the seal on the domination of the capitalist over the worker' (Marx, 1976, 899, 'Bloody legislation against the expropriated', emphasis added).

Once the seemingly neutral play of market forces ensured the dominance of capital in a sequence of production and reproduction, the force of the state or of law was made secondary. Let us quote a key passage from Capital where Marx was graphic in his description:

> The capital-relation presupposes a complete separation between the workers and the ownership of the conditions for the realization of their labour. As soon as capitalist production stands on its own feet, it not only maintains this separation, but reproduces it on a constantly extending scale. The process, therefore, which creates the capital-relation can be nothing other than the process which divorces the worker from the ownership of the conditions of his own labour; it is a process which operates *two transformations*, whereby the social means of subsistence and production are turned into capital, and the immediate producers are turned into wage-labourers. So-called primitive accumulation, therefore, is nothing else than the *historical* process of divorcing the producer from the means of production. It appears as 'primitive' because it forms the *pre-history* of capital, and of the mode of production corresponding to capital. (Marx, 1976, 874–75, emphases added).

Two transformations, as Marx showed, were central to primitive accumulation after it delinked labour from its means of production: Turning the social means of labour into capital and turning the producer into a wage labour. The 'primitive' nature of such accumulation is derived from the fact that it constituted capital's pre-history. Both these 'twin transformations' and 'historicity', as we shall see shortly, generated major debates among the Marxians in their bid to interpret multiple instances of capitalism and its global spread.

Capital's past?

One gets a strong suggestion in Marx's writing that primitive accumulation of capital does not stand as capital's present, but as a prerequisite of its becoming, as a condition anterior to capital's rise. However, the antecedent of capital's rise can only be understood 'retrospectively', that is, once capital has become self-sustaining in an expanded mode of production. (Althusser and Balibar, 1970, 276, 'Primitive accumulation: a prehistory'). In other words, the salience of primitive accumulation can only be appreciated after capital has arrived and reached its fullness. The moment is immanent in capital in transit, though capital on arrival is transformed beyond recognition. In Grundrisse, Marx compares primitive accumulation with the making of a city. When a city emerges into a complex web of administrative, financial, cultural, productive and leisurely activities, the conditions of its making get erased:

> While e.g. the flight of serfs to the cities is one of the historic conditions and presuppositions of urbanism, it is not a condition, not a moment of the reality of developed cities, but belongs rather to their past presuppositions, to the presuppositions of their becoming which are suspended in their being.

So a 'temporal cleavage', so to say, divides the making of a city and a city that is made; the conditions that went into the city's making become visible as belonging to the past only from the vantage point of a developed city. Likewise, for capital,

> The conditions and presuppositions of the becoming, of the arising, of capital presuppose precisely that it is not yet in being but merely in becoming; they therefore disappear as real capital arises, capital which itself, on the basis of its own reality, posits the conditions for its realization (Marx, 1993, 459, emphases original).

This formulation has a dual possibility. While the past here is separated from the present, so much so that the past is recognisable as pre-history of the present only after the present gets delinked from the past and is transformed into an entity independent of the past, it also inheres that the past as an antecedent of the present stores infinite possibilities as long as 'it is not yet in being but merely in becoming'. While two cities, on arrival, are unmistakably recognized as cities, no two cities are identical, they have different pasts recognisable as different only after they become or emerge as different cities. Like the universal city, universal capital can also emerge as different entities in different historical instances, an idea (of 'different universal') that we follow later in the context of primitive accumulation in postcolonial conditions.

If primitive accumulation indeed causes painful dislocations for capital's rise, the central question is how to manage the social disquiet that it brings in its aftermath. In India's representative democracy the authoritarian option of using the state's sovereign force to suppress popular resistance, as widely used in pre-democratic Europe or in contemporary China, cannot be exercised with complete impunity. It requires a far more sophisticated and compliant management in recognition of the fact that despite industrialization and urbanization at a rapid scale, a vast majority of Indians still draw their subsistence from agro-based rural economy and almost the entire workforce operates in the informal sector. In developing an appropriate technology of management, especially from the perspective of leftwing politics, it is vital to have a clear understanding of the cost of economic transformation, its different interpretations and its specific forms in the postcolonial economic that adheres to the compulsions of both profit and populism.

One-off episode

Capital's rise found a polemical twist in the way Vladimir Ilyich Lenin characterized agrarian transformation in Russia. Lenin's formulations, as we shall see, had considerable influence on West Bengal's governmental left a century down the line. 'In historical development of capitalism', Lenin noted, 'two features are important'. They are, first, the transformation of natural economy of the direct producers into commodity economy and, second, the transformation of commodity economy into capitalist economy (Lenin, 1960–70, 93). Lenin considered them as 'natural' and 'spontaneous' stages, which could be guided toward socialism. Writing *Development of Capitalism in Russia* from his Siberian exile in 1897, he was convinced that the capitalist mode of production was increasingly dominating the 'pre-capitalist' rural economy. This, for Lenin, was good for the cause as it was consistent with his goal of transcending capitalism by a revolutionary alliance of the working class and the peasantry (consisting of the hyper-exploited rural proletariat and the economically distressed middle peasants).

Lenin preferred capitalism over 'village community' which the Narodniks idealized believing that capitalism was 'foreign' to Russia, imported by the state. Against such romanticism Lenin claimed that capital's penetration in Russia reveals the presence of 'all those contradictions' inherent in every capitalist order like

> competition, the struggle for economic independence, the grabbing of land (purchasable and rentable), the concentration of production in the hands of a minority, the forcing of the majority into the ranks of the proletariat, their exploitation by a minority through the medium of merchant's capital and the hiring of farm labourers' (Quoted from Le Blanc, 2008, 94).

The Narodniks wanted to preserve the peasant communities as an antidote to capitalism, for Lenin the peasantry was the 'deepest and most durable foundation' of capitalism in Russia (quoted from Le Blanc, 2008, 95).

By welcoming capital's transformation of the peasantry, Lenin maintained, one does not become an 'apologist for capitalism'.[7]

> The Narodniks usually shut their eyes to this fragmentation [of agricultural holdings], and when the Marxists express the view that the splitting up of the peasantry is progressive, the Narodniks confine themselves to hackneyed outcries against 'supporters of land dispossession', thereby covering up the utter fallacy of their views about the pre-capitalist countryside (Le Blanc 2008, 99, words in parenthesis added).

More than hundred years later, in defending the Left Front government's action against the mounting criticisms of the human rights activists, the environmentalists, and the radical left protectors of subsistence peasantry, the CPI(M) amply borrowed from Lenin's arsenal.

As defending the peasant community is still in fashion, so the need to make a case for its destruction. David Harvey, for instance, says that the destruction is a 'necessary though ugly stage through which the social order had to go in order to arrive at a state where both capitalism and some alternative socialism might be possible' (Harvey, 2003, 163). To make an omelette you must break the eggs, he insists. No doubt that 'class violence is abhorrent', there are many positives too. Forces that destroy the peasant community also obliterate feudal relations, liberate creative energies, open up society to strong currents of technological and organizational change, and overcome a world based on superstition and ignorance and replace it with a world of scientific enlightenment with the potentiality to liberate people from material want and need (Harvey, 2003, 162–63).

The bottom-line is clear – primitive accumulation is coercive, but there's no point in being nostalgic about what it wipes out because it opens the path for social progress. Besides, as Marx implied, primitive accumulation is a necessary as well as conclusive stage in capital's rise without which some alternative socialist form cannot be imagined.

While few doubt that the rise of capital in Europe involved painful dislocations, the Marxists differ in their opinion on whether primitive accumulation has actually concluded as a stage or continues as a process. Continuity, some suggest, is unavoidable because capitalism is never self-sustaining, extraction and circulation of capital always requires its 'other'. Others think that primitive accumulation continues because the antecedents of capital never completely yield to a capitalist production, but they keep resisting, disrupting or upsetting in ways that are not yet sufficiently understood. If indeed primitive accumulation is incapable of subsuming all that is outside capital once and for all and of charting an unequivocal social progress, then it goes without saying that the leftwing agenda cannot be a replication of the Leninist one. A more nuanced response to capitalist transformation is required.

Ongoing process

'[A]t some times Marx's analysis of primitive accumulation... seems to be a process that ceased with the establishment of capitalism. At other times, it seems to be more of an ongoing process' wrote Michael Perelman (2000, 28). Dipesh Chakrabarty also suggested that some 'remnants' of 'vanished social formations' may remain 'partly still unconquered' even after capital had arisen signalling that 'a site of 'survival' of that which seemed pre- or noncapitalist could very well be the site of an ongoing battle' (Chakrabarty, 2000, 65, emphasis added). Indeed, Marx did not deny that 'extra-economic force is still of course used' after the emergence of capital, but he was quick to add that it happened 'only in exception cases'. 'In the ordinary run of things', he maintained, 'the worker can be left to the "natural laws of production"', i.e., on the perpetual dependence on wages (Marx, 1976, 899).

If Marx could not discount the possibility for extra-economic measures to survive, why was he not more explicit about the continuity of primitive accumulation? Perelman had an answer. He thought that Marx's principal focus was not so much the brutalities associated with primitive accumulation, but the viciousness underneath the apparent civility of market societies, a reality that classical political economy sought to conceal under an 'invisible hand'. In his effort to reveal the hidden dynamics of the economic with all its cruelty, Marx underplayed the theme of continuity of primitive accumulation as that could risk 'throwing readers off track' in believing 'that measures to eliminate 'unjust' instances of primitive accumulation might suffice to bring about a good society' (Perelman, 2000, 30). This, for Perelman, was vindicated in a letter that Marx wrote to chastize 'suprahistorical presentation of primitive accumulation' devoid of any 'concrete historical analysis'.[8] In this letter Marx tended to underplay the importance of 'primitive accumulation' in his Capital as merely a 'historical sketch' that 'does not claim to do more than trace the path by which in Western Europe, the capitalist economy emerged from the womb of the feudal economic system'. (Marx, quoted in Perelman 2000, 27). So Marx's take on primitive accumulation, in his own words, was specific to 'Western Europe' and 'sketchy', a point that we will return to when we visit the Indian debate on the subject.

To say that the coercive extra-economic aspects of primitive accumulation are not only antecedents of capital, but also its constituents, one has to show why capital required it even after becoming capital, even after attaining self-sufficiency or the capacity for extended reproduction. For Rosa Luxemburg, accumulation had 'two different aspects'. One concerned the relation between capital and wage-labourer within the capitalist mode of production, the other was made of the relationship between capitalist with non-capitalist modes of production. While the first followed the classical model of extended reproduction, a coercive exchange with non-capitalist modes of production was necessary as the workers in the capitalist economy, who earned less than the value produced, could not create the effective demand for manufactured commodities. To resolve this problem of so-called 'overproduction', she pointed out, capitalism's 'predominant methods are colonial policy, an international loan system – a policy of spheres of interest – and war. Force, fraud, oppression, looting are openly displayed without any attempt at concealment' (Luxemburg, 2003, 432). Drawing on this, Hannah Arendt argued that the imperialist principles of politics reflected the bourgeois economic principles: unlimited accumulation of power mirrored the unlimited accumulation of capital (Arendt, 1976, 125 in Fine, 2001, 116).

That primitive accumulation was necessary for capital's global extension found acceptance in dependency and world system theories as well. They considered colonialism and neo-colonialism as political tools available for resolving capital's crisis of accumulation. Andre Gunder Frank, a principal proponent of this position, argued that of all the responses to the crisis of accumulation in late eighteenth century England

> by far the most important reactions and consequences for world history were, on the one hand, the plunder of Bengal (that was subsequently extended to other parts of India) in a drive for primitive accumulation not witnessed since the Spanish conquered America and established slave plantations in the Caribbean; and, on the other hand... the Industrial Revolution (Frank, 1978, 179–80).

Capitalism turned into a world system by keeping peripheral capital (both its 'ancient' and 'modern' sectors) in a state of perpetual dependency so that extra-economic accumulation could continue outside the geographical limits of metropolitan capital. Within the frame of this unequal exchange, therefore, development of the metropolitan centres was perceived as an effect of continuing primitive accumulation in the peripheral economies.[9]

Post-welfare capitalism, David Harvey pointed out, does not maintain any spatial distance between extended reproduction and primitive accumulation anymore, rather they are fused together. Marx's general theory of accumulation was based on some key liberal assumptions – such as free market, competition, private property, juridical individualism, freedom of contract etc. 'The disadvantage of these assumptions', for Harvey, 'is that they relegate accumulation based upon predation, fraud, and violence to an 'original state' that is considered no longer relevant or… as being somehow 'outside' of capitalism as a closed system'. But the reality is different. Capitalism possesses an insatiable appetite for assets outside of itself. 'If those assets, such as empty land or new raw material sources, do not lie to hand, then capitalism must somehow produce them'. Therefore, it is necessary for Harvey to re-evaluate 'the continuous role and persistence of the predatory practices of 'primitive' or 'original' accumulation'.

Since it is odd to call an ongoing process 'primitive' or 'original', Harvey prefers to call it 'accumulation by dispossession' (Harvey, 2003, 143–44). He agrees with Lenin that in spite of its horrific costs primitive accumulation had many 'positives' going for it. Accumulation by dispossession, by contrast, is all negative (Harvey, 2003, 162–4). It only reveals neoliberal capital's attempts to surmount the problem of over-accumulation by investing at home and abroad to privatize public assets, appropriate commons, and dismantle welfare. This cannot be challenged by a homogenizing agency of the dispossessed such as Hardt and Negri's 'multitude', nor can this be combated by strategies that are entirely country-specific. The task of the traditional left, according to Harvey, is to connect worldwide struggles against expanded accumulation with accumulation by dispossession by inventing an organic linkage between the two (Harvey, 2003, 176–77).

One cannot but be somewhat selective in concurring with dependency theorists or with Harvey. While dependency theory overstressed the structural imperatives in capital's circulation underrating the potentials of periphery to act as an agent of transformation, Harvey by drawing a rather indiscriminating picture of a 'post-welfare state' as a common target for creative destruction in both the global North and the South, ended up offering an inadequate account of the vital differences between the two. Nonetheless, the German social democrats, the Latin American radicals and the European critics of neoliberal enterprises converged on a common ground – they all agreed that capital's extra-economic coercion over its 'other' representing either the colonized, or the dependent or the commons did not terminate after capital came into being, but continued as its constitutive present. As a contrarian to the Leninist perspective on industrialization, as we shall see below, this argument could potentially have useful insights for the Indian left.

'Passive revolution', India

Since mid-1980s the importance of capital's political and ideological implications found a discursive salience in the analyses of some Indian political scientists and economists who tried to explain the peculiar cohabitation of pre-capitalist and capitalist social formations in postcolonial conditions. They liberally used Gramsci's idea of 'passive revolution' to get a grip of the nature of dialectic underway in India's late capitalist transformation (Kaviraj, 1988; Bardhan, 1984; Sen, 1988; Chaudhuri, 1988; Chatterjee, 1988; and Datta Gupta, 1988). Passive revolution for Gramsci was a process in which a social group occupied power not by rupturing the social fabric (like the Jacobins in France or Bolsheviks in Russia) but through adaptation and gradual transformation in the mode of what he calls 'war of position' (Forgacs, 2000). Gramsci made use of this idea diversely to explain the nineteenth century movement for national liberation (Risorgimento), the restoration of society after upheavals during the First World War, Fascism and the entire spectrum of liberal-constitutional movement in Italy. As a mode of 'revolution-restoration', passive revolution sets in places where the revolutionary classes cannot overthrow the preceding order to establish their complete supremacy, instead take recourse to prolonged negotiations, adjustments, compromises etc. attempting to establish a moral and cultural hegemony.

In India, passive revolution signified the compulsions on capital to accommodate pre-capitalist modes of production. During its fight against colonialism, India's national bourgeoisie represented popular interests within a broad 'equivalential chain', the effects of which lingered for several years after Independence. As part of the ruling coalition the bourgeoisie could not detach itself from the pre-capitalist social forces, nor could it forcibly install an economic regime of expanded reproduction on a great majority of peasant population. Universal suffrage and a democratic constitution placed serious constraints on the bourgeoisie's ability to act purely after its narrow instrumental rationality. In the postcolonial economic, therefore, the clash of thesis (pre-capital) and antithesis (rising capital) did not find resolution in a Hegelian synthesis (domination of capital), rather it produced a 'surrogate synthesis', a seemingly neutral space to enact compromises (Chatterjee, 1988). The Nehruvian state, with its bureaucratic apparatus and ideology of development, was the political form of such surrogacy. Clearly, the new Indian state, the state of passive revolution, could not afford to inflict an unrestrained extra-economic coercion if it were to legitimize capital.

In the late 1980s, Sudipta Kaviraj found the state in India faced with a 'structural crisis' in view of fresh challenges mounted by communal and regional forces. In its attempt to overcome these challenges, private corporate capital now broke free from the erstwhile compact of class forces, and started asserting its independence, indicating that passive revolution was 'lapsing into failure'. The structural crisis of the Indian state, paradoxically, was now correlated with the 'successes' of Indian capitalism (Kaviraj, 1988, 2441). What, then, was its aftermath? What happened in the following two decades when India's economy took a pronounced neoliberal turn with capital more stridently asserting its autonomy? Did the state now face a weaker resistance of the pre-capitalist forces? Could it now undertake an unrestrained primitive accumulation to facilitate an expanded reproduction of capital without inviting any political crisis? In other words, did private capital now reach a hegemonic stage from which it could unleash a rapid material expansion for building urban and industrial infrastructure even if that meant destruction of the peasant economy at an unprecedented scale? We shall see shortly that capital's hegemony in India's economic transformation was never unchallenged; it was incessantly contested by popular politics. The governmental left, we shall further see, drove straight into a political quagmire by allowing itself to be seduced by a hegemonic image of neoliberal capital. This eventually had a grossly paralytic effect on the left's ability to explore alternatives in the postcolonial economic.

Postcolonial economic

Kalyan Sanyal, for one, raised misgivings about the handling of passive revolution by the Gramscians calling their assumptions 'historicist' and 'stagist'. Though they attempted to 'break away from the stagist paradigm of historical materialism that reduces the peripheral capitalism to a mere case of failure', he argued, a 'full-scale capitalist transformation, i.e., the classical case, as a possibility, remains embedded in the framework as a reference point'. As a result, while the postcolonial case was treated as a 'successful passive revolution by the bourgeoisie, producing capitalism of a different kind', the analysis 'remains implicitly anchored in the trajectory of capitalist development implied by the framework of historical materialism' (Sanyal, 2007, 36). The story of passive revolution in India, therefore, is one of injunction on a full scale capitalist development since 'the need for legitimization in a framework of representative democracy does not allow the society to pass through this crucial stage' (Sanyal, 2007, 37). Kaviraj's observation of its 'failure' in the face of capitalism's 'success' illustrates vividly how the Gramscian readings of Indian politics – despite claims to the contrary – effectively presented a narrative of transition. The absence/presence of the narrative, Sanyal claimed, was internal to 'passive revolution' itself. '[F]or an understanding of postcolonial capital', according to Sanyal, 'we must break with the historicism that marks the Gramscian concept of passive revolution' (Sanyal, 2007, 38).

Starting here, Sanyal presented a radically contrarian thesis on capital's journey in the postcolonial economic rejecting any narrative of transition from pre- or non-capital to capital altogether. 'Isn't it possible to see capitalism as necessarily a complex of capitalist and non-capitalist production residing in the commodity space?' he asked. That is, capitalist development in these conditions not only presents a case in which capital combines with non capitalist economic processes, but more significantly it also 'necessarily produces' and 'brings them into existence' (Sanyal, 2007, 7, emphasis original). Sanyal, however, was not in agreement with those who believe that the pre-capitalist sector is preserved because it subsidizes 'capital's need' by supplying cheap labour and raw materials, by keeping wages at a minimum, by allowing subsistence village economy to partially shoulder the cost of reproducing labour power, or by providing a market in the 'natural economy' to transform surplus value into profit. The main problem with the 'capital's need' theory is that it does not explain how such need can continuously be met within a dynamic model of expanded reproduction where the 'outside' of capital, the sphere of non-capital, is by definition static. The only way such a model can survive for long is by a supersession of non-capital by expanded production – by universalizing capital – a possibility as we have seen was theoretically dismissed even by the Gramscians. Then what? Sanyal here took a critical turn, departing from Marx's own take on primitive accumulation.

For Marx, as already noted, primitive accumulation made capital's pre-history when pre-capitalist labour, dislocated and dispossessed, got absorbed as proletariat in the new mode of production. The 'outside' of capital could be internalized through such extra-economic coercions as it accompanied territorial expansion of imperial economies, settlements in colonial geographies of power, large manufacturing units using labour intensive technology and, above all, no instances of universal suffrage or a global discourse of rights. By contrast the postcolonial economic is radically different. It cannot push its workers to other lands, its capital intensive technologies promote a 'jobless growth', and the international standards of human rights set a limit on its ability to use repression for dispossessing the population in natural economy. Therefore, primitive accumulation in the postcolonial economy, according to Sanyal, does not eliminate capitals 'outside'; rather it leaves the domain of pre-capital partly unabsorbed into capital. Direct producers do get estranged from their means of production, 'but not all those who are dispossessed find a place within the system of capitalist production'. With no access to means of labour, they are left with labour alone; with no access to the wage economy, they cannot put their labour on sale as commodity. 'They are condemned to the world of the excluded, the redundant, the dispensable, having nothing to lose, not even the chains of wage-slavery' (Sanyal, 2007, 53).

But capital cannot let the 'outside' die, as that creates a crisis for its legitimacy. Therefore, 'capital's political and ideological conditions of existence require that the dispossessed producers inhabiting the outside be reunited with means of labour so that they can subsist by engaging in economic activities outside the domain of capital'. Parts of the means of labour appropriated by capital are sent back from the domain of capital to its outside 'where producers are reunited with the means of production to engage in non-capitalist production'. This 'decapitalization' of means of labour is what Sanyal called 'reversal of primitive accumulation' (Sanyal, 2007, 59). Such a complex unity of capital and non-capital, of primitive accumulation and its reversal, of expanded reproduction and self-subsistent need economy, of a reserve army of wage labour and a surplus labour in the economic 'wasteland' are what characterize the 'arising' of capital in the postcolonial economy.

> Seen thus, the postcolonial capital never becomes in the Hegelian sense...Like the proverbial Sisyphus, capital is engaged in a task that it never accomplished: its arising is never complete; its universality never fully established; its being forever postponed...(It is condemned) to a perpetual state of becoming (Sanyal, 2007, 61, emphases original, parenthesis added).

Universal/local

Despite its analytical precision, Sanyal's thesis raises a nagging doubt: while the compulsion to maintain the need economy is palpable, can that be external to capital? Or, can we instead perceive the so-called 'non-capital' as integral to capital's constitution? In chapter 2 ('The Two Histories of Capital') of his *Provincializing Europe*, Dipesh Chakrabarty had anticipated this problem. He argued that there can be two histories of capital, both universal and both can be written retrospectively after the arrival of capital. The first, which he called History 1, draws upon those antecedents which capital posits as its own being, i.e., those elements of capital's pre-history which lend themselves to capital's logic of reproduction. The second or History 2 is based on antecedents that do not make capital's life process but causes disruption for capital's self-reproduction. Chakrabarty used Marx's method, as opposed to his formulations, to uncover the intimate struggle between these two histories. While History 1 is dominant, it is not omnipotent, it cannot erase History 2 completely. 'But Marx does not himself think through this problem, although his method, if my analysis is right, allows us to acknowledge it' (Chakrabarty, 2000, 67). History 1 'is the universal and necessary history we associate with capital' and it 'forms the backbone of the usual narratives of transition to the capitalist mode of production' (Chakrabarty, 2000, 63). History 2, therefore, opens the possibility to interrogate what 'universality of capital' and the 'narrative of transition' signify in the present context.

By placing these two sets of distinction on one another, capital/non-capital and History 1/History 2, it seems History 1 alludes to capital as a 'universal' entity and History 2 to the 'local' instances of non-capital. Capital, on its part, symbolizes such virtues as law and efficiency, profit and property, rationality and modernity. Non-capital imbibes impulses like customs and rites, spatial practices and lethargy, commons and affect. As Michael de Certeau reminded us, the latter elements make everyday human practices 'beneath the fabricated and universal writing' of capital remaining illegible and subterranean, and giving 'the illusion, in neighbourhood or village, of immobility' (de Certeau, 1984, 200–01). The elements of non-capital make an 'illusionary inertia', their differences notwithstanding in reality they remain a part of capital's constitution. By lending themselves to difference, therefore, they don't proclaim an externality. 'Difference, in this account, is not something external to capital. Nor is it something subsumed into capital. It lives in intimate and plural relationships to capital, ranging from opposition to neutrality' (Chakrabarty, 2000, 66). Capital's utopia is to subsume all differences into its own logic, to delete every mnemonic trace having potentials to harm its extended reproduction; primitive accumulation is the method by which capital seeks to accomplish it.

'Different universal'

We have seen that primitive accumulation is an ongoing campaign, rather than an episodic conjuncture to mark capital's arrival. It is a campaign that illustrates capital's attempt to conquer non-capital and non-capital's constant resistance, in myriad forms, to submission. Politics is the lifeblood of this disruptive encounter. Capital, contrary to what Sanyal suggested, cannot 'reverse' primitive accumulation, as one cannot undo ageing, it can only hope to minimize its impact. Once inside the modern theatre of production and circulation, the so-called 'non-capital' can never reclaim its pristine externality. So rather than conceptualizing a split between capital and non-capital, Partha Chatterjee's way of distinguishing 'corporate' and 'non-corporate' capital, and his suggestion that the political management of capital calls not for an undoing of primitive accumulation but a reversal of its effects, seems a more accurate rendition of the changing landscape (Chatterjee, 2008).

What makes postcolonial capital stand out, therefore, is not that it is in a constant state of becoming, a capital disrupted. When read with the tools that Chakrabarty introduced, even the capital of 'full-scale reproduction' appears as permanently in the making, in negotiation with elements of non-capital. What makes postcolonial capital different is the manner in which corporate capital relates to its non-corporate counterpart, the texture of their interaction. The texture belongs to a history markedly different from that of metropolitan Europe, so it is neither derivative of, nor translatable to, the latter. Here the narrative of transition is discarded not because postcolonial capital is perpetually condemned to a state of incompleteness, as Sanyal suggested, but because it is yet unknown what kind of future it can posit for itself within the field of its historical and social differences. That future, in India's economic transformation, necessarily hinges on an accommodation of non-corporate capital in corporate scheme of things, of the logic of commons in that of profit, of the intent of distribution in that of accumulation. Such a social compact, however, is founded not on any moral goodwill, but on the strategic compulsion of political management, of undoing or minimizing the impact of corporate accumulation on the peasants, the unemployed, the informal workforce, the so-called 'dangerous classes'. While corporate entities possess the power of the elevated state having access to coercive apparatuses, the non-corporate segment wields the power of the embedded state emboldened by its number. It is the art of managing an exchange between the two by keeping their frontiers blurred that largely defines governance in India's postcolonial polity. It is the art of hemming popular demands in an equivalential chain to disrupt any societal equilibrium that constitutes the political in postcolonial democracy.

Such differences and uncertainties make the story of postcolonial capital both connected to a universal story of capital yet different from that in a dynamic, constitutive sense. It offers a narrative of capital's transition, albeit a narrative not reducible to the transition associated with classical primitive accumulation. This distinction is vital to understand how elements of difference and universality internal to capital combine to make something like a 'different universal', how large-scale dispossession in India is countered by symbols of re-possession, how non-corporate capital finds a place within capital's extended reproduction as a politico-economic necessity. In absence of an understanding of these distinctive and dynamic attributes of India's postcolonial political economy, where the priorities of the elevated state can work only as responsive to the politics of the embedded state, any economic policy is bound to falter in the face of popular resistance or administrative floundering.

Protests in Nandigram and Singur, and the responses of the parliamentary left, particularly of the CPI(M), laid bare an innocence typical of misjudging this reality. As a leftwing coalition its task was clearly to begin from the beginning, from the non-corporate popular segment at the ground level, sharpening its interests and heightening its anxieties in every available forum. Instead, it started with the premise that industrialization, as 'natural' and 'desirable', should get priority over every other consideration for economic transformation. As a result, in its effort to become a facilitator for industry, the left turned into an apologist for corporate capital mouthing the latter's rhetoric of development and sharing the latter's utopia of an uncomplicated transition. For a great majority of West Bengal's highly politicized small peasant population, sharecroppers and agricultural workers this indicated not just a threat to their longstanding balance with powerful economic interests, but more dramatically a betrayal by the left on which it had traditionally kept faith for evolving a grammar of government that combined the elevated and the embedded domains of state-power through meticulous mediations on their behalf. A careful scrutiny of the empirical events, as we shall take up later, would show that the early demand of the rural poor was not to put a stop on industry or SEZ, but to be taken on board for deciding the terms of exchange, to be consulted for identifying the land to be taken, labour to be employed, compensation to be paid.

Why on earth did the left in West Bengal depart from its 'government as practice' and decide to put a programmatic thrust for rapid industrialization disregarding decades of its pragmatic politics? The reasons are to be located in the changing landscape of the state's politics, of its party society, and in the felt compulsions as well as opportunities in India's neoliberal economy. The political part we have discussed earlier in the book and will return once more to it towards the end of this chapter. The economic compulsions, which we now turn to, resulted largely from a felt need to attract capital in the hope of arresting decades of industrial decline and to bridge the budgetary gap between revenue and social spending, both now considered necessary as well as possible in a market-driven economy. To get a clearer understanding we briefly recount the story of West Bengal's industry in the last five decades.

State of industry

Between 1946 and 1965, as industrial census figures show, West Bengal topped the list in employing people in manufacturing industries, and was second only to Maharashtra in terms of value added (Dasgupta,

1998; Banerjee, 1982; Das Gupta, 1994). During the same period, however, Maharashtra received more industrial licenses from the central government. Higher value addition with lower employment means more efficiency and addition of non-wage value leading to higher profitability. West Bengal's low labour productivity relative to many other states could be due to old industries, low skill level, low literacy rate and a precarious industrial base severely impaired after the partition (Bagchi, 1998). One of the reasons for West Bengal's top slot in engineering industry was evidently its location advantage – proximity to coal and mineral producing regions in eastern India.

The location advantage, however, was eliminated by the freight equalization policy for steel that the central government introduced in the mid-1950s. Its impact was immediate on West Bengal, as during the next several decades the state started losing out to other regions in obtaining licenses for industries that required steel. In 1966 alone, 35 steel-based industries were de-licensed, which was a fatal blow to West Bengal's traditional advantages in manufacturing. Curiously, no such equalization was introduced by New Delhi for other materials, such as raw cotton, which could have offered the state an opportunity to grow in a different direction. This coincided with the period of stagnancy in the agricultural sector, which meant slow expansion of market for industrial produce within the state barring those items produced for consumption of government or of other industries. Though the central government made the highest industrial investments in West Bengal (13.3 per cent of its total investment) between 1947 and 1968, the slide of the state's industrial production could not be stopped.

The situation got even worse between mid-1960s and mid-1970s. The Indo-Pakistan war in 1965, and two consecutive years (1965–67) of harvest failure spiralled into an industrial recession, most adversely affecting the metal products and transport goods industries. The immediate fall out of the recession was massive retrenchment of industrial workers in the period 1966–69 of which West Bengal was among the worst hit. Between 1965 and 1968, out of eight major industrialized states in the country total employment in manufacturing increased for all states barring West Bengal and Gujarat. With the organized left anxious to protect the interest of the worker, West Bengal in this period experienced an unprecedented rise in labour militancy causing record loss in workdays. The crisis got deepened as harvest failures in 1965–67 caused food shortage (especially of Bengal's staple rice) leading to outbreaks of food riots and agitations. With the United Front elected to power in 1967, aggressive working class agitation reached a new peak. Between 1961 and 1968, West Bengal remained witness to a steep decline in the number of licenses for new industries (from 62 to 6) and for expansion of existing units (from 66 to 15). Investment of capital in new ventures came down from ₹ 21 crore in 1966–67 to ₹ 9 crore in 1969–70 (Sreemanta Dasgupta, 1988, 3051). During 1970–77, West Bengal shared the country's sluggish industrial growth (except 1976) and its procurement of industrial licenses grew only marginally, while it now started falling behind other states, particularly Gujarat. Between January 1970 and December 1977 a paltry sum of ₹ 213 crore was invested in West Bengal.

On assuming office, the Left Front government adopted an industrial policy in its bid to increase employment in the industrial as well as agricultural sector (GoWB, 1978e). It placed new emphasis on 'lessening the stranglehold' of monopoly houses and multinational firms in the state, encouraging small and cottage industries, and gradually expanding public sector enterprises. Admitting that 'it is not possible to leave out altogether the multinational corporations and the big industrial houses in the immediate period', it resolved to make efforts so that these companies re-invested major part of their profit for generation of employment in the state. However, '[t]here can be no question of allowing new multinational units to come in' its document clearly stated.

The industrial slump continued. The number of industrial licenses issued for West Bengal over 1977–87 was as low as 438 (compared to 1254 for Maharashtra and 2042 for Gujarat). Even the licenses issued were not of equal value for substantial expansion of industry. For example, in 1984 West Bengal received 93 licenses of which only five were for new units and eight for substantial expansion (Sreemanta Dasgupta, 1988, 3053). In the first 10 years of the Left Front government, the average annual investment in industrial projects was as low as ₹ 86 crore. In 1977–78 the state's share of the total employed in industries across the country was 15 per cent and of the total value added 12.2 per cent, in 1987–88 they both came down to 9.4 per cent and 8.9 per cent respectively. West Bengal's employment figures in factory sector in 1987–88 were lower than even the 1970–71 census figure that, again, was below the 1965–66 figures due to recession. So the downhill journey of the state in big manufacturing industry continued unabated despite a clear reduction in the workers' militancy during the first 10 years of the Left Front.

In fact, during the better part of 1980s the state saw a series of industrial closures as old and sick units of jute, cotton and manufacturing industries started to shut down, workers were laid off with unions agreeing to terms of settlements, inconceivable in the heady days of labour unrest. By the late 1980s, the industrial situation was so bad in the state that the working class practically lost its bargaining power vis a vis capital which made the situation, ironically, a good time to invest.[10] Things started changing as the Congress was unseated from the central government in 1989, and successive coalitions gave the left some leverage in the centres of power. In 1988 the state attracted ₹ 73.4 crore in investment that jumped to ₹ 136.54 crore in 1989 and ₹ 230.19 crore in 1990. Two important changes took place as Congress returned to power in the early 1990s: almost total scrapping of the licensing system for setting up industries and partial annulment of the freight equalization for steel.

Jyoti Basu was quick to welcome the removal of these regulations and announced his resolve to restore West Bengal's status as a leading industrial state. This had an immediate impact on West Bengal, which was now open to private corporate investment and advanced technology. In September 1994, the government announced its New Industrial Policy which declared that:

> apart from the presence of large Indian industrial houses…a number of Multi-national Corporations (MNCs) have long been successfully operating in the state… A welcome development is that a good number of Non Residents Indians, MNCs directly or through foreign governments and Indian industrial houses have…shown

special interest in coming to West Bengal (GoWB, 1994, Section 4.4, 7).

This approach, as one recognizes without any difficulty, was very different from the one followed in the early days of the Left Front government.

Once the government adopted the new policy, West Bengal saw a relative surge in investment (Sinha, 2006, 156-7). Between 1991 and 1997 the state stood only third (after Maharashtra and Tamil Nadu) in its share of proposals for Foreign Direct Investment (FDI) among major Indian states (Sinha, 2004, 78; 2006). To manage the changing industrial climate a semi-autonomous WBIDC was set up with Somnath Chatterjee, a CPI(M) leader and a close confidant of Jyoti Basu, at its helm. Clearly, the party and its labour wing were deliberately kept aside from the new discourse of development in which industry – capital-intensive and privately owned – were to play a big role. Credibility was an issue in the new scenario. The investors had to be convinced that the state government was sincere in its commitment to maintain industrial peace and that there was no imminent threat to their investment. Left Front's basic constituencies had to be convinced that by inviting big capital the state government was not capitulating to the new economic regime dictated by New Delhi, on the contrary it was trying to re-establish the economic autonomy of the regional state. Within the party forums as well as outside in public meetings and media interviews Jyoti Basu and Somnath Chatterjee repeatedly argued that there was no other alternative to this policy if the state government was to survive in the new economy: where, else, is the money? The central committee of the CPI(M) stood firmly behind the goverment stating, among other things: 'it is upto the Left Front government to initiate steps to attract capital investment in West Bengal. This can be done only by allowing greater investment of private capital in various sectors' (quoted in Karat, 2002).

A number of left critics were quick to take up an issue with the governing left on this point. They argued that the new industrial policy marked a departure from class politics and was dangerously close to the one adopted by the central government (Das Gupta, 1995). They wanted the state government to adopt a more cautious and graded approach, and stick to its commitment of confining private investments only core and essential sectors. Most importantly, the critics wanted the government not to trade the interests of the working classes in its eagerness to procure private investments. Such cautioning was prompted by analyses suggesting that in India's post-liberalization economy states with pro-worker legislations – such as West Bengal – had a slower pace of growth for their industrial units than those with pro-employer laws. (Aghion, et al., 2008). Interestingly, the informal labour market and acquisitions of agricultural land – which would subsequently emerge as the most contentious issues – were yet to gain prominence in the debate over investments of private capital.

2001 onward there was a consorted attempt to project Buddhadeb Bhattacharjee, who took the mantle of the state on the eve of an assembly election from the octogenarian Jyoti Basu, as an investment-friendly, pragmatic and unorthodox leader of the left with whom the investors could do business. In the mainstream newspaper a new coinage – 'Brand Buddha' – made rounds, a brand that seemingly 'sold' well in the neoliberal marketplace (Das, 2013, 246–56; Basu, 2007, 288–306). During the better part of 1990s the CPI(M) had veered around courting private capital for West Bengal's 'development'. With the advent of Buddhadeb three simultaneous processes started. The government started asserting its autonomy from the party. The party toned down its anti-capitalist rhetoric. 'Efficiency' and 'image-correction' became the buzzwords in the administrative and media circles. Highlighting its stable government, industrial peace, strategic location, and a fairly workable bureaucracy, the state now sought to emerge as a major destination for domestic and global capital (Pedersen, 2001, 665).

After the CPI(M)'s Congress in 2002, it seems, the social democratic emphasis of the parliamentary left got overshadowed by a more pro-liberalization perspective, despite misgivings within the party (Das, 2013, 246). The signs of this change did not go unnoticed in the industrial circles. In 2009 the general secretary of the Associated Chamber of Commerce and Industry of India (ASSOCHAM), the apex business body, remarked:

During the last five-six years, there has been a tremendous change in the perception about West Bengal among the investors outside the state... Today there is hardly any large industrial house which has no presence in West Bengal, while till about five-seven years back talking about investing there was a joke (quoted in Das, 2013, 250).

Some substantial investments were made in iron and steel sector, followed by chemicals, petrochemicals and food processing. Haldia started off with an initial investment of ₹ 60 billion, 'in 2006–07 the figure stands at ₹ 300 billion'. Mitsubishi chemicals were looking to open a second unit there after investing ₹ 1.7 billion, Jindals showed interest to set up a steel plant by investing ₹ 35.5 billion in West Midnapore, Videocon proposed a white goods factory in the north. 'IBM, Cognizant, and GE Capital have evinced interest in investing in the IT sector and we need their units'. (Bhattacharjee, 2007). It was with such exuberance that the Left Front government, emboldened by a massive election win in 2006 for the seventh time without a break, driven by its ideological conviction in the 'objective necessity' for a 'painful transition', and – as discussed earlier – largely innocent of the specificities of capital in India's transforming political economy, decided to go for an all out campaign to set up industries on vast tracts of agricultural land in Singur and Nandigram.

Contestations

The atmosphere was getting edgy in Singur in the post-monsoon months of August and September 2006 as the sowing period was ending. Wherever the government officials went to issue acquisition notice, they faced stiff resistance by the KJRC workers and beat a retreat. On 22 August, the Block Development Officer (BDO) arranged a public hearing of grievances, which was foiled by the KJRC demonstrators who gheraoed his office. In the last week of August, the Calcutta High Court allowed a writ petition that challenged the legality of land acquisition in Singur, which encouraged the protesters. In early September, an international fact finding team went to Singur and, following its meetings with the affected peasants, sent a hard hitting letter to the state government, with a copy to the United Nations Commission on Human Rights (UNCHR) and posted its findings on the internet. Rezzak Mollah, the land and land reforms minister, now admitted that Singur presented a 'complicated scenario'. Only 'a third' of the affected landowners had consented to acquisition, and a litany of litigation threatened to stall the project unless the government managed to quickly plug 'several legal loopholes'. Situation turned worse on 20 September as the government suddenly announced that the land which was notified earlier under the Land Acquisition Act of 1894 had now been vested in the government 'without any encumbrance'. In lay terms it meant that the land belonging both to 'willing' and 'unwilling' owners now changed from private to the government's ownership. Some eminent personalities, including the former Prime Minister V. P. Singh, urged the government to wait till the end of the harvesting season before imposing eviction.

Eager to pay up compensation money to the consenting peasants, the government decided to issue cheques from the BDO's office on 25 September. This, again, was foiled as five thousand villagers, almost half of them women, thronged the BDO's office and stopped anyone from collecting the cheques, thus paralysing the process. A night-long sit-in continued as Mamata Banerjee and Rabindranath Bhattacharjee joined the protesters. In the wee hours next day, the government deployed the Rapid Action Force, which arrested 78 protesters and bundled both Banerjee and Bhattacharjee out of Singur. The reaction was far reaching. Mamata Banerjee called for a 12-hour Bengal bandh (general strike) on 9 October with a section of the Congress now supporting her. Next day, on 27 September, Congress leaders Subrata Mukherjee, Somen Mitra and Sudeep Bandopadhyay shared stage with her for the first time in many years. Though Priya Ranjan Dashmunshi, the union minister of information and broadcasting, still backed the state government, there was no denying that support for Mamata was rising. Dashmunshi asked the government to call an all-party meeting, which the government readily accepted.

With the government relying on law and force to clear the space for

191

industry in Singur, the opposition focused on building a moral case against eviction. In early October, a former chief justice of the Supreme Court and several judges made an appeal to Ratan Tata to relocate his project in view of the ongoing agitation. On the auspicious night of Bijoya Dashami, the final day of the Durga Puja celebration, the bulk of Singur residents turned off lights and stayed in the dark as a mark of protest. The government-sponsored all-party meeting on 4 October fell through, as the TMC refused to attend, following which the government declared that it soon would take physical possession of the entire land before handing it over to the Tatas. Meanwhile, the central government gave approval to a number of SEZs in the country, the one in Nandigram included. Sensing that the state government was firm in its resolve to oppose her movement against eviction, Mamata declared that she would never allow the government to implement its plan for setting up a SEZ in Nandigram.

Unfazed by these developments, on 11 October Buddhadeb declared that the government had completed its legal possession in Singur, and was ready to give the land to the Tatas. He took pain to explain how difficult it was to get the Tatas invest in the state over Uttarakhand and Himachal Pradesh. West Bengal offered the 'best package', of which the location was one. An editorial in *Ganashakti*, the CPI(M)'s Bengali daily, thanked the Tatas for agreeing to invest in West Bengal. Nirupam Sen assured the detractors that the land was not being given outright to the Tatas, but leased out for 99 years. While the government agreed to spend ₹ 148 crores to compensate those affected, the Tatas promised to invest ₹ 1000 crores for the factory. The Tatas insisted that if they obtained possession of the land by December, the first car would roll out in 2008. As protests were brewing and getting sharpened, both the government and the industrial house gave the impression that the course of events was entirely under their control.

Seeds of protest

The state government's Statistical Handbook prior to the acquisition indicated that Singur was a block with a thriving agri-business whose 83 per cent land was irrigated with a whopping 220 per cent crop density. Paddy and potato were the main crops in the region, jute and several vegetables were also grown. A survey conducted in November 2006 by a civil society initiative, 'Sanhati Udyog', revealed that the 997 acres assigned for the factory contained more than 11,000 landholdings of around 2 bighas (0.66 acres) or less per holding on average, feeding around 6,000 families, of which 3,500 were subsistence farmers and 1,200 unrecorded bargadars. Singur also attracted migrant workers from the arid districts of West Bengal and from Jharkhand. Cultivation apart, 400–450 were cycle cart drivers, 200 odd families relied primarily on animal husbandry, 150 or so sold vegetables and roughly 500 were employed by five cold storages in neighbouring Ratanpur. These figures, however, were grossly at variance with those supplied by the CPI(M) or the state government.[11]

Was the Singur movement against land acquisition from the beginning? A large section of civil society organizations as well as the opposition parties were convinced that it indeed was with its anti-industry stridency. On the other hand, for the government, the locals were misled by the opposition into believing that they stood only to lose once their land was given for the factory, disregarding the 'unlimited' opportunities that the new economy promised to offer. The seeds of protest, it seems, were sown somewhere in between. Initially, the locals were opposed – not so much to the factory – as to their exclusion from the process of fixing compensation and the price for their land. Those with unclear legal standing – such as unrecorded bargadars or landowners without proper papers – were uncertain about their prospect of getting compensated at all. They also suspected that the government tended to lower its estimate of double-cropped holdings in order to reduce its compensation liabilities. Their early demonstration against the Tata officials perhaps signalled an acute disapproval of these uncertainties. The message was that the locals better not be taken for granted by the company, which the unilateralism of the state government was seen as encouraging. But the government's perpetual apathy, and the CPI(M)'s lethargy, rapidly changed the situation and made Singur a fertile ground for a movement *against* the factory, which Mamata Banerjee eventually lapped up. Mamata, on her part, should be credited for accurately sensing the opportunities she was offered by the left's blunder. When Nirupam Sen, the industry minister, finally went to Singur to explain the government's compensation package and the benefits that the project could bring, the KJRC activists organized a sizable crowd waving black flags at the minister.

By mid-October 2006 it became clear that the protesting farmers, encouraged by the KJRC to sow potato seeds as a sign of their determination to continue possession over the land, would not budge without a fight. On its part, the KJRC now portrayed the clash between the government and the 'unwilling' landowners as not one for adequate compensation, but for the life and livelihood of people against an insensitive administration eager to appease big business. The peasants' moral case got strengthened as the local administration allegedly committed some petty acts of retribution such as damaging the local pumping station in Madhyapara, thus blocking a vital source of irrigation. Powerful 'non-partisan' voices like those of the social activist Medha Patkar and the noted writer Mahasweta Devi now extended their support for the movement as they attended a KJRC meeting on the Bajemelia hospital ground in end-October. They warned the state government that it solely would be responsible should law and order collapse in Singur following its attempt to evict the peasants and take possession of the land. They also held a public hearing against acquisition in which Dudh Kumar Dhara, a member of the village panchayat, complained that the government did not bother to consult the panchayat before issuing the acquisition order. No gram sabha was convened, the locals were not taken into confidence, and the government worked its way only through those belonging to the ruling party. The parliamentary left, it seems, violated every protocol of its governmental mode evolved in the 1980s, when special care was taken by the mediatory party and mass organizations to make higher administrative policies comply with ground level popular interests.

Signs of a desperate policy adopted at the top and thrust unilaterally with little space for strategic manoeuvrings upon a population on the edge, started affecting the unity of the Left Front. A heated debate reportedly sparked off on the last day (30 October) of a state committee meeting of the CPI(M), where a clear division was registered on land acquisition.[12] Jyoti Basu 'cautioned' the government especially in matters of seizing multi-crop land and advised that 'enough' compensation be paid to the land losers. He was getting jittery as other left partners – the CPI, the RSP and the Forward Bloc – complained about a distinct lack of transparency in the actual terms of the state government's contracts with the Tatas, the Salim Group and the Reliance. That Basu took these criticisms seriously was evident when he insisted that he would attend the Left Front meeting slated for 3 November despite his poor health. In the middle of this, the rural comrades of the CPI(M) began to push the alarm bell. Leaders from Howrah, Hooghly and South 24 Parganas urged the party top leadership to 'prepare comprehensive policy guidelines on land acquisition as well as compensation and rehabilitation to clear the contradictions within the government, the party and the front'. On a more desperate note a representative from Hooghly district, where Singur is located, spelt out that the acquisition there 'should be treated as an exception rather than a rule'.

As the growing dispute between the peasants and the government was taking a political toll and the principal opposition party successfully throwing its weight behind the agitated peasants, a section within the left demanded that the state government should stay clear of land acquisition for private corporate houses, and instead allow the latter to go for a direct purchase of land from owners. Against this the CPI(M) leadership argued that in the fertile regions of rural West Bengal, where land reforms generated a preponderance of middle and small peasant proprietors, a direct purchase of land for big factories or townships would require prolonged negotiations with numerous landholders, which no potential investor can find attractive. Besides, a big corporation, if it were to purchase directly, would rely on the local land dealers and powerful interest groups, players who definitely would make a killing before handing such lands over to the buyer. This would severely increase, not reduce, the vulnerability of the rural poor. In addition, the government supposedly had the 'most accurate' land records to ensure that price and compensation were correctly determined and delivered to the actual landowner, not any fictitious claimant.

Little did these arguments reflect the changed property and political equations at the ground level. In the commercially active and highly fertile southern districts of West Bengal, *de facto* operational rights over land were often transferred behind the government's back, with no records of such part-sales or lease deeds kept with the block administration. These arrangements, secured by firm 'verbal contracts', involved no transaction cost or complicated dealings with the bureaucracy. As a result, when the government announced compensation for the legal landowners, the absentee landowners with little stake in the land were among the first to collect their cheques, and the actual cultivators or informal lease holders swelled the rank of the protesters. Moreover, though the government wanted to cut the 'middlemen' out, in the changed configuration of rural power, these middlemen or 'contractors' – as discussed in previous chapters – now established their control over available organs of the local party units. These chieftains, local and not-so-local, expected to make it big from the proposed industrial transformation. Their enthusiasm for big capital investments was often in conflict with the interests of the poor and self-cultivating peasants.

Intensification

Early November onward, the confrontation between government and the protesting peasants in Singur got further intensified. Government wanted to close the legal formalities as quickly as possible, and hand over the site to the Tatas so that the latter could take up construction work immediately. It was expected that once the construction started job-opportunities would open up and training for the local youth would begin. With such a 'positive' drift in the local economy it would be difficult for KJRC or TMC to sustain their protest. So the focus was on efficacy, on quick collection of 'consent letters' from the landholders willing to sell their property as smoothly and securely as possible. The site was cordoned off to enable the building of a boundary wall, visits by outsiders prohibited and any public announcement on the other potential hotspot, Nandigram, was kept suspended for the time being.

On its part, the protest movement did not have much of a legal case going for it, and given the smallness of the Opposition in the state's legislature, it had little option but to take up a fight with the administration by mobilizing mass action, and building a moral case against the regime. Cultivators not willing to part with land in Singur were indeed victims of injustice, but that did not make a big enough cause to attract wider public attention. Besides, it was important for leaders like Mamata Banerjee not to appear as creating obstacles for West Bengal's economic revival an accusation that the government routinely made. The Opposition was not just fighting a government, but also the 'pro-poor' image of the left electorally endorsed through decades. To undermine the government Mamata had to attack this image first. She had to harden her stance, step up her stakes, and do everything possible to get the regime reveal its 'real' face, a face – according to her – of violence and machination, of cold brutality and downright pretension. On 5 November she issued her 'final ultimatum', demanding that the government must return all land seized to the farmers by 17 November.

With no concession from the government, Mamata brought out a 'dandi march' in Kolkata on the day her ultimatum expired. Two days later the KJRC took out a protest march from the Bajemelia hospital ground in Singur. The march ended in Khaserberi where Becharam Manna, the convenor of KJRC, addressed a well attended meeting in presence of representatives from the CPI(ML), SUCI, CPI(ML)-New Democracy, and APDR. On 30 November, the state government announced its plan to detain any political leader visiting Singur and imposed a 'prohibition order' under the section 144 of the Code of Criminal Procedure (CrPC).

On the same day Mamata Banerjee headed for Singur. She was stopped near Maitipara in Hooghly, allegedly 'pushed, shoved, and bundled into a car', and sent straight back to Kolkata.[13] Reaching the city, she and her supporters marched into the premises of the state legislature, ransacked whatever they found, and smashed the furniture. Blind rage got the better of any sensible agitation, giving the government a chance to call her 'fascistic'. The Speaker kept the House open for public display of the broken furniture as exhibits. Biman Bose, the chairman of the Left Front, remarked that Indian democracy never saw an MP vandalizing a state legislature, indicating that Mamata's movement had hit a moral dead-end. Undeterred, next day (1 December) the TMC called for a 12-hour flash strike to protest her arrest. The strike, however, received little public support, forcing Mamata to withdraw halfway through.[14]

It seemed that the movement was now slipping out of Mamata's hands. She pledged to stop the acquisition, yet the government paraded the 'willing' landholders happily collecting their cheques. The government made special police arrangement for fencing the site and cut up all routes from Kolkata, stopping leaders trying to reach Singur. This made the government a target of Opposition ire for being thoroughly 'undemocratic' and 'authoritarian'. The TMC, after its vandalism, found its position severely compromised. The onus now fell on Mamata Banerjee to find a way to jack up her credibility. A veteran in playing with populist passion she took a moral route to demonstrate her 'sacrifice' for the cause. On 4 December, she launched an 'indefinite hunger strike' from a platform set up at the heart of central Kolkata. This proved a turning point in reinventing her political fortune.

Claims, counter-claims

As Mamata Banerjee was on fast in Kolkata, a war of conflicting claims raged over the government's compensation package, and over the number of landowners who had 'consented'. An editorial of the CPI(M)'s national mouthpiece *People's Democracy* claimed that the government had received voluntary consent for 950 out of 997.11 acres and the owners had collected their compensation.[15] In the remaining land consent could not be procured because the owners were not local residents. Countering the Opposition's claim that substantial part of land taken by the project was highly fertile and multi-crop in character, the editorial stated that 90 per cent was mono-crop. 'The compensation package worked out by the Left Front government after elaborate consultation with the local population' was also considered more than adequate. Mono-crop land was purchased at ₹ 8.6 lakh/acre, double-crop at ₹ 12 lakh/acre, 'one and half times more than the market price'.[16] The government not only compensated 237 recorded sharecroppers, but also included 170 odd unrecorded ones though it was not legally mandatory. They got 25 per cent of what was given to the landowners which was on average ₹ 2 lakhs per cultivator of mono-crop and ₹ 3 lakhs per cultivator of double crop land.

Compensation aside, according to Nirupam Sen, the Minister of Industries, the factory in Singur made good economic sense. In a press briefing he claimed that land in any case was losing its agricultural character, being sold for industrial use at a frantic pace after the construction of the expressway.[17] A centrally imposed moratorium on such transactions was lifted just a year ago. The situation changed so drastically in these months that more than half of the sales deeds that the government drafted were with 'non-agricultural' landholders scattered over five maujas. 'So it is clear', according to the minister, 'that the farmers in Singur sold their land long before the government started acquisition for the factory'. A cold storage, two petrol stations, a ceramic factory and a condom factory had already come up in the locality. With the government spending ₹ 140 crores and the Tatas a total of ₹ 1500 crores, he claimed, 10,000 jobs would be created in the area, an 'immensely good sign' for the state's flailing industrial economy.

The farmers, according to Sen could get a better return from bank interests than what they possibly earned from agriculture. 'We have already created 4,500 workdays in Singur as 1,500 men and women were employed in the construction of the boundary wall, many of whom would be employed for guarding the factory'. Though employment cannot be guaranteed in the 'new economy', he assured that greater job opportunities would open up for the locals. On 10 December, the SUCI, a constituent of the KJRC, released a rival list at a press conference in Beraberi Purba Para of Singur. This list claimed that the government was yet to get consent from owners of nearly 344.91 acres spread over several maujas, and less than half of the government's compensation money could so far be disbursed.[18] This perhaps was the first detailed rebuttal of the figures that the government routinely furnished.

In the midst of this war of words, on 18 December a young woman, Tapasi Malik, the daughter of a sharecropper who lost his land in the project site, was murdered in Singur.[19] Her burning body was discovered in a pit inside the fenced off area of the project. Mamata Banerjee claimed that Tapasi was a KJRC activist and she was raped and murdered by the 'CPI(M) goons' employed as security guards at the site. She wasted no time to call a 48-hour bandh – the fourth strike within a month and an unusually long one even by West Bengal standards – from her fast. Mamata's fast and Tapasi's death turned Singur into an intense emotional wrangle, way beyond the calculus of economic losses and gains that the state government had pitched its strategies on. The movement now gained a national if not a global recognition, and it was impossible for the state government to shut the opposition out the way it could even few weeks back. Mamata called off her fast on 28 December, after she received a letter from A. P. J. Abdul Kalam, the President of India. On the same day, another announcement was made with far-reaching political consequences. The Haldia Development Authority issued a pithy note stating that agricultural land would be acquired in Usmanchak, Jadubarichak and two more mauzas in Khejuri for the construction of an industrial complex.

Nandigram imbroglio

In Nandigram, several anti-CPI(M) outfits had for quite some time been active in their attempt to convince the local people that they should be prepared against a plan chalked out by the state government to seize a vast tract of agricultural land for setting up the SEZ to be funded by the Salims. The locals had no idea about the scale of the project. When they enquired with the members of the CPI(M)-run village panchayat, they were assured that no such plan was in the offing, and it was just another example of falsehood spread by desperate opposition parties. People, indeed, had reasons to be concerned. They had memories of the 'Jelligram Project' for which in 1977 the Calcutta Port Trust and Burn Standard acquired some 400 acres in nearby Gangachar. Only few land losers were given a paltry compensation, that too after a prolonged court case in Kolkata. Only a handful of locals got jobs which they eventually lost as, after few years of difficult running, the factory was shut down in 1989. The factory land was not returned to the peasants but was transferred to the Zilla Parishad for 'social forestry'.

On 29 December, Lakshman Seth, the CPI(M) MP and the party's local satrap, organized a public meeting near the Nandigram Bus Stand. In the meeting he spoke at length on how wonderfully the place would change once the proposed SEZ metamorphosed into an urban-industrial complex far bigger than neighbouring Haldia, considered a feather on the left government's cap. He read out an inventory of 27 mauzas slated for acquisition in Nandigram-1 block. Until now the villagers thought that the project would be limited to just two – Usmanchak and Jadubarichak – and had no idea that the government's proposal extended over a much larger area affecting almost the entire population of the region. So the anti-government campaigners were right, the villagers were literally shell-shocked. The local CPI(M) leaders lost whatever was left of their credibility as villages after villages now hardened their resolve not to yield. On that cold winter night a political vacuum was created in Nandigram inciting an immediate response.[20]

Within a couple of days Seth's claims got the look of an official approval in a notice that the Haldia Development Authority, under the aegis of Seth himself, issued on 2 January 2007, enlisting two maujas of Khejuri along with 27 named earlier for the project at the 'initial stage'. The Salim Group's 'mega chemical hub' was to take 10,000 acres, and Pawan Ruia's 'ship building and repairing' unit another 2,500 acres. Together the land required here was several times larger than in Singur. The notice was delivered to all village panchayats in the region asking them to get ready for the acquisition. It proved highly contentious triggering off a series of incidents that spiralled out of the administration's control. Eventually, the chief minister Buddhadeb Bhattacharjee had to call the notice 'patently illegal' and ask people to treat it as 'a scrap of paper for the waste bin'. By then, however, the major damage was done, and thousand of CPI(M) party workers were driven out of their villages lest they collaborated with the government's 'anti-peasant' moves. The question is, why did Seth, despite being a member of a disciplined party, take such a hurried and risky action?

The answer probably lay in Seth's interpretation of the political conjuncture. He saw that the government pushed itself into a corner in Singur, it would be difficult to resolve the situation there without a thorough and difficult negotiation with the TMC. He also sensed the uneasiness of his South 24 Parganas comrades, led by none other than Rezzak Mollah, over the proposed acquisition in their district for an expressway and a couple of large townships along the route. The expressway was supposed to connect Kolkata with Haldia by a bridge to be built over the Hooghly River, and so investment in Nandigram was conditional upon access to land on the other side of the river. Apprehensive that dillydallying by the local party units there coupled with indecisions at the top might push such an 'attractive' investment in and around Haldia – his sphere of influence – off its track, he judged that the time was just right to show the world how eager the region was for 'development'. In his smug overconfidence, little to be surprised, he overlooked how the local mood in Nandigram had changed over the last several months, and how a vast section of the peasantry was determined not to give in to a regime whose local agents had lost its confidence.

Effects of the notice were brought home next day (3 January). A meeting was underway in the panchayat office in Garchakraberia when it was attacked by some 3,000 villagers. They ransacked the office and set two police vehicles on fire. The meeting, the panchayat functionaries claimed, was to prepare for a central team's visit to the village for declaring it 'nirmal' (clean) in recognition of its improved sanitation facilities. The attackers, however, were agitated by a rumour that the meeting was for finalizing a detailed plan for land acquisition. They gathered activists of the TMC, the SUCI, the Jamiat Ulema-i-Hind and the CPI(ML)-Liberation. In response, the administration sent an additional 350 policemen which included the Rapid Action Force.

The locals in Sonachura, Osmanchak, Jalpai, Garchakraberia and other places decided to deny the police an entry into the villages. 'As the night fell, the villagers began digging up roads to cut off police and officials. Armed with bows and arrows and swords, around 2,000 villagers held vigil near approach roads.'[21] In all probability these were not spontaneous actions, they were preceded by months of preparation by the anti-SEZ activists in the locality. That it took the ruling party completely off guard only proved its flailing sense of the popular pulse. 'The government has not yet started the spadework in Nandigram, but the violence is a grim reminder of the challenges that lie ahead when the acquisition eventually begins', wrote a newspaper.[22]

Divided heads

In Kolkata, a subtle war of words broke out on the same day between CPI(M)'s general secretary Prakash Karat and West Bengal chief minister Buddhadeb Bhattacharjee. The occasion was a public meeting for the 40th foundation day of *Ganashakti*, the party's Bangla daily, and the bone of contention was SEZ. Karat had for some time been persuading the United Progressive Alliance government in New Delhi to revise its SEZ policy, especially the provisions related to land use for non-productive purposes. The CPI(M), he said, was against 'land grabbing in the name of special economic zones' and West Bengal was no exception. State-specific compulsions made it difficult for the party to launch a broadside against SEZ, which was necessary for its ideological coherence. Bhattacharjee, on his part, was on the defensive. He said West Bengal would limit the number of SEZs to 'four-to-five' and allow them only in core sectors such as petrochemicals. Defending his policy Bhattacharjee said that the SEZ's are 'coming up across the country, we can't say no to them'.[23] He claimed that West Bengal had the 'best compensation package' and that 'history will not spare' the left if it failed to seize this opportunity. With 62 per cent of the state's population dependent on agriculture that had a mere 27 per cent share in the state's total income (a shade higher than industry, 24 per cent), his choices apparently were limited.[24]

Indications were that the left government in West Bengal was now staring at its first major blunder with the new industrial strategy. Its lack of clarity generated differences not just in the Left Front, but also within the CPI(M). Prakash Karat tried to explain why the Left Front was pro-SEZ in West Bengal, and why land acquisition in Singur was different from coercive acquisition in other states. While he endorsed government initiatives in Singur, when asked on the raging anti-SEZ protests in Nandigram, Karat reportedly 'kept mum'.[25] CPI(M)'s allies, however, refused to be so discreet. Asoke Ghosh, the Forward Bloc leader, asked why the CPI(M) failed to share the 'relevant documents' on its SEZ policy despite its 'assurance in the last Left Front meeting'. D. Raja of the CPI warned that the state government should 'learn a lesson from Singur and not take hasty steps in Nandigram and other SEZ projects'. Both these parties insisted that 'in letter and spirit' the state government should follow the note on SEZ that they jointly prepared for the United Progressive Alliance. Karat, in reply, said 'we have made various proposals in the joint left note all of it cannot be feasible everywhere at one go, neither have we reached conclusions on all issues'.

With the Opposition revived, the protesters up in arms, the coalition of the left divided and the CPI(M) confused, the ground beneath the left's feet started to slide. The state government pushed itself into a political quagmire, and as violence in the countryside escalated with the rise in police brutalities and partisan clashes, the parliamentary left found it morally difficult to defend itself as a 'leftwing' force anymore. The Left's 'pro-poor' and 'pro-peasant' image now stood in tatters, exposing its grassroots workers to the most vicious popular wrath. Scores of CPI(M), Krishak Sabha and Centre of Indian Trade Unions' (CITU) offices were vandalized, torched, locked up, occupied or taken over by the rival political organizations. Within hours of Lakshman Seth's notice in Nandigram more than 250 party workers and their families were flushed out of Garchakraberia, Sonachura and Rajaramchak.[26] In Kalicharanpur protesters blocked the roads leading to the village panchayat, preventing the RAF entering the village. 'The villagers' frenzy had left even the organisers of the protests against land acquisition flummoxed', reports a newspaper. Apprehension grew among the local leaders of the TMC, the Congress, the SUCI and the Jamiat Ulema-i-Hind about 'whether they would be able to hold on to the reins for long'.[27] Some members of the CPI(ML-Liberation), a Naxalite outfit, were also arrested in Nandigram in early January.[28] Ashok Guria, the CPI(M) leader from East Medinipur, alleged that 'they are the brains behind cutting up roads and blowing up bridges'. While the villagers were fighting to protect their farmlands, Guria complained that the Naxalites (and eventually the Maoists) were 'saying we won't allow the Salims to enter'.[29] Little did Guria and his ilk realize that in its effort to protect few thousand acres for the Salims and the Tatas their party was losing its basic constituency, which it had sutured for decades by hard work and sacrifice of hundreds of dedicated comrades.

Events in both Nandigram and Singur slowly but steadily rolled out of the government's hands. In the first week of January the TMC leaders dashed to Nandigram where, with other resistant groups, the Bhumi Uchchhed Pratirodh Committee (BUPC, or the committee for resistance against eviction from land) was constituted. The BUPC, with the TMC at its helms, played a decisive role in organizing the anti-acquisition farmers against the CPI(M). By the end of the week, violent clashes broke out between the CPI(M) and the BUPC workers. With the CPI(M) receiving administration's support, the BUPC decided to cut off the villages that it controlled by digging ditches, felling trees and breaking bridges to keep the police off, and to flush out the families supporting the ruling party. By fanning out of Sonachura, it forced the CPI(M) families take refuge in makeshift camps of Khejuri and Tekhali across the Talpatti Bridge.

Incidents of killings filled newspapers and news channels every day, sound of gunfire and bombs enveloped the air. What started as a protest against a shocking announcement for land acquisition now turned into a turf-war between two principal political positions. When the administration finally woke up and sent police to break the resistance on 14 March, large scale violence erupted and fourteen villagers got killed. In Singur the KJRC continued its attacks on the factory, playing hide and seek with the police and the security staff. After the police firing in

Nandigram, it was a matter of days before the Tatas had to depart from Singur for Sanand in Gujarat leaving a strategically bewildered and morally famished Left Front staring at its imminent electoral trounce.

Flawed analytics

Was it a mistake for the parliamentary left to invite the likes of the Tatas and the Salim Group to West Bengal? I do not think so, because to run a state government it is imperative to create jobs, and there can be little doubt that despite its capital intensive character the big industries do create opportunities in ancillary manufacturing units in addition to jobs created in the burgeoning service sector. It is for this reason that attracting investments by outbidding others has become common for a state government in India's new economic environment; standing out of this race may sound radically authentic, but cannot be a sustainable governmental option in purely financial terms. Was the mistake, then, in seeking to acquire agricultural land for industries and townships? Does not seem so either, for in intensively cultivated West Bengal which had just 1 per cent fallow land it was unlikely that large tracts could be found for industrial or urban infrastructure leaving agriculture unaffected. Besides, as discussed earlier, agriculture itself had hit an impasse as cost of inputs rose, advances dried up, government subsidies diminished, agricultural holdings fragmented, infrastructure remained poor, and intermediaries gobbled a chunk of profit in a highly uneven and uncertain market. In places like Singur, as we have seen, a good number of plots changed hands from cultivators to non-farm owners within a year of lifting the central moratorium on land transaction that was imposed after the adjacent expressway started its operation.

It takes a Narodnik to imagine that a class of small holding peasant hinging at the subsistence level of economy fought the police and the ruling party agents because its class interest rested on protecting its class existence. Peasants in Singur or in Nandigram hardened their stand and expressed their unwillingness to part with their lands because they had genuine problems with losing property at terms decided (Singur) or to be decided (Nandigram) by the government without them in the picture. The local panchayat representatives or the local leaders of prominent political parties, traditional bearers of relevant information in West Bengal's party society, as we have seen, were kept more or less outside the loop. In clear violation of its 'government as practice', which carefully weighed programmatic objects of policy with the pragmatic interests of the population by establishing a dynamic link between the elevated and the embedded domains of state through the mediation of a disciplined political outfit, the left leaders took the population for granted and, therefore, indulged in smug unilateralism. The peasants were up in arms against precisely this violation, this deviation from mutually agreed practices, because it made them highly suspicious of the government's intent, which they had genuine reasons to perceive as bent in favour of protecting big corporate interests than those of the peasant classes.

It is pertinent to ask, why did the left deviate from its traditional governmental protocols? Leaving aside the contingent and less compelling reasons such as the left's electoral triumphalism, its arrogant sense of invincibility, misreading of the popular mandate, immaturity of top leadership, enchantment with 'Brand Buddha' etc. which were just surface symptoms, it is important to locate the foundational malaise in the left's understanding of India's politico-economic reality. I think the mainstream left parties, the CPI(M) in particular, failed to appreciate three imperatives of India's political economy of transformation: to identify the distinct logic of capital in the postcolonial economy, to recognize the logic of popular politics in an economically backward yet politically animated democracy, and to reconcile the logic of capital with that of popular politics in a rapidly changing society.

The logic of capital in the non-western world, as we have already shown, does not necessarily follow the classical pattern of capitalist development in which pre- or non-capitalist economic forms get subsumed into capital's expanded mode of production. Instead, vital elements of capital's 'other' are retained in the 'texture' of the economy since the 'twin transformation' that Marx spoke about – of social means of subsistence and production into capital and of immediate producers into proletariat – are impossible to accomplish in the present state of technology and geopolitics. Hence, primitive accumulation instead of signifying a rapturous transition to capitalism, presents itself as an ongoing process in which the 'pain' of accumulation demands a different order of long-term management. The governmental left, operating within the Leninist framework of transition, failed to see these complexities integral to the postcolonial economy. It was rather fused to a programmatic certainty that industry was a 'natural' and pressing outcome of its achievements in land reforms, for which the cultivators would either give up their property willingly, or they should be convinced to make a one-time 'sacrifice' for their own good. Because, after all, 'agriculture is our foundation', the left proclaimed its certitude in a widely circulated slogan, 'industry our future'.

The ongoing character of 'suffering' due to primitive accumulation is further complicated by the existence of universal suffrage in an electoral democracy. In the European countries until the late nineteenth century, or nearer home in Korea, Malaysia, Indonesia and Thailand, or more recently in China, large scale dispossession of the primary producers was dealt by the authoritarian state in ways that are unthinkable in India. Here the state cannot afford to banish myriad forms of lives and livelihoods belonging to the realms of non-corporate capital by force, rather it must find ways to accommodate them with the support of government subsidies and distributive social policies. This involves a gradual and calibrated process of negotiations both within the departments of the government as well as between the government and different stakeholders such as political parties, civil society associations, judicial bodies and the mass media for reaching a minimum agreement. In states like West Bengal, which had a working structure of local representation and highly agile popular politics, the need for such conversations to precede any announcement for large scale dispossession was even greater. This was completely ignored by the left. Not just that, driven by a moral conviction that it was playing a historically progressive role of a 'deliverer' of modern industry to a backward agrarian economy, some left leaders displayed their fondness for a deeply authoritarian mindset. For example, Benoy

Konar, a central committee member of the CPI(M) preferring to treat Nandigram as a 'mere law and order problem' sent a chilling message: 'If they (the protesting peasants) want to do things democratically, we shall reciprocate. But if they want to make things difficult for us, we are prepared to make life hell for them'.[30] This was the farthest one could deviate from managing the adversities of primitive accumulation in an electoral democracy.

The governmental left not only failed to form an effective strategy to deal with complex demands of capital and of popular politics, its analysis of 'neo-liberal globalization' also went well off the track. In its attempt to distract attention from its policy muddles and bureaucratic missteps, it went to the absurd extent of suggesting that its alignment with the Tatas and the Salim Group in West Bengal was actually an effort to wage a fight against neo-liberalism. 'In the present age of globalisation', wrote a CPI(M) member of parliament, 'the major direction of neo-liberal policies is aimed at de-industrialisation in the third world economies. In the face of this, industrial development, particularly in manufacturing and processing sectors, is, in itself, a struggle against those policies'.[31] However, the man considered the chief architect of India's integration with the neoliberal global order made no mistake in recognizing his ally in India's economic transformation. 'I do sincerely believe', remarked Prime Minister Manmohan Singh in his reply to a motion of thanks on the presidential address in the Rajya Sabha, 'that my friend Buddhadeb is right when he says the time has come in this country to work steadfastly to rapidly industrialise the economy'.[32] The Indian left's historic blunders in Singur and Nandigram will stand as a compelling evidence of how a flawed analysis leading to a strategic miscalculation can transfer an otherwise well-intended initiative to the side of its political adversaries. This in the end pushed the left to stare helplessly at its 'government as practice' imploding in a world upside down where, like the chiastic chants of the witches, fair seemed foul, and foul appeared deceptively as fair.

Endnotes

1. For a detailed legal status of the disputed land up to September 2011 see http://www.indiakanoon.org/doc/496064/, accessed on 24 March 2013, 7:22 AM. For a sequential discussion on the legislative and public debate over the Act of 1894 and its right of 'eminent domain' preceding 2006, see Ghosh, Abhijit (2007, especially chapter 3, 47–94).

2. For one of many accounts of the press meet see 'Journey starts in people's car', *The Telegraph*, Kolkata, Friday, 19 May 2006.

3. *The Telegraph*, 'Why Queries Basu', Kolkata, 27 May 2006.

4. *The Telegraph*, Friday, 16 June 2006.

5. *Anandabazar Patrika*, Friday, 16 June 2006.

6. 'We are facing a transitional period of development; from agriculture to industry...I am very clear about what we are trying to do...Another point being raised is that industrialisation means capitalist development...If you want industry you have to ask all industrial houses including big business to invest ...' 'It is high time we move from agriculture to industry': Interview with Buddhadeb Bhattacharjee, *The Hindu*, 27 February 2007, quoted in Das, 2013, 247.

7. 'It is the Narodniks – who exert every effort to show that an admission of the historically progressive nature of capitalism means an apology for capitalism...'. See *The Development of Capitalism in Russia* in Le Blanc, 2008, 109.

8. Perelman, 2000, 26–27. The letter mentioned was written by Marx to the editorial board of *Otechestvenniye Zapitsky* (November 1877) critiquing Nokolai Mikhailovsky's mechanical application of his analysis of primitive accumulation for predicting Russia's future, in Karl Marx and Friedrich Engels, *Selected Correspondence*, 1975, 291–94, Progress Publishers, Moscow.

9. Frank, 1966, 18. Frank also suggests: 'Underdevelopment is not due to the survival of archaic institutions and the existence of capital shortage in regions that have remained isolated from the stream of world history. On the contrary, underdevelopment was and still is generated by the very same historical process which also generated economic development: the development of capitalism itself', quoted in Peet and Hartwick, 2009, 168.

10. 'Between 1980 and 1991, factory employment in West Bengal fell from 8,75,000 to 7,79,000; the trend seems to have been reversed, but only very mildly since then: from 7,78,000 in 1990 the factory employment rose to 9,21,000 in 1995. Between 1980 and 1995, employment in coal mines fell from 1,28,000 to 96,000, and in tea plantations it stagnated between 2,43,000 and 2,58,000'. (See Bagchi, 1998, 2977).

11. The CPI(M)'s claim was that there were 237 sharecroppers in the affected area of whom only 170 were unrecorded. See the Editorial, 'Singur: Myth and Reality', in

People's Democracy, 20(50), 10 December 2006. For a rebuttal of Sanhati figures by Brinda Karat ('Singur: Just the facts, please', *The Hindu*, 13 December, 2006) and ensuing debate joined in by Pashchim Banga Khet Mazdoor Samiti and Meher Engineer see the blog 'Development Dialogues', available at http://development-dialogues.blogspot.in/2007/02/singur-just-facts-please-brinda-karat.html, accessed on 24 March 2013, at 12:49 PM.

12. *The Telegraph*, 'Basu sermon to Buddha', Tuesday, 31 October 2006.

13. *Anandabazar Partrika*, 'Akta bhul chaley-i boomerang: Fascist tokma Mamata-r gay-e', Friday, 1 December, 2006.

14. *Anandabazar Patrika*, : 'Bhikkhe kore tool-table firiye dite chan Mamata', Saturday, 2 December, 2006.

15. *People's Democracy*, 'Singur: Myth and Reality', 30(50), 10 December 2006.

16. *Anandabazar Patrika*, Jayanta Ghoshal, 'Singur-e onnay hoini: Nathhi diye bojhaben Nirupam', Monday, 11 December 2006.

17. *Anandabazar Patrika*, Jayanta Ghoshal, 'Singur-e onnay hoini: Nathhi diye bojhaben Nirupam', Monday, 11 December 2006.

18. For details see Majdoor Mukti Publication, 'A Timeline of Singur', available at http://dasasis.wordpress.com/2008/06/18/singur-timeline-18-may-2006-15-june-2008/, accessed on 30 March 2013 at 17:46 hrs.

19. *The Telegraph*, 'Young girl's body, aflame', Tuesday, 19 December 2006.

20. The importance of the meeting of 29 December 2006 cannot be overemphasized. During my field-trip in the area in early 2008 several interviewees confirmed how 'shocked' and 'bewildered' they were following the announcement by Lakshman Seth that evening.

21. *The Telegraph*, 'False alarm sparks clash', Thursday, 4 January 2007.

22. *The Telegraph*, 'False alarm sparks clash', Thursday, 4 January 2007.

23. *The Telegraph*, 'Bengal limits number of SEZs: cut-off at four to five plans', Thursday, 4 January 2007.

24. *Anandabazar Patrika*, 'Pashey-i aachhe dal: Kolkatay eshe Buddher shilpayone shilmohor Karat-er', Thursday, 4 January 2007.

25. *The Telegraph*, 'Karat assurance on SEZs – Village up in arms', Friday, 5 January 2007.

26. *The Telegraph*, Simi Kamboj and Naresh Jana, 'Land backlash takes life of its own', Saturday, 6 January 2007.

27. *The Telegraph*, Simi Kamboj and Naresh Jana, 'Land backlash takes life of its own', Saturday, 6 January 2007.

28. *The Telegraph*, 'SEZ zone seethes, government stalls – naxalite twist with JNU link', Friday, 5 January 2007.

29. *Ananda Bazar Patrika*, 'Singur thheke Nandigram: oshantir jonno CPM dushchhe Naxalder-i', Saturday, 6 January 2007.

30. *The Telegraph*, Naresh Jana, 'Mobilization and mayhem hitback men and motive', Monday, 8 January 2007. He also reminded the detractors of Keshpur, a place in West Medinipur district, where the CPI(M) could establish its 'complete control' following a turf battle with the TMC in which more than 50 workers belonging to both parties got killed between 1998 and 2000.

31. Niotpal Basu, 'Singur, Nandigram and industrialization of West Bengal – II', *People's Democracy* 31(4), 28 January 2007.

32. *The Economic Times*, 'Beleaguered Buddhadeb gets prime support in SEZ war', 9 March 2007. See also Times News Service, 9 March 2007, available at http://articles.economictimes.indiatimes.com/2007-03-09/news/28482303_1_industrialisation-jyoti-basu-support, accessed on 4 April 2013 at 5:00 PM.

APPENDIX I

THE LEFT THROUGH ELECTIONS

This section looks at the Left Front in West Bengal through five successive elections – the Lok Sabha (LS) or the national parliament in 2004 and 2009 and the Vidhan Sabha (VS) or the state legislature in 2001, 2006 and 2011 – during the last decade of its governance. While the elections of 2001, 2004 and 2006 reflected the left's undisputable dominance in the state, in 2009 the left received its first serious challenge from a buoyant Trinamul Congress–Congress alliance, which eventually unseated it from power in 2011. Here, we trace the left's transformation from a seemingly invincible political force to the one defeated by focusing on the changing dynamics of its electoral constituency.

In the pages below we attempt to find answers to the following questions: Who voted for the left? What constituted the left's electoral base in West Bengal in terms of economic classes, social categories, age groups or locations? Had there been any significant change in these characteristics over the last decade of the Left Front in power? What did the left's changing electoral fortune actually signify in terms of its broader political effects or its capacity to represent the poor and the marginal? In what way was the left's governmental performance responsible for its electoral decline? What can we make of the social outlook of the left voters? Is it markedly different from the rest?

In taking up these questions, we make use of the massive pre- and post-poll surveys conducted in the course of the National Election Survey

(NES) by Lokniti, a group of political and social scientists attached to various academic institutions in India who have done an exemplary work since the mid-1990s of studying voters' identities and opinions in the course of periodic elections at both state and national levels. The surveys are based on significantly large data sets developed from scientific sampling techniques and structured questionnaires, carried out by a dedicated crop of coordinators and investigators spread in every district of the country. In terms of its meticulous planning, time-bound execution, and comprehensive coverage, the NES has no parallel in India. Here, we use fragments of such data collected in West Bengal in the course of 2001 VS, 2004 LS, 2006 VS, 2009 LS and, finally, 2011 VS. Our use of the data is geared to the need of responding to the specific set of queries mentioned above only to get a glimpse of the left and its changing fortune in West Bengal. For clarity's sake, to bring the object of our study to a sharper focus, here we have clubbed all political parties and coalitions in two neat categories: the 'left' and the 'non-left'. While the former denotes the Left Front, the latter refers to all political parties outside the Front including TMC, the Congress and the Bharatiya Janata Party (BJP).

Table A1.1: Percentage of votes polled and seats won (percentage rounded off) by the CPI(M), the Left Front, and the opposition/non-Left Front parties in LS and VS elections in West Bengal from 2001–11

		2001 VS	2004 LS	2006 VS	2009 LS	2011 VS
CPI(M)	Vote share	36.6	38.6	37.1	33.1	30.8
	Seat share	49	62	60	24	14
Left Front	Vote share	49.1	50.7	50.2	43.3	41.1
	Seat share	68	83	80	34	21
Opposition/ non-Left Front	Vote share	50.9	49.3	49.8	56.7	58.9
	Seat share	32	17	20	66	79

Source: Compiled from Election Commission sources.

In Table A1.1 we find a dramatic change in the CPI(M)'s and the left's electoral standing during the last decade of its rule. As evident, the highest vote share of the CPI(M) in these five elections was 38.6 per cent (2004 LS), and of the Left Front as a whole 50.7 per cent (the same election). In fact, the average vote share of the Left Front from 1977 to 2011 (18 elections) was 47.92 per cent, the highest being 54 per cent (1980 LS) and the lowest 34.3 per cent (1977 LS). This clearly shows that the majority of West Bengal's electorate had consistently been against the left, which nonetheless got elected due to the solidity of its alliance and the fragility of opposition unity. This had been such an important factor in the first past the post system that if one takes the last (2011 VS) election in which the left faced a defeat out of consideration, the coalition on an average won 77.7 per cent seats in seven elections to the state legislative assembly since 1977, and the CPI(M) itself got 58.6 per cent. This gave the party a comfortable majority in the House, and the coalition more than two-third seats. Between 2006 VS and 2011 VS, however, the prospect of the Left Front and the CPI(M) took a severe beating, the vote share of the coalition dropped by a massive 9 per cent point, and that of the CPI(M) by almost 7 per cent point, causing a sharp decline in the share of seats from 80 to 21 per cent point for the Left Front. The scale of the decline, and its decisive character, can possibly be measured by the fact that never before since 1977 the CPI(M)'s and the Left Front's share of votes dropped continuously for four successive general elections as it did from 2004 to 2011.

The LS election in 2004 stands out as one of the best performances by the left in its three and half decades of rule in West Bengal. At the national level this was a remarkable election because it saw a reassertion of the marginal social classes – the SCs, the STs and the OBCs – challenging the National Democratic Alliance (NDA) government led by the BJP. In this context, the fact that the Left Front in the state pulled off 50.7 per cent votes, highest since the 1989 LS, with the CPI(M) getting 38.6 per cent on its own, highest since the 1980 LS, turned the alliance into a big player in New Delhi's power struggle. Out of 42 seats in the state, the Left Front won 35, of which the CPI(M) won 26, the CPI 3. The Congress got six seats (14.6 per cent votes), and the TMC – in alliance with the BJP – just one seat (21 per cent votes). It was mainly on the strength of its numbers in West Bengal that the left reached the parliament with an unprecedented 61 MPs. Its support to the Congress-led United Progressive Alliance as an ally proved critical for the survival of the government and for some social policies it adopted in rapid succession. However, such dominance of the left, both in New Delhi and in West Bengal, was short-lived.

It is well known that the left's electoral dominance was the result of its control over rural West Bengal, home to more than 70 per cent of the state's electorate. We have discussed the major distributive policies (Chapter 2) and mediatory politics (Chapter 3) of the Left Front, which enabled it to expand influence, and then maintain it by means of a fairly extended organizational network (Chapter 4). This was evident in the share of left votes in the rural areas, which tended to be greater than in the urban constituencies (see Table A1.2).

Table A1.2: Left vote share in rural and urban constituencies

	2001 VS	**2006 VS**	**2011 VS**
Rural	52	50	43
Urban	40	50	34

Source: NES 2001, 2006 and 2011 weighted data set.
Note: All figures in rounded up percentage points

Between 2001 and 2011, the left steadily lost its rural popularity, at a slower rate between 2001 and 2006 (by 2 per cent point), at a much faster rate in the following five years (by 7 per cent point between 2006 and 2011). By contrast, urban votes moved more unevenly, peaking by 10 per cent points between 2001 and 2006, thereafter dropping even faster by 16 per cent point between 2006 and 2011. The election of 2006 VS, which marked the largest victory for the 'reformist' chief minister Buddhadeb Bhattacharjee, promised a rapid industrialization and growth for the state's ailing economy, which might have enchanted a good number of the urban voters inducing them to vote the left. The failure to deliver on such promises might have had a damaging impact on the left's acceptability in 2011, more so in the urban constituencies than the rural ones.

Next, we look into the overall electoral base of the left.

Table A1.3: Left vote share: Different economic classes

	2001 VS	**2004 LS**	**2006 VS**	**2009 LS**	**2011 VS**
Poor	56	56	54	45	43
Lower	48	52	50	39	42
Middle	40	48	47	41	41
Upper	33	41	51	49	36

Source: NES 2004, 2006, 2009, 2011 weighted data set.

Note: All figures percentage points rounded up. Category names changed to make comparable across the years without altering their relative positions within the scale.

As Table A1.3 shows, until 2006, more than 50 per cent income poor voters voted the left parties. Since 2009, however, the trend changed with a majority of the poor voting the non-left parties.

Among the 'lower middle' and 'middle middle' income groups, the left vote had a similar decline. Here the left's popularity first went up from 2001 to 2004, and then went down again. The years 2004-06 may be considered the most 'optimistic' time in the state, when the economic climate was thought to be improving with the government taking a pro-active role in inviting direct capital investments in services and manufacturing from both domestic and global entrepreneurs. Such optimism, as seen in chapter 5, was nonetheless not sustainable, as peasant protest against the government's land acquisition policies coupled with a series of political and administrative bungling sent the government's credibility for a toss. Post-2009, therefore, the optimism of the recent past was found missing which might have caused some erosion also in the left's support base consisting of the 'lower-middle' and 'middle-middle' segments.

Upper 'class' support for the left was highest in 2006, which can be considered as Buddhadeb Bhattacharjee's most successful election. The left could attract a large section of well to do voters as Bhattacharjee was promising an economic regeneration to utilize the state's supposed educational and intellectual capital. The upper classes kept their support alive till 2009, but once the left's exit was seen as imminent, they quickly switched sides (sliding by 13 per cent points). Between 2009 and 2011, when the left votes either declined or remained unchanged for other class segments, support from the 'lower middle' stratum, however, rose marginally. It could have been because this segment – with some technical skills and education – hoped to improve its economic condition if the left's industrialization were to succeed.

When we look at the rural-urban divide and disaggregate the electorate in different economic groups, we get an interesting texture of the left's constituency of support:

Table A1.4: Shifting support for the Left: Rural and urban segments

Segments	Occupational groups	Vote share of the left in 2009	Change of the vote share since 2004
Rural	Agricultural workers	46	–2
	Skilled and semi-skilled workers	30	–16
	Marginal farmers and sharecroppers	44	+1
	Self-cultivators	31	–26
	Salaried classes	62	+23
Urban	Professional and salaried	44	–3
	Business	39	–15
	Skilled and semi-skilled workers	57	+3

Source: Compiled from NES 2009 and 2004 in Jyotiprasad Chatterjee and Suprio Basu, 26 September 2009: 'West Bengal: Mandate for Change', *Economic and Political Weekly* XLIV(39): 152–56 (153).

Despite decline in support within the rural segment, the backing of agricultural workers for the left parties did not dip by any significant degree. The decline was by only 2 per cent point. Also, in rural West Bengal, as shown in Table A1.4, the support of the marginal farmers and sharecroppers went up by a shade (1 per cent point) in 2009. So, although most commentators hold the opposite view, the poorest segment in rural West Bengal maintained its support for the left even during the period of its terminal crisis. However, support for the left parties dropped most dramatically from two different groups in five years after the 2004 LS: the skilled and semi-skilled rural workers (by 16 per cent points) and self-cultivating peasants. These categories together make the 'middle' stratum of households in West Bengal countryside that had aspirations for – and the ability to – establishing its control over the left's peasant organizations since the late 1980s. Such dominance, as we pointed out already in Chapter 2, had an adverse effect on the voice of the poor peasants and agricultural workers, whom the party was ideologically committed to represent. It seems from the data that when the left was faced with a defeat these middle class elements returned in large number from the left to the non-left parties (particularly, to the TMC). One gets here perhaps a concrete illustration of the lateral shift of the local patronage structure that we analysed in some detail in Chapters 1 and 4.

Surprisingly, the left enhanced its support among the salaried segment in rural West Bengal. These were mostly school teachers and lower government officials, constituting the educated base of the rural society. These households were not primarily dependent on land, so they offered no great resistance to the government's acquisition policy. Rather, some of them considered the government's industrial thrust as beneficial for the economy, for the mobility of the young in their families who were reluctant to take agriculture as a profession. Politically, the influence of these segments cannot be emphasized enough, though such influence was by no means uniform or permanent (see Chapter 3). It will be interesting to see what role these elements can play in a changed political landscape, how they influence the outlook and opinion of the rural population in the coming years and decades.

The left's support had also gone up among the urban skilled and semi-skilled workers. The reason seems obvious: with no agricultural land

and so no threat of losing out in the acquisition process, these segments stood to benefit from an increased job opportunity if urbanization or industrialization were to materialize. Such a surge in support was important for at least two reasons. These classes depended a great deal on the ruling political combination for meeting their livelihood demands in the informal economy. Though we do not have any comparable data from 2011 VS, it will not be inaccurate to argue that for the urban poor engaged in high risk economies (such as street hawking, auto-rickshaw or taxi driving, working as daily wagers in construction industry etc.) the safest option was to quickly shift their allegiance from the left to the TMC immediately after the 2009 LS election, when it became rather obvious that the left was unlikely to return in 2011 VS. On the other hand, there was no such dilemma for the urban middle classes – salaried and in business. They did not constitute a great support base for the left during the entire stint of the left regime; their opposition only got more pronounced and determined through the last few years of the Left Front government.

Table A1.5: Left vote share: Different social classes

	2001 VS	2004 LS	2006 VS	2009 LS	2011 VS
General	38	46	48	41	38
OBCs	48	55	53	43	42
SC	49	57	55	53	42
ST	67	41	55	50	45
Muslims	58	45	46	36	42

Source: NES 2001, 2004, 2006, 2009 and 2011 weighted data set.
Note: All figures in rounded up percentage points.

The left got a solid block of support from the OBCs, the Dalits, the Adivasis and the Muslims. In comparison, its support from the upper castes was rather mute. In 2004 LS and 2006 VS, the OBC support shot up to close to 55 per cent and then fell sharply in 2009 and 2011 (Table A1.5). Dalit support also waned in 2011 VS, after peaking in 2004 LS, and remaining more or less stable above the halfway mark through 2006 VS and 2009 LS. Muslim votes, which traditionally favoured the left, went sharply down to 36 per cent point in 2009 LS – following the publication of the Sachar Committee Report (which painted the condition of Muslims in West Bengal in pretty poor light) and the left's exit from the UPA on the issue of Indo-US nuclear deal – before picking somewhat up to 42 per cent point in 2011 VS. It is also clear that the left's support was steadily declining among the tribal population since the 2004 LS election. The left cannot but take the slide in the support of these segments seriously if it hopes to retain social justice as among its principal ideological aims. The signs were rather ominous for the left as both OBC and SC support reached an all time low in 2011 VS election.

Age is an important factor in profiling the electorate. Every political party seeks to have more of its voters from the 'young' not just because they outnumber the 'old' in India, but also because the young offer a more durable support base as well as a larger catchment group for active party workers.

Table A1.6: Distribution of age among left and non-left voters

	Left		Non-left	
	2006 VS	**2011VS**	**2006 VS**	**2011 VS**
Up to 25 years	14	16	11	19
26–35 years	28	24	30	25
36–45 years	25	26	26	24
46–55 years	18	17	20	16
55 + years	15	17	13	16
	100	100	100	100

Source: NES 2006 and 2011 weighted data set.
Note: All figures in rounded up percentage points.

Looking at the age profile of the left and non-left voters, we do not get a very different picture between the sets. The left had a slight edge over the non-left in 2006 among the youngest group (up to 25 years), which it lost in 2011. The maximum drop in support base between 2006 and 2011 for both the left and the non-left had been in the group 26–35 years, by 4 per cent point in the former case and 5 per cent point in the latter. While the profile of the voters for the left and non-left parties do not differ dramatically across these two VS elections, we get a different picture when we profile the age groups and account for the changes in their political affiliations.

Table A1.7: Changes in political affiliation by age

	Left		Non-Left		
	2006	**2011**	**2006**	**2011**	
Up to 25 years	56	36	44	64	100/100
26–35 years	48	40	52	60	100/100
36–45 years	49	43	51	57	100/100
46–55 years	48	42	52	58	100/100
55 + years	53	43	47	57	100/100

Source: NES 2006 and 2011 weighted data set.
Note: All figures in rounded up percentage points.

Table A1.7 shows that the left vote dropped by at least 6 per cent points among all age groups, but among the youngest group (up to 25 years) the drop between the 2006 VS and 2011 VS was significantly high. Here the left's share got reduced by 20 per cent points, from 56 to 36. Correspondingly, that of the non-left went up sharply. Similar change took place in the next youngest group (26–35 year), in which the left lost by 8 per cent point. Taking Tables A1.6 and A1.7 together, one gets a clearer picture. While the age distribution of voters did not change much across political divides, there had been an exodus of young voters from the left to non-left parties in 2011, which probably remains a far more pertinent feature of the left's defeat than simply its reduced share of votes.

It is also important to find out how the electorates' general evaluation of the Left Front government conditioned their partisan preference during the election. In other words, did the experience of governance matter in elections and, if it did, how?

Table A1.8: Party support and assessment of
Left Front government's performance

	2004 LS		2009 LS		2011 VS	
	Left	Non-Left	Left	Non-Left	Left	Non-Left
Fully satisfied	12	19	52	8	38	5
Somewhat satisfied	35	34	34	29	45	21
Somewhat dissatisfied	12	14	4	18	5	23
Entirely dissatisfied	17	18	4	38	3	35
Can't say	24	15	6	7	9	16
	100	100	100	100	100	100

Source: NES 2004, 2009 and 2011 weighted data set.
Note: All figures in rounded up percentage points.

Table A1.8 shows the level of satisfaction (and dissatisfaction) of left and non-left voters in the performance of the Left Front government over a period of stability (2004) as well as turmoil (2009 onward). Note how those 'fully satisfied' with the government's performance among the left voters increased from 12 (2004 LS) to 52 per cent point (2009 LS) before sliding to 38 per cent points (2011 VS) as the left entered a period of crisis. Similarly, note how the non-left voters, who nonetheless were generally high in satisfaction with the workings of the left government, dropped from 19 (2004 LS) to 8 (2009 LS) to 5 (2011 VS) per cent points over the same period. Also, the proportion of voters who voted the left despite their uncertainties on the quality of its governance declined rapidly from the period of stability to that of crisis (from 24 to 6 and 9 per cent points). These trends indicate two things at once:

- The left voters tended to more or less affirm their faith in the Left Front in an act of closing their ranks and standing by the government when it started sliding down the popularity curve. The trend was also evident among those left voters who were 'entirely dissatisfied' with the workings of the government; their proportion dipped from 17 (2004 LS) to 4 (2009 LS) to 3 (2011 VS).

- The satisfaction level of the non-left voters as regards the character of left governance was considerable when the regime was stable (a fifth confirming that they were 'fully satisfied'), yet it rapidly declined as the prospect of actually replacing the government became imminent. Still, remarkably more than a quarter of the non-left voters affirmed 'full' or 'moderate' satisfaction with governance even in the years preceding the election of 2011.

Taking these figures together one gets the impression that:

- The left evoked a good deal of positive response on its governmental performance from not just its own constituency, but also from those who voted against it.

- Opinion on the quality of governance got increasingly polarized as the political situation entered from a stable to a turbulent phase when the defeat of the three and a half decade old regime deemed probable.

- Governance did not play a very significant role in shaping voters' choice. In other words, 'good governance' did not appear here as sufficient for enlisting electoral support, nor was the idea of 'good' independent of the larger ambience within which people made up their choices.

Our next point of interest is to gather how the electorate evaluated Jyoti Basu and Buddhadeb Bhattacharjee. Jyoti Basu was the Chief Minister of the Left Front government from 1977 to 2001. It was during his tenure that West Bengal accomplished land reforms and decentralization of administration, attained agricultural growth, and maintained 'social peace'. Jyoti Basu also supervised a steady de-industrialization of West Bengal, flight of capital from the state, and growth in unemployment figures. As Buddhadeb Bhattacharjee took over after Basu's retirement, the state attempted a complete image makeover from an industrial laggard to a new destination for capital. The initial years of Bhattacharjee delivered some quick gains. They, however, were short-lived and soon conflict between corporate interests and popular constituencies made grounds for violent clashes in rural West Bengal, sending the apparent coherence of his administration for a spin (see Chapter 5). Consequently, people's relative evaluation of these two leaders changed.

Table A1.9: Change in voters' evaluation of Jyoti Basu (1977–2001) and Buddhadeb Bhattacharjee (2001–11) as chief ministers

	Left voters		Non-Left voters	
	2006 VS	2011 VS	2006 VS	2011 VS
Buddhadeb Bhattacharjee better	44	14	28	5
Jyoti Basu better	17	37	14	40
Both equally good	28	34	11	7
Both equally bad	3	1	28	22
Can't say	8	14	19	26
	100	100	100	100

Source: NES 2006, 2011 weighted data set.
Note: All figures in rounded up percentage points.

Table A1.9 shows the high expectation of the voters in Buddadeb Bhattacharjee in 2006 VS elections, and its rapid erosion by the 2011 VS election. In 2006, 44 per cent left voters preferred Bhattacharjee to Basu, by 2011 it dropped to mere 14 per cent point. In 2006 only 17 per cent left voters thought that Basu was better than Bhattacharjee, by 2009 their proportion swelled to 37 per cent point. Some left voters who preferred Bhattacharjee over Basu in 2006 revised their opinion drastically in a matter of five years.

The erosion of Bhattacharjee's appeal was more profound among the non-left voters; it dropped from 28 to 5 per cent point. Correspondingly, Basu's approval shot up from 14 to 40 among the non-left voters. Such changes of approval for Bhattacharjee and Basu among the left as well as the non-left voters clearly indicate that the early optimism in Bhattacharjee disappeared quickly with the government's inability to deliver on its promises.

If approval or disapproval of political personalities revealed such sharp variations at the time of elections – when the pitch of campaigns by contending forces reached its peak – it remains of interest to get a sense of how the voter engages with public and political affairs during the ordinary times. For that, we may turn to Table A1.10.

Table A1.10: Party support and usual interest in politics and public affairs, leaving aside the period of elections

	2004 LS		2009 LS	
	Left	Non-left	Left	Non-left
Intense	12	13	11	6
Somewhat	50	47	33	29
Nil	29	31	51	60
Can't say	9	9	5	5
	100	100	100	100

Source: NES 2004, 2009 weighted data set.

Note: All figures in rounded up percentage points.

While in 2004 intense political interest of the non-left voters was surprisingly a notch higher than their left counterparts, in 2009 interest among the left was found twice as big as that of the non-left. The importance of these data, however, consists in the overall decline of interest in political and public affairs among *both* left and non-left voters. Only 29 per cent of left and 31 per cent of non-left voters were indifferent to civic affairs in 2004, the proportion shot up to 51 per cent and 60 per cent respectively by 2009. This happened at a time when the left was losing its grip over the state's politics and the non-left was clearly on the rise. So emergence of the non-left was accompanied not by an absorbing civic or partisan engagement of its constituency, rather what we find here are growing signs of indifference and alienation.

If voting preference changed so rapidly one wonders if they affected all political parties equally, or whether the left voters showed more stability in their political choice than those who voted other parties such as the Congress, the TMC or the BJP? The NES in 2004 LS sought to know whether the voters voted the same party in that election which they traditionally supported. Keeping in mind that it was perhaps the best election for the left in the decade, one can draw a few inferences from Table A1.11.

Table A1.11: Traditional party support and voting in the Lok Sabha, 2004

Party	Congress alliance	NDA	Left Front	Others	
Congress	67	13	16	3	100
BJP	15	65	16	4	100
TMC	8	74	13	5	100
Left Front	3	7	85	5	100
Floating voters	12	29	51	8	100
Others	14	34	40	11	100

Source: NES 2004, weighted data set.
Note: All figures in rounded up percentage points.

These figures indicate that an overwhelming 85 per cent of left voters voted the left parties in 2004 LS, way above 74 per cent of TMC (which was in alliance with BJP in NDA) voters, 67 per cent Congress voters and 65 per cent BJP voters who voted along their partisan loyalty. That the left also received 51 per cent votes from the floating voters, far more than its rivals, was a testimony to its credibility in the state. 16 per cent of BJP voters and 13 per cent of TMC voters, at a time when two were in alliance, switched their preference to the left. Attracting a good number of voters from the traditional supporters of rival parties can have a flip side too. They can easily drift when the political conjuncture is markedly different, as the left's vote-share dipped when its defeat was largely perceived as imminent.

Another indicator of the voters' steadfastness was whether she or he voted the same party in the local (such as municipal or panchayat), regional (such as VS) and the national (LS) elections. In local elections the candidates are often more familiar than they are in the state/regional or national elections, so individual or group based affiliations may play a more critical role in them. Some parties may not contest in local elections at all. For example, the BJP did not have its footprint in every village panchayat constituency in West Bengal. Some parties were also too small to contest meaningfully above the village level. While some smaller socialist outfits routinely fielded candidates in panchayat elections, they remained almost invisible in the higher segments. Some parties contested one another only at the local level but maintained electoral alliance at the regional or national level. Also, the poll-issues differed between national and state/regional levels, calling for different electoral priorities.

Table A1.12: Voters' support and voting preference in local, state and national elections

	Left	**Non-left**
Same Party	70	61
Different Party	17	25
Can't Say	13	14
	100	100

Source: NES 2004, weighted data set.

Note: All figures in rounded up percentage points.

In 2004, as shown in Table A1.12, the left voters demonstrated considerable consistency, 70 per cent of them affirmed their support for the left at every level of representation. For the non-left voters, a quarter voted different parties at different levels, in which considerations such as a party's availability in a particular constituency, alliance strategy, personal image of a candidate, winning possibilities etc. must have played key roles.

At the height of the left's organizational strength, local administrative institutions assumed tremendous importance, especially for the rural voters. The village panchayat played a pivotal role in the political consolidation of the population. Until the 2008 election to the panchayat, the left parties controlled 66 per cent of village panchayat segments, 74 per cent of panchayat samiti (at the block level) and 87 per cent of zilla parishad (district panchayat) seats. The dominance of the left in these bodies was so overwhelming that in many places the distinction between 'the party' (by which people referred to the CPI(M)) and the panchayat got blurred. Several analysts of West Bengal's politics attributed the source of the left's enduring strength to its control over the panchayat. One would obviously be curious to know, notwithstanding their political salience, did the people indeed perceive the panchayat as central to their lives.

Table A1.13: Party support and whom the rural respondent contacts when in difficulties

	Congress+	BJP+	Left	Others	N
Panchayat	47	35	44	53	227
Block office	4	1	4	3	19
Peasant Organization	7	3	4	0	27
Local clubs	1	3	2	3	14
Local important person	17	33	24	14	164
Religious leader	1	0	0	0	2
Party office	8	8	10	8	61
NGOs	2	1	1	0	8
Others	12	14	11	21	82
	100	100	100	100	604

Source: NES 2004, weighted data set.
Note: All figures in percentage points.

As Table A1.13 based on the 2004 survey shows, most people (38 per cent) turned to the panchayat in their moments of crisis, the next popular destination being a locally important person (27 per cent). The party office came next (10 per cent), followed by the peasant organization (4 per cent). Anybody with some experience of fieldwork in rural West Bengal knows that chances are that a locally influential person is almost always a political leader. In sum, a vast majority of the state's electorate (almost 80 per cent) turn to a *political* entity in search of help, which marks a distinctive feature of rural West Bengal's social life.

Finally, the NES data help us to obtain some sense of the social outlook of the left voters, in comparison to those who voted for the non-left parties. One wonders if more than three decades of left rule in West Bengal made any significant impact upon the opinion of voters on some critical social issues such as gender equality. We present here data collected in 2004 and 2009 about how the voters responded to the question of women's education, the extent of their disagreement or agreement with the proposition that 'too much education is not good for women'.

Table A1.14: Political affiliation and reaction to the statement: Too much education is not good for women

	Fully disagree		Somewhat disagree		Somewhat agree		Fully agree		No opinion		
	2004	2009	2004	2009	2004	2009	2004	2009	2004	2009	2004/ 2009
Left	60	47	9	12	5	14	17	17	9	10	100/ 100
Non-left	63	58	8	19	5	5	18	11	6	7	100/ 100

Source: NES 2004, 2009 weighted data set.

Note: All figures in rounded up percentage points.

The data in Table A1.14 do not allow a room for much optimism for the left parties on the question of gender equality. In 2004, though around 70 per cent left voters expressed their full or moderate disagreement with the typically patriarchal proposition, a good number of left voters – 30 per cent more or less – agreed with it. By 2009, the disagreement of the left voters dropped by about 10 per cent points. By contrast, among those who voted for non-left parties, disagreement with the proposition was a notch higher in 2004 than their left counterparts. By 2009, the difference between these two sets of voters appeared more striking; almost 10 per cent more non-left voters fully disagreed with the statement, showing a greater sensitivity to gender equality. Going by these figures, the left cannot have much to celebrate about the social outlook of its constituency.

Rather there is a cause for concern if one looks at the 'regressive' trends from 2004 to 2009.

So the fall from eminence of the left had shades not visible to one blinded by the quantum of vote- and seat-shares – and their changes – in the national or the state elections. To get a clear sense of the character of the left's political tendencies, a deeper probe is necessary. This section, with the aid of a large set of data collected in the course of successive NES, sought to dispel some common myths about West Bengal politics. Here, we saw that popular support for the left was rarely a majority support, that the urban and rural poor did not *necessarily* vote for the left during the last few years of its rule, that the deepest erosion that the Left Front suffered by 2011 was among the Dalit and Backward voters, that the slide in Muslim votes was not yet as decisive as it is commonly assumed, that support for the left had actually risen among the urban skilled workers, the poor and marginal peasants and the sharecroppers in 2009, and that its quality of governance before the beginning of rural turbulence in the state received a wide endorsement even from those who voted against it. The data also revealed that one of the greatest achievements of the left in West Bengal was its ability to retain a steady block of core voters, which was not prone to switch sides, and it helped the coalition consolidate its gains for years against the fragmentary opposition. Despite its long tenure, however, the left made doubtful *social* impact as evident from the 'conservative' response of its voters on a gender sensitive issue. The left also failed to retain support from the younger voters, as indicated by an alarming shift of preference for those below 35 years of age from the left to non-left parties between 2006 and 2011.

APPENDIX II

LOCAL GOVERNANCE AND ELECTABILITY

The panchayat election in 2008 was a watershed election in West Bengal. That year the left met its first serious challenge in the countryside after 30 years of uninterrupted domination. In the preceding panchayat election (2003), the Left Front had won in 85 per cent Panchayat Samiti seats, which came down to 57.45 per cent in 2008. In 2003, of the total 3,220 Gram Panchayat the Left Front had won 2,311 or 71.77 per cent; in 2008 the number was 1,625, or 50.47 per cent (Chattopadhyay, 2008). As the 2008 panchayat election launched an unmistakable power-shift in West Bengal's rural politics, a trend that continued even in 2013 and beyond, one was obviously curious about what actually made people vote so differently in it in comparison to the previous local elections. The media in general attributed the left's land acquisition policy as primarily responsible for its setback. We wanted to find out, more specifically, if there was any correlation between the electorate's perception of the quality of local governance and their voting preference. For this we placed a set of governance-related data drawn from a large sample of Gram Panchayats in 2005-06 against the outcome of the 2008 panchayat election in the same localities. The exercise gave us some results which may have interesting implications.[1]

The pre-2008 data were collected in the course of a baseline survey conducted by a team of researchers on the impact of the state government's policy of 'Strengthening Rural Decentralization' (SRD), a policy initiated with the financial assistance of the British Department for International Development (DFID).[2] The study had a wide coverage: it included all 18 districts of rural West Bengal with a sample size of 162 Gram Panchayats (or 5 per cent of the total number of Gram Panchayats excluding the Darjeeling Gorkha Hill Council) and was based arguably on one of the country's largest surveys of households (37,000 plus) for evaluating the performance of Gram Panchayats in any state. For sample selection, a two-stage sampling method was employed. In the first stage, all blocks were grouped into four quartiles according to their degree of 'backwardness' based on three principal indicators drawn from the Census of 2001: percentage level of illiteracy, percentage of SC/ST population in total population, and percentage of agricultural labourer in total population. Thereafter, in each quartile 5 per cent Gram Panchayats were selected by method of random sampling, and 5 per cent households from each *sansad* (represented by an elected member) of each Gram Panchayat were sampled.

Two types of questionnaires were administered in 2005–06: one specifically for the head of each household or his/her replacement by any other adult member in case of absence, the other for the *pradhan* of the Gram Panchayat who often spoke in the presence of the panchayat secretary or members of the party that s/he belonged to. For the woman *pradhan*, her husband almost always accompanied her during the interview. Based on data collected through interviews and other official sources (such as the audited annual accounts of the Gram Panchayats), we measured each Gram Panchayat along six different indices: accountability and transparency index, service delivery index, decentralization index, well-being index, participation index and financial sustainability index. This apart, we kept a record of the political composition of each of these 162 Gram Panchayats, whether they were ruled by the left or non-left parties, the nature of the coalition in power, the relative strength of the ruling party/coalition etc. We did a repeat collection of information on the political composition of these Gram Panchayats after the 2008 election. (Tables below are computed from data supplied by the survey of 2005-06 and information on the political profile of each of the surveyed Gram Panchayats following the 2008 panchayat election).

The electoral shift between 2003 and 2008 panchayat election was fairly well reflected in the 162 sampled Gram Panchayats. At the time of the survey, 115 (70.99 per cent) of these 162 Gram Panchayats had left parties at the helm. In the 2008 election, the number of sampled Gram Panchayats ruled by the left parties dropped to 88 (54.32 per cent). Correspondingly, the number of non-left Gram Panchayats increased from 29.01per cent to 45.68per cent (Table A2.1). We also observed that of the 53 (32.72per cent) sampled Gram Panchayats that had a change of guard (Table A2.2), an overwhelming majority (40 out of 53 or 75.47per

Table A2.1: Overall distribution of parties in power
in 2003 and 2008

Party in power / Year	Left	Non-left
2003	70.99 % (115)	29.01% (47)
2008	54.32 % (88)	45.68% (74)

Source: Collaborative survey conducted by the author

Table A2.2: Percentage of Gram Panchayats with a change in the regime

Regime shift		Frequency	Per cent
Change	Left to non-left	40	24.69
	Non-left to left	13	8.02
	Total	53	32.72
No change		109	67.28
Total		162	100

Source: Collaborative survey conducted by the author

Table A2.3: Distribution of Gram Panchayats (per cent) and regime change

Regime	Party in power / Year	Left	Non-left
Change	2003	75.47	24.53
	2008	24.53	75.47
No change	2003–08	68.81	31.19

Source: Collaborative survey conducted by the author

cent) shifted loyalty from left to non-left (Table A2.3). These data will now allow us to look for a possible correlation between regime change in a Gram Panchayat in 2008 and its position in terms of different indices of governance that we had computed earlier. The idea is to find out the relative strength of those indices and their correlation with the change of electoral verdict in the sampled Gram Panchayats.

Among the six indices originally selected four are relevant for this analysis – (a) accountability and transparency; (b) service delivery; (c) decentralization; and (d) participation. For the sake of simplicity we split these indices along their median value: those above the median were 'better performers', those below 'poor performers'. This, we understand, allows us to trace the strength of correlation between the quality of governance and regime-change for four relevant indices within a simple matrix. Our interest is in understanding the relative importance of these four indices and their pattern of occurrence in Gram Panchayats that voted the same party/parties to power as compared to those which changed loyalty. Of those which changed, we are keen to know how the governmental indices varied across Gram Panchayats that switched from left to non-left as compared to those from non-left to left. To mention once more, our purpose is to find out whether quality of governance had any correspondence with electoral preference of the voters, and if it had then to what extent. Some of the results may indeed have counter-intuitive implications, as they seem to indicate a rather complicated relationship between governmental performance and electoral outcome in the local democratic institutions.

First, to find out how far the index of accountability and transparency induced a change of regime at the Gram Panchayat level in 2008 we find that the Gram Panchayats that were above the median value (or those performed well) had regime change in 31.76 per cent cases, and those

Table A2.4: Accountability and Transparency Index and regime change

	Position of the Gram Panchayat	Regime change	Left to non-left	Non-left to left
Accountability and transparency index	Below median	33.77	24.68	9.09
	Above median	31.76	24.71	7.06

Source: Collaborative survey conducted by the author

below had such changes in 33.77 per cent cases (Table A2.4). On the other hand, among those Gram Panchayats which elected the same parties in 2003 and 2008, 66.23 per cent faired rather poorly in the survey on this count. So it can be claimed that the voters did not vote out any political party in the Gram Panchayat due to any lack of accountability and transparency in its workings. In fact, it reinforces the point made earlier in chapter 1, that voters did not necessarily depend on the formal channels of local government mechanisms to obtain administrative information. They had many informal ways of knowing things, which made the index 'accountability and transparency' rather inadequate as a measure of good governance in rural West Bengal.

Second, we tested the possible impact of service delivery index on regime change at the Gram Panchayat level. This is crucial, because since the inception of the panchayat system in 1978, service delivery is recognized as a key function of the local government. Some researchers argued that the left's long duration in power depended largely on a patron-client relationship it developed through the panchayat by skillfully manipulating its service delivery mechanism. We find in our survey that those Gram Panchayats, which had better records of service delivery, experienced regime change in 22.92 per cent cases, and those with poor records voted out the party in power in 46.97 per cent cases (Table A2.5). So the difference between two sets of Gram Panchayats in this case had indeed been significant. We also look for which bloc of parties, the left or the non-left, was more adversely affected due to poor service delivery in their respective Gram Panchayats. This, we think, would enable us to say whether the left, which was in power at the state level, was more often punished for its poor performance at the local level than the non-left, which was in the opposition in 2008. We get interesting results here. The rate of regime change from left to non-left among Gram Panchayats both above and below the median was higher than the rate of change from

Table A2.5: Service Delivery Index and regime change

Gram Panchayats ordered by service delivery index	Regime change	Left to non-left	Non-left to left
Below median	46.97	31.82	15.15
Above median	22.92	19.79	3.13

Source: Collaborative survey conducted by the author

non-left to left. However, the ratio of regime change from left to non-left as compared to non-left to left was significantly lower (approximately, 2:1) among Gram Panchayats with poor service delivery records than the ratio (approximately, 6:1) among Gram Panchayats with better records. In other words, though service delivery was highly correlated with regime stability, poor service delivery in a Gram Panchayat affected the party running the local government more when the party belonged to the non-left bloc than the left bloc. While service delivery, a component of patron-client relationship, was important for the left and the non-left parties alike, the left's dependence on such means for electoral renewal at the local level – as long as it was the ruling party in the state – was almost a third of that of the non-left.

Third, the index of decentralization is important, as it stands for the degree of autonomy a Gram Panchayat has in relation to higher bodies in the panchayat hierarchy as well as to the line departments of the state administration. Here we found that the Gram Panchayats which performed better, that is, those above the median value for decentralization index, had significantly lower (21.65 per cent) cases of regime change than those which fared poorly on this score (49.23 per cent) (Table A2.6). This apart, we also found that the ratio of regime change from left to non-left as compared to non-left to left was significantly higher (approximately,

Table A2.6: Decentralization Index and regime change

Gram Panchayats ordered by decentralization index	Regime change	Left to non-left	Non-left to left
Below median	49.23	33.85	15.38
Above median	21.65	18.56	3.09

Source: Collaborative survey conducted by the author

6:1) among the better performing Gram Panchayats than among the underperforming Gram Panchayats (approximately, 2.2:1). So the Gram Panchayats that stood higher on the scale of decentralization (i.e., which had greater autonomy) were significantly less likely to vote the incumbents out of power than those dependent on commands from above. Also, among the Gram Panchayats high on decentralization index the chances of regime change from left to non-left were significantly (almost three times) higher than the Gram Panchayats lower on decentralization. Decentralization also had a strong correlation with service delivery index, in fact the highest between all the indices taken together. So a Gram Panchayat with more autonomy was likely to be a better deliverer of services, and more likely to elect the incumbent back to office. However, the electoral advantages in such Gram Panchayats were not evenly spread between left and non-left parties. The electoral data from 2003 and 2008 panchayat election seems to indicate that the non-left parties stood to gain more than the left parties in electoral terms in Gram Panchayats carrying higher decentralization indices.

Fourth, the level of popular participation in Gram Panchayat activities had an intriguing relationship with voting pattern. In Gram Panchayats, which recorded a high degree of participation, the incidents of regime change between 2003 and 2008 were also higher than those where the degree of participation was low (37.65 per cent and 27.27 per cent respectively) (Table A2.7). However, the ratio of change from left to non-left parties was significantly lower in Gram Panchayats with high

Table A2.7: Participation Index and regime change

Gram Panchayats ordered by participation index	Regime change	Left to non-left	Non-left to left
Below median	27.27	22.08	5.19
Above median	37.65	27.06	10.59

Source: Collaborative survey conducted by the author

participation index in comparison to Gram Panchayats where the index of participation was low (approximately, 2.5:1 and 4.2:1 respectively). Thus, though a high level of participation increases the chances of regime change, the non-left parties face more difficulties than their left counterparts in dealing with such eventualities. This difference is significant in view of the generally negative impact of participation on regime stability. It is possible that a high degree of participation takes place where competition between contending political parties is also high, and in 2008 it did not affect the left parties as adversely as it affected the non-left parties due to the left's as yet better organizational control over public participation.

In sum, from the set of data collected before and after the panchayat election of 2008, we can state that the relationship between some key indices of governance and local electoral mandate had been anything but straightforward. Accountability and transparency, though crucially important for 'good governance', had a negligible impact on regime stability (or regime change), perhaps due to the overall atmosphere of proximity and informality at the Gram Panchayat level. While the electorate was found to be generally sensitive to the quality of service delivery, they were less punishing when the incumbent in the local government had been the left (which was also the ruling party in the state in 2008) compared to when the local incumbent was a non-left party. The probability of regime-change in a local government body that had larger autonomy (or a higher index of decentralization) was less than those that were more susceptible to control from above. However, when change did occur, the left was hit harder than the non-left in those places where the autonomy was high rather than low. This offered a mixed signal for the dominant party in the panchayat; an allowance of larger local autonomy was good for continuity in general, but the dominent party (left) had higher chances of losing in places where the local government had enjoyed greater autonomy. The data also showed that intense popular participation is no guarantee against regime change. Rather Gram Panchayats that were actively participatory were more prone to change the locally governing party. However, the impact of participation on a political bloc seemingly depended on its level of coherence and organization. In an overall climate of large-scale shift towards the non-left in 2008, the left could retain its position proportionately better in localities with a proactive rather than a submissive electorate.

Endnotes

1 The correlations presented here were estimated together with my colleague Pranab Kumar Das. I am grateful to him for allowing me to publish our collaborative findings here.

2 The data were drawn from a survey conducted in 2005–06 by a team from the Centre for Studies in Social Sciences, Calcutta, that included Partha Chatterjee, Pranab Kumar Das, Dhrubajyoti Ghosh, Manabi Majumdar, Surajit Mukhopadhyaya and myself. The team also included Jahan Ali Biswas, Sourav De, and Prosenjit Roy as field supervisors and data analysts, and hundreds of field investigators who were recruited locally.

BIBLIOGRAPHY

Acharya, Poromesh. 'Education: Politics and Social Structure'. *Economic and Political Weekly* 20(42) (19 October, 1985): 1785–89.

Aghion, Philippe, Robin Burgess, Stephen J. Redding and Fabrizio Zilibotti. 'The Unequal Effects of Liberalization: Evidence from Dismantling the License Raj in India'. *The American Economic Review* 98(4) (September, 2008): 1397–412.

Agro-Economic Research Centre. 'An Evaluation of the Programme of Barga Operation in West Bengal', mimeographed. Santiniketan: Visvabharati, 1986.

All India Kisan Sabha (AIKS). *Forward to United Struggle*. New Delhi, 1984.

_____. *General Secretary's Report and Statement of Policy* (approved by the Thane Meeting of the Central Kisan Committee). 26–28 September, 1986.

_____. 'Land to the Tiller', (by M. Basavapunnaiah). *Souvenir.* 24th Conference, Medinipur, 8–11 November, 1982.

_____. *Proceedings and Resolution.* 24th Conference, Medinipur, 8–11 November, 1982.

_____. *Report of the General Secretary.* 26th Conference, Khammam, Andhra Pradesh, 27–30 April, 1989.

_____. *Statements.* 29th Session of the Medinipur District, 2–4 November, 1990.

_____. *Towards a Country-wide Peasant Struggle: Proceedings, Resolutions, General Secretary's Report and Statement of Policy* (approved by the Thane Meeting of the Central Kisan Committee). 26–28 September, 1986.

Althusser, Louis and Étienne Balibar. *Reading Capital*, Part-1. Translated by Ben Brewster. London: New Left Books, 1970.

Arendt, Hannah. *The Origins of Totalitarianism*. New York: Harvest, 1976.

Bagchi, Amiya Kumar. 'Studies on the Economy of West Bengal since

Independence'. *Economic and Political Weekly* 30(47/48) (21 November, 1998): 2973–78.

Banaji, Jairus Sukumar Muralidharan, Dilip Simeon, Satya Sivaraman and Rohini Hensman. 'End of the Left in India?', Letter to EPW. *Economic and Political Weekly* 46(23) (June, 2011): 4–5.

Bandyopadhyay, D. *Land Reforms in West Bengal*. Calcutta: Government of West Bengal, 1980.

Bandyopadhyaya, Nripen. 'Operation Barga and Land Reforms Perspective West Bengal: A Discursive Review'. *Economic and Political Weekly* 16(25/26) (20–27 June, 1981): A38–A42.

Bandyopadhyaya, Nripen and N. Krishnaji. 'Evaluation of Land Reform Measures in West Bengal: A Report'. Unpublished report, Centre for Studies in Social Sciences, Calcutta, programme sponsored by ILO (ARTEP), 1983.

Bandyopadhyay, Sarbani. 'Caste and Politics in Bengal'. *Economic and Political Weekly* XLVII(50) (15 December, 2012): 71–73.

Bandopadhyay, Sekhar. *Caste, Culture and Hegemony: Social Domination in Colonial Bengal*. New Delhi: Sage Publications, 2004.

Banerjee, Abhijit V., Paul J. Gertler and Maitreesh Ghatak. 'Empowerment and Efficiency: Tenancy Reform in West Bengal'. *Journal of Political Economy* 110(2) (April, 2002): 239–80.

Banerjee, D. 'Industrial Stagnation in Eastern India: A Statistical Investigation'. *Economic and Political Weekly* 17(8/9) (20 and 27 February, 1982): 286–98 and 334–40.

Banerjee, Sumanta. *India's Simmering Revolution: The Naxalite Uprising*. London: Zed Books, 1984.

———. *In the Wake of Naxalbari: A History of the Naxalite Movement in India*. Calcutta: Subarnarekha, 1980.

Bardhan, Pranab. 'Political Clientelism and Capture: Theory and Evidence from West Bengal, India', 27 August 2012. Available at Dilip Mookherjee website: http:// people.bu.edu/dilipm/wkpap/index.html, accessed on 26 September, 2014.

———. *Political Economy of Development*. Delhi: Oxford University Press, 1984.

Bardhan, Pranab and Dilip Mookherjee. 'Pro-poor Targeting and Accountability of Local Governments in West Bengal'. *Journal of Development Economics* 79(2006): 3013–327.

Bardhan, Pranab, Dilip Mookherjee and Neha Kumar. 'State-led or Market-led Green Revolution? Role of Private Irrigation Investment vis-à-vis Local with Government Programs in West Bengal's Farm Productivity Growth'. *Journal of Development Economics* 99(2) (2012): 222–35.

Bardhan, Pranab, Sandip Mitra, Dilip Mookherjee and Abhirup Sarkar. 'Political Participation, Clientelism and Targeting of Local Government Programs: Results from a Rural Household Survey in West Bengal, India', 2011 (revised 4 October). Available at Dilip Mookherjee website: http://people.bu.edu/dilipm/wkpap/index.html, accessed on 26 September, 2014.

Bardhan, Pranab, Sandip Mitra, Dilip Mookherjee, and Anusha Nath. 'Changing Voting Patterns in Rural West Bengal: Role of Clientelism and Local Public Goods'. *Economic and Political Weekly* xlix(11) (15 March, 2014): 54–62.

Basu, Partha Pratim. '"Brand Buddha" in India's West Bengal: The Left Reinvents Itself'. *Asian Survey* 47(2) (March–April, 2007): 288–306.

Basu, Saroj Kumar and Santosh Kumar Bhattacharyya. *Land Reforms in West Bengal: A Study in Implementation*. Calcutta: Oxford Book Company, 1963.

Basu, Subho and Auritro Majumder. 'Dilemmas of Parliamentary Communism: The Rise and the Fall of the Left in West Bengal'. *Critical Asian Studies* 45(2) (2013): 167–200.

Bhaduri, Amit. 'Alternatives to Industrialisation'. *Economic and Political Weekly* 42(18) (5 May, 2007): 1597–601.

————. 'An Analysis of Semi-feudalism in East Indian Agriculture'. *Frontier* 6(25/27) (29 September, 1973): 11–15.

————. 'Development or Development Terrorism?'. *Economic and Political Weekly* 42(7) (17 February, 2007): 552–53.

————. 'The Economics and Politics of Social Democracy'. In *Development and Change: Essays in Honour of K. N. Raj*, edited by Pranab Bardhan. Bombay: Oxford University Press, 1993.

————. 'A Study in Agricultural Backwardness Under Semi-feudalism'. *Economic Journal* 83(329) (March, 1973): 120–37.

Bhalla, G. S. and Gurmail Singh. *Indian Agriculture: Four Decades of Development*. New Delhi: Sage Publications, 2001.

Bhattacharjee, Buddhadeb. 'On Industrialisation in West Bengal'. *The Marxist* 23 (1) (January–March, 2007). Available at: http://www.cpimwb.org.

in/upload_all_docs/pdf/lf_govt/On_Industrialisation_in_W.B._-_
Buddhadeb_Bhattacharjee.pdf, accessed on 26 September, 2014.

Bhattacharya, Dipankar. 'New Challenges for Bengal Left: Panchayat Election Pointers'. *Economic and Political Weekly* XXVIII(29/30) (17–24 July, 1993): 1491–94.

Bhattacharya, Malabika. 'English to Return to Bengal's Primary Schools'. *The Hindu*, Wednesday, 15 October, 2003.

Bhattacharyya, Asit Kumar. 'An Examination of Land Reforms with Special Reference to West Bengal'. In *Land Reforms in Eastern India*, edited by Manjula Bose, 183–93. Calcutta: Planning Forum, Jadavpur University, 1981.

Bhattacharyya, Dwaipayan. 'Agrarian Reforms and Politics of the Left in West Bengal'. Ph.D thesis, University of Cambridge, 1993.

_____. 'Civic Community and its Margins: Schoolteachers in Rural West Bengal'. In *Interrogating Social Capital: The Indian Experience*, edited by Dwaipayan Bhattacharyya, Niraja Gopal Jayal, Bishnu N. Mohapatra and Sudha Pai, 139–64. New Delhi: Sage Publications, 2004.

_____. 'Limits to Legal Radicalism: Land Reforms and the Left Front in West Bengal'. *The Calcutta Historical Journal* 16(1) (January–June, 1994): 57–100.

_____. 'Making and Unmaking of Trinamul Congress'. *Economic and Political Weekly* 39(14/15) (2 April, 2004):1529–37.

_____. 'Of Control and Factions: The Changing "Party-Society" in Rural West Bengal'. *Economic and Political Weekly* 44(9) (28 February, 2009): 59–69.

_____. 'Politics of Middleness: The Changing Character of the Communist Party of India (Marxist) in Rural West Bengal (1977-1990)'. In *Sonar Bangla? Agricultural Growth and Agrarian Change in West Bengal and Bangladesh*, edited by Ben Rogally, Barbara Harriss White and Sugata Bose, 279–300. New Delhi: Sage Publications, 1999.

_____. 'West Bengal: Permanent Incumbency and Political Stability'. In *Electoral Politics in Indian States: Lok Sabha Elections in 2004 and Beyond*, edited by Sandeep Shastri, K. C. Suri and Yogendra Yadav, 326–45. New Delhi: Oxford University Press, 2009.

Bhattacharyya, Dwaipayan and Kumar Rana. 'Politics of PDS Anger in West Bengal'. *Economic and Political Weekly* 43(5) (2 February, 2008): 63–69.

Bhattacharyya, Maumita and Sudipta Bhattacharyya. 'Agrarian Impasse in West Bengal in the Liberalization Era'. *Economic and Political Weekly* 42(52) (29 December– 4 January, 2007): 65–71.

Bhaumik, Sankar Kumar. 'System of Land Tenure, Allocative Efficiency and Agrarian Development: A Study of Agriculture in West Bengal'. PhD dissertation, Centre for Regional Development, School of Social Sciences, Jawaharlal Nehru University, New Delhi, 1989.

Bourdieu, Pierre. *Distinction: A Social Critique of the Judgement of Taste*. Translated by Richard Nice. Cambridge: Polity Press, 1984.

_____. 'The Forms of Capital', Chapter 1. In *The Routledge Falmer Reader in Sociology of Education*, edited by Stephen J. Ball. London: Routledge Falmer, 2004.

_____. *Homo Academicus*. Translated by Richard Nice. Stanford, California: Stanford University Press, 1988.

_____. *The Logic of Practice*. Translated by Richard Nice. Stanford: Stanford University Press, [1980] 1990.

_____. *Outline of a Theory of Practice*. Translated by Richard Nice. Cambridge: Cambridge University Press, [1972] 1977.

_____. *Rules of Art*. Translated by S. Emanuel. Cambridge: Polity, [1992] 1996.

_____. 'Social Space and Symbolic Power'. *Sociological Theory* 7(1) (Spring, 1989): 14–25.

Brockling, Ulrich, Susanne Krasmann and Thomas Lemke, eds. *Governmentality: Current Issues and Future Challenges*. New York and Oxford: Routledge, 2011.

Burawoy, Michael. 'For a Sociological Marxism: The Complementary Convergence of Antonio Gramsci and Karl Polanyi'. *Politics & Society* 31(2) (June, 2003): 193–261.

Centre for Monitoring Indian Economy (CMIE). *Performance of Agriculture in Major States 1967-68 to 1991-92*. Bombay, July, 1993.

Centre for Studies in Social Sciences (CSSSC). 'SRD Programme: Design of Purpose-Level Indicators and Baseline Measurement in West Bengal Districts'. *Draft Final Report*. Calcutta, April, 2006.

Certeau, Michel de. *The Practice of Everyday Life*. Translated by Steven Rendall. Berkeley: University of California Press, 1984.

Chakrabarti, Prafulla. *The Marginal Men: The Refugees and the Left Political Syndrome in West Bengal*. Kalyani, West Bengal: Lumière Books, 1990.

Chakrabarty, Dipesh. *Provincializing Europe: Postcolonial Thought and Historical Difference*. Princeton: Princeton University Press, 2000.

Chandra, Uday and Kenneth Bo Nielsen. 'The Importance of Caste in Bengal'. *Economic and Political Weekly* XLVII(44) (2012): 59–61.

Chatterjee, Partha. 'Democracy and Economic Transformation in India'. *Economic and Political Weekly* 43(16) (19 April, 2008): 53–62.

_____. 'Historicising Caste in Bengal Politics'. *Economic and Political Weekly* XLVII(50) (15 December, 2012): 69–70.

_____. 'On Gramsci's "Fundamental Mistake"'. *Economic and Political Weekly* 23(5) (30 January, 1988): PE24–26.

_____. *The Politics of the Governed: Reflections on Popular Politics in Most of the World*. New Delhi: Permanent Black, 2004.

_____. *The Present History of West Bengal: Essays in Political Criticism*. Delhi: Oxford University Press, 1997.

Chattopadhyay, Apurba Kumar. 'Distributive Impact of Agricultural Growth in Rural West Bengal'. *Economic and Political Weekly* 40(53) (31 December, 2005): 5601–10.

Chattopadhyay, Suhrid Sankar. 'Wake Up Call'. *Frontline* 25(12) (7 June, 2008). Available at: http://www.frontline.in/static/html/fl2512/stories/20080620251203300.htm, accessed on 11 September, 2014.

Chaudhuri, Ajit. 'From Hegemony to Counter-hegemony: A Journey in a Non-imaginary Unreal Space'. *Economic and Political Weekly* 23(5) (30 January, 1988): PE19–PE23.

CMIE. *Performance of Agriculture in Major States 1967–68 to 1991–92, July*. Bombay: Centre for Monitoring Indian Economy, 1993.

Cooper, Adrienne. *Sharecropping and Sharecroppers' Struggles in Bengal 1930–1950*. Calcutta: K. P. Bagchi and Company, 1988.

CPI(M). *Central Committee Resolution on Certain Agrarian Issues and an Explanatory Note by P. Sundarayya*. Calcutta, 1973.

_____. *The Political Organisation Report*. 2nd Session, Keshpur Local Committee No. 1, 17–18 June, 1984.

_____. *Programme*. Adopted at the 7th Congress of the CPI, Calcutta, 31

October to 7 November 1964, with Amendments by the 9th Congress in Madurai, 27 June to 2 July, 1972. New Delhi: CPI(M) Publication, 1989.

_____. *Report on the Present Political Situation*. Central Committee, 2–7 February, 1970.

Crook, Richard C. and James Manor. *Democracy and Decentralization in South Asia and West Africa*. Cambridge: Cambridge University Press, 1998.

Das, Arup Jyoti. *Kamtapur and the Koch Rajbanshi Imagination*. Guwahati: Montagemedia, 2009.

Das, Ritanjan. 'History, Ideology and Negotiation: The Politics of Policy Transition in West Bengal, India'. Doctoral dissertation, London School of Economics and Political Science, January, 2013.

Das Gupta, Ranjit. 'Industrial Development Policy: A Critical View'. *Economic and Political Weekly* 30(30) (29 July, 1995): 1896–901.

_____. *Labour and Working Class in Eastern India: Studies in Colonial History*. Calcutta: K. P. Bagchi, 1994.

Das Gupta, Sreemanta. 'West Bengal and Industry: A Regional Perspective'. *Economic and Political Weekly* 33(47/48) (24 November–4 December, 1998): 3049–60.

Dasgupta, Biplab. *The Naxalite Movement*. Calcutta: Allied Publishers, 1974.

_____. 'Monitoring and Evaluation of the Agrarian Reform Programme of West Bengal', mimeographed. Calcutta, December, 1987.

_____. 'Sharecropping in West Bengal from Independence to Operation Barga'. *Economic and Political Weekly* 19(26) (30 June, 1984): A85–A96.

Dasgupta, Rajarshi. 'The CPI(M) "Machinery" in West Bengal: Two Village Narratives from Kochbihar and Malda'. *Economic and Political Weekly* 44(9) (28 February, 2009): 70–81.

Dasgupta, S. and A. Singh. 'Will Services be the New Engine of Indian Economic Growth?'. *Development and Change* 36(6) (2005):1035–57.

Datta, Prabhat.. *Panchayats, Rural Development and Local Autonomy: The West Bengal Experience*. Kolkata: Dasgupta and Company Pvt. Ltd, 2001.

Datta Gupta, Sobhanlal. 'Understanding Gramsci: Some Exploratory Observations'. *Economic and Political Weekly* 23(32) (6 August, 1988): 1620–22.

Davidson, Alistair. 'Gramsci and Lenin, 1917–1922'. In *Antonio Gramsci: Critical Assessments of Leading Political Philosophers*, edited by James Martin. London: Routledge, 2002.

Desai, M., S. H. Rudolph and A. Rudra, eds. *Agrarian Power and Agricultural Productivity in South Asia*. New Delhi: Oxford University Press, 1984.

Desai, Manali. 'Party Formation, Political Power, and the Capacity for Reform: Comparing Left Parties in Kerala and West Bengal, India'. *Social Forces* 80(1) (September, 2001): 37–60.

Dreze, Jean and Amartya Sen. *An Uncertain Glory: India and its Contradictions*. London: Allen Lane, 2013.

Dutt, K. 'Operation Barga: Gains and Constraints'. *Economic and Political Weekly* 16(25/26) (20–27 June, 1981): A58–A60.

Eco, Umberto. 'Political Language: The Use and Abuse of Rhetoric'. In *Apocalypse Postponed*, edited by Robert Lumley. London: Fleming,1995.

Echeverri-Gent, J. 'Public Participation and Poverty Alleviation: The Experience of Reform Communists in West Bengal'. *World Development* 20(10) (1992): 1401–22.

Erlenbusch, Verena. 'The Place of Sovereignty: Mapping Power with Agamben, Butler, and Foucault'. *Critical Horizons* 14(1) (2013): 44–69.

Ettlinger, Nancy. 'Governmentality as Epistemology'. *Annals of the Association of American Geographers* 10(3) (2011): 537–60.

Field, John Osgood and Marcus F. Franda. *Electoral Politics in the Indian States: The Communist Parties of West Bengal*. New Delhi: Manohar Book Service, 1974.

Fine, Robert. *Political Investigations: Hegel, Marx, Arendt*. London: Routledge, 2001.

Forgacs, David, ed. 'Passive Revolution, Caesarism, Fascism', Chapter 8. In *The Gramsci Reader: 1916–1935*. New York: New York University Press, 2000.

Foucault, Michel. 'Governmentality'. In *The Foucault Effect*, edited by Graham Burchell, Colin Gordon and Peter Miller. Hertfordshire: Harvester Wheatsheaf, 1991.

_____. *Security, Territory, Population: Lectures at the Collège de France, 1977–78*. Translated by Graham Burchell. Hampshire/New York: Palgrave Macmillan, 2009.

Frank, Andre Gunder. 'The Development of Underdevelopment'. *Monthly Review* 18(4) (September, 1966): 17–31.

_____. *World Accumulation, 1492–1789*. New York: Algora Publishing, 1978.

Frankel, Francine R. *India's Green Revolution: Economic Gains and Political Casts*. Princeton: Princeton University Press, 1971.

Ganguly, Bodhirupa. 'Operation Barga in West Bengal: A Case Study', mimeographed. Santiniketan: WIDER Project on Rural Poverty, Social Change and Public Policy, 1990.

Ganguly, Rajat. 'Poverty, Malgovernance and Ethnopolitical Mobilization: Gorkha Nationalism and the Gorkhaland Agitation in India'. *Nationalism and Ethnic Politics* 11(4) (Winter, 2005): 467–502.

Ghatak, Maitreesh and Maitreya Ghatak. 'Recent Reforms in Panchayat System in West Bengal: Toward Greater Participatory Governance?'. *Economic and Political Weekly* 37(1) (2002): 45–58.

Ghosh, Abhijit. *Land, Law and the Left: The Saga of Disempowerment of the Peasantry in the Era of Globalization*. New Delhi: Concept Publishing Company, 2007.

Ghosh, Anjali. *Peaceful Transition to Power: A Study of Marxist Political Strategies in West Bengal 1967–77*. Calcutta: Firma KLM Private Limited, 1981.

Ghosh, Anjan. 'Cast(e) out in West Bengal'. *Seminar* 508 (December, 2001). Available at: http://www.india-seminar.com/2001/508/508%20anjan%20ghosh.htm, accessed on 30 April, 2014.

_____. 'Gorkhaland Redux'. *Economic and Political Weekly* 44(23) (6–12 June, 2009): 10–13.

_____. 'The Role of Rumour in History Writing', unpublished paper. 2007.

Ghosh, Ratan. 'Agrarian Programme of the Left Front Government'. *Economic and Political Weekly* 16(25–26) (20–27 June, 1981): A49–A55.

Ghosh, Tushar Kanti. 'Assessment of Operation Barga: Case Study of Burdwan District in West Bengal', mimeographed. Calcutta, 1981

_____. 'Introduction of Integrated Set-Up of Land Reforms Administration in West Bengal', mimeographed. Calcutta, May, 1985.

_____. 'Land Reforms in West Bengal: Legislation and Achievement'. In *Land Reforms in Eastern India*, edited by Manjula Bose, 142–70. Calcutta: Planning Forum, Jadavpur University, 1981.

_____. *Operation Barga and Land Reforms*. Delhi: B. R. Publishing Corporation, 1986.

Gopal Iyer, K. *Report on the Empirical Study of Land Reforms in India*. Mussourie: Lal Bahadur Shastri National Academy of Administration, 1990.

Government of Bengal (GoB). *Report of the Land Revenue Commission*. Chairman: F.L.C. Floud, Vol. 1. Alipore: B.G. Press, 1940.

Government of India (GoI). *Annual Report 2006–2007*. New Delhi: Ministry of Rural Development, 2007.

_____. *National Human Development Report, 2001*. New Delhi: Planning Commission, March, 2002.

_____. 'National Programme of Nutritional Support to Primary Education, 2006: Guidelines'. New Delhi: Ministry of Human Resource Development, Department of School Education and Literacy, September, 2006.

_____. *West Bengal Development Report*. New Delhi: Planning Commission, Academic Foundation, 2010.

GoWB.*An Alternative Approach to Development: Land Reforms and Panchayats*, (by Surya Kanta Mishra, Minister of Panchayat and Rural Development). Calcutta: Information and Cultural Affairs Department, 1991.

_____. 'Bargadars and Institutional Finance', (by N. Banerjee, Officer on Special Dutys), mimeographed. West Bengal: Directorate of Land Records and Surveys, 15 January, 1973.

_____. 'Bargadars of Salihan: A Case Study of the Operation of the Law Relating to the Protection of Bargadars (share-croppers) in a Village in West Bengal', (by D. Bandyopadhyay, Indian Administrative Service), mimeographed. New Delhi: Public Administration Case Workshop, Administrative Staff College of India, 20–23 December, 1971.

_____. 'Debates on the West Bengal Panchayat Bill'. Extracts from the *Proceedings of the Meeting of the West Bengal Legislative Assembly* held on 9 September, 1969. Calcutta, 1969.

_____. *Economic Review, Year 1989-90*. Statistical Appendix. Calcutta: State Planning Board, 1989.

_____. *An Evaluation of Land Reforms in West Bengal with Special Reference to Operation Barga*. Calcutta: Statistical Cell, Board of Revenue, 1981.

_____. 'Evasion of Ceilings in West Bengal', (by K. L. Mukhopadhyay), mimeographed. 1973.

_____. *Fourth Workshop on Land Reforms (23-24 June): Operational Decisions.* For Official Use Only. Calcutta: Board of Revenue, 1981.

_____. 'The Gram Panchayats in West Bengal and their Activities', mimeographed. West Bengal: Survey and Evaluation, Economic Planning Stream, Town and Country Planning Department, July, 1980.

_____. 'Guidelines on Implementation of Ceiling Provisions under W. B. L. R. Act, 1955', Confidential. West Bengal: Directorate of Land Records and Surveys, 1990.

_____. 'Indra Lohar and the Due Process of Law: A Case Study of the Constraints to the implementation of Law Relating to Protection of Bargadars', (by D. Bandyopadhyaya, Secretary to the Department of Labour, Government of West Bengal), mimeographed. 1972.

_____. 'Industrial Policy of West Bengal'. *Social Scientist* 6(6–7) (January–February, 1978): 103–08.

_____. *Information on West Bengal Panchayats, Their Members and Functionaries after the Panchayat General Election 2008 and 2009 (Siliguri).* Kolkata: Panchayat and Rural Development Department, 2010.

_____. 'Kanungos of Midnapore District: Case Studies of Bargadars', mimeographed. For Official Use Only. January, 1977.

_____. 'Land Reforms: A Package Programme', (by P. Bandyopadhyay), mimeographed. For Official Use Only. 24 Parganas: Settlement Office, 1983.

_____. *Land Reforms in West Bengal,* (by D. Bandyopadhyay, Indian Administrative Service). Calcutta, 1980.

_____. *Land Reforms in West Bengal: Statistical Report.* West Bengal: Statistical Cell, Board of Revenue, March, 1981.

_____. *Land Reforms in West Bengal: Statistical Report III.* West Bengal: Statistical Cell of the Board of Revenue Land and Land Reforms Department, 8 March, 1980.

_____. *Land Reforms in West Bengal: Statistical Report IV.* West Bengal: Statistical Cell, Board of Revenue, 22 September, 1980.

_____. *Land Reforms in West Bengal: Statistical Report VI.* West Bengal: Statistical Cell, Board of Revenue, 19 September, 1981.

_____. 'Land Reforms Work in Burdwan: A Critical Analysis', (by S. K. Sarkar, Settlement Officer, Burdwan-Bankura and Additional District Magistrate,

LR, Burdwan), mimeographed. For Official Use Only. Burdwan: Land Reforms Offices, 1985.

———. *Memorandum for the Fifth Finance Commission*, Chapter 1. Calcutta, 1968.

———. 'Monthly Report of the Progress of Work for the Month of November, 1990', mimeographed. Calcutta, West Bengal: Directorate of Land Records and Survey, 1990.

———. 'Monthly Report of the Progress of Work for the Month of December, 1990', mimeographed. Calcutta, West Bengal: Directorate of Land Records and Survey, 1990.

———. 'A Note on Implementation Agency for Land Reforms', (by D. Bandyopadhyay and B. Sarkar, Indian Administrative Service), mimeographed, no other detail available. 1971

———. 'Operation Barga in West Bengal: An Introduction', (by N. K. Raghupathy, Secretary, Board of Revenue). West Bengal: Board of Revenue, 1991.

———. 'Policy Statement on Industrial Development'. 23 September, 1994.

———. 'Ramdhan Tudu: A Tribal Bargadar in District Hooghly', (A Case Study) (by Bikram Sarkar, Director of Land Records and Surveys), mimeographed. West Bengal: Directorate of Land Records and Survey, 1978.

———. *Reports on the Land Reforms Reorientation Camp of Belda (Narayangarh P.S.) in Midnapore District*. Midnapore: Settlement Office, 11–13 May, 1978.

———. 'Report of the Mukherjee-Maitra Commission', mimeographed. Calcutta, 1973.

———. *A Report on the Reorientation Camp at Bagmundi (Purulia)*. Purulia: Settlement Office, 1979.

———. *A Report on the Reorientation Camp: Malandighi*. Burdwan: Settlement Office, 1978.

———. 'Report of the State Education Commission', mimeographed. Calcutta. August, 1992

———. 'Statistics of Bargadars and Extent of Barga Cultivation in West Bengal: An Analytical Study', (by P. K. Datta), mimeographed. West Bengal: Directorate of Land Records and Survey, May, 1981.

———. 'A Study on Evasion of Land Ceiling-I under the West Bengal Estates

Acquisition Act 1953', (by P. Bandyopadhyay), mimeographed. Calcutta, 1983.

———. 'A Study of Evasion of Land Ceiling-II under the West Bengal Estates Acquisition Act 1953', (by P. Bandyopadhyay), mimeographed. Calcutta, 1983.

———. 'Statistical Handbook on Bargadars of West Bengal', mimeographed. West Bengal: Research and Training Cell, Directorate of Land Records and Surveys, April, 1985.

———. *Supreme Court Judgment Dated the 9thMay, 1980. Upholding Ceiling on Land Prescribed Under the West Bengal Land Reforms Act 1955*. West Bengal: Board of Revenue, 23 July, 1980.

———. *Third Workshop on Land Reforms (September 15-16, 1980): Operational Decisions*. For Official Use Only. West Bengal: Board of Revenue, 1980.

———. Speech by Tribhuvan Narayan Singh, Governor of West Bengal, West Bengal Legislative Assembly. 7 February, 1979.

———. *The West Bengal Land Reforms Act, 1955 and the Rules Framed There under*. Calcutta: Directorate of Land Records and Surveys, 1989.

———. *West Bengal Panchayat Act, 1973*. Alipore: Government of West Bengal Press, 1973.

———. *The West Bengal Panchayat Act, 1973: As Modified up to 31st January, 2004*. Kolkata: Law Department, 2004.

———. 'What Happened to Vested Land?', (by B. K. Sarkar and R. K. Prasannan), mimeographed. Calcutta: Directorate of Land Records and Survey, 1976.

———. *Workshop on Land Reforms (June 23–24, 1978): A Few Operational Decisions*. West Bengal: Board of Revenue, 1978.

Gramsci, Antonio. *Selections from Prison Notebooks*. Edited and translated by Quintin Hoare and Geoffrey Norwell Smith. London: Lawrence and Wishart, 1971.

———. 'Some Theoretical and Practical Aspects of Economism'. In *The Gramsci Reader: Selected Writings 1916–1935*, edited by David Forgacs. New York: New York University Press, 2000.

Grindle, Merilee S. 'Good Enough Governance: Poverty Reduction and Reform in Developing Countries'. *Governance: An International Journal of Policy, Administration and Institutions* 17(4) (October, 2004): 525–48.

Gupta, Bhupesh. *Masterpiece of Left Opportunism: Critique of CPM Draft Political Resolution*. New Delhi: Communist Party of India, May, 1972.

Guruswamy, Mohan, Kamal Sharma and Jeevan Prakash Mohanty. 'Economic Growth and Development in West Bengal: Reality versus Perception'. *Economic and Political Weekly* 40(21) (21 May, 2005): 2151–57.

Halder, Srijan. 'Caste–Class Situation in Rural West Bengal'. In *Caste and Class in India*, edited by K. L. Sharma. New Delhi: Rawat Publications, 1994.

Harris, John. 'Reflections on Agrarian Change in India Since Independence: Does "Landlordism" Still Matter?'. Draft paper presented at Yale Conference on new questions concerning land in modern India, Yale University, 27–29 April, 2012

_____. 'What is Happening in Rural West Bengal? Agrarian Reform, Growth and Distribution'. *Economic and Political Weekly* XXVII(24) (1993): 1237–47.

Hart, H. C. 'Political Leadership in India'. In *India's Democracy: An Analysis of Changing State Society Relations*, edited by Atul Kohli. Princeton, New Jersey: Princeton University Press, 1988.

Harvey, David. 'From Managerialism to Entrepreneurialism: The Transformation in Urban Governance in Late Capitalism'. *Geografiska Annaler, Series B, Human Geography* (The Roots of Geographical Change: 1973 to the Present) 71(1) (1989): 3–17

_____. *The New Imperialism*. Oxford: Oxford University Press, 2003.

Herring, Ronald J. *Land to the Tiller: The Political Economy of Agrarian Reform in South Asia*. New Delhi: Oxford University Press, 1983.

Karat, Prakash. 'Left Front Government: Bastion of Left Democratic Forces'. *The Marxist* 18(2) (April–June, 2002). Available at: http://www.cpim.org/marxist/2002-WB-LG-Govt-PK.pdf, accessed on 25 September, 2014.

Kaviraj, Sudipta. 'A Critique of Passive Revolution'. *Economic and Political Weekly* (Special Number) (November, 1988): 2429–44.

_____. 'The Splits in the Communist Movement in India', Doctoral Thesis. New Delhi: Jawaharlal Nehru University, 1979.

Khasnabis, R. 'Operation Barga: Limits of Social Democratic Reforms'. *Economic and Political Weekly* 16(25/26) (20–27 June, 1981): A43–A48.

Kohli, Atul. *Democracy and Discontent: India's Growing Crisis of Governability*. Cambridge: Cambridge University Press, 1990.

_____. *Poverty amid Plenty in the New India*. Cambridge: Cambridge University Press, 2012.

_____. *The State and Poverty in India: The Politics of Reform*. Cambridge: Cambridge University Press, 1987.

Konar, Harekrishna. 'The Problems of Land Reform and its Solution'. In *Agrarian Problems of India*. Calcutta: Harekrishna Konar Memorial Agrarian Research Centre, 1979.

Laclau, Ernesto. *On Populist Reason*. London: Verso, 2007.

Lahiri, Ranjit Kumar. 'Land Reforms in West Bengal: Some Implications'. In *Land Reforms in Eastern India*, edited by Manjula Bose, 108–20. Calcutta: Planning Forum, Jadavpur University, 1981.

Le Blanc, Paul, ed. *Lenin: Revolution, Democracy, Socialism: Selected Writings*. London: Pluto Press, 2008.

Leiva, Fernando Ignacio. 'Toward a Critique of Latin American Neostructuralism'. *Latin American Politics and Society* 50(4) (Winter, 2008): 1–25.

Lenin, Vladimir I. *Collected Works*, Volume 42 (October 1917–March 1923). Moscow: Progress Publishers, [1969] 1977.

_____. 'On the So-called Market Question'. In *Collected Works*, Volume 1 (1893). Moscow: Foreign Languages Publishing House, 1960–70.

Levien, Michael. 'India's Double-Movement: Polanyi and the National Alliance of Peoples' Movements'. *Berkeley Journal of Sociology* 51 (2007): 119–49.

Lieten, G. K. 'Depeasantisation Discontinued: Land Reforms in West Bengal'. *Economic and Political Weekly* 25(40) (1990): 2265–71.

Lipton, Michael. *Land Reform in Developing Countries: Property Rights and Property Wrongs*. Oxon: Routledge, 2009.

Luxemburg, Rosa. *Accumulation of Capital*. Translated by Agnes Schwarzschild with a new introduction by Tadeusz Kowalik. London: Routledge, 2003.

Majumdar, Asok. *Peasant Protest in Indian Politics: Tebhaga Movement in Bengal*. New Delhi: NIB Publishers, 1993.

_____. *The Tebhaga Movement: Politics of Peasant Protest in Bengal 1946– 1950*. New Delhi: Aakar, 2011.

Majumdar, Manabi. 'Democracy in Praxis: Two Non-Left Gram Panchayats in West Bengal'. *Economic and Political Weekly* 44(9) (28 February, 2009): 82–93.

Majumdar, Tapas. 'An Education Commission Reports'. *Economic and Political Weekly* 28 (19) (8 May, 1993): 919–20.

Mallick, Ross. *Indian Communism: Opposition, Collaboration and Institutionalization.* New Delhi: Oxford University Press, 1994.

Marx, Karl. *Capital: A Critique of Political Economy*, Volume 1. Translated by Ben Fowkes. Harmondsworth: Penguin Books (in association with New Left Review), 1976.

_____. *Grundrisse: Foundations of the Critique of Political Economy* (Rough Draft). Translated with a foreword by Martin Nocolaus. London: Penguin Books (in association with New Left Review), 1973] 1993.

Mehrotra, Santosh, ed. *The Economics of Elementary Education in India.* New Delhi: Sage Publications, 2006.

_____. 'Reforming Elementary Education in India: A Menu of Options'. *International Journal of Educational Development* 26 (2006b): 261–77.

_____. 'What Ails the Educationally Backward States?'. In *The Economics of Elementary Education in India*, edited by Santosh Mehrotra. New Delhi: Sage Publications, 2006a.

Middleton, Townsend. 'Anxious Belongings: Anxiety and the Politics of Belonging in Subnationalist Darjeeling'. *American Anthropologist* 115(4) (December, 2013): 608–21.

Midnapore Planning and Development Society. *Participatory Gram Panchayat Planning under Convergent Community Action: Salboni Pilot Project.* Kalyani: State Institute of Panchayat and Rural Development, 2002.

Miller, Peter and Nicholas Rose. *Governing the Present.* Cambridge: Polity Press, 2008.

Mitchell, Timothy. 'Everyday Metaphors of Power'. *Theory and Society* 19(5) (October, 1990): 545–77.

Mitra, Sumit. 'Language Barrier: West Bengal Schools Churn out Students with Poor English, Parochial Policies Need Rethink'. *India Today*, 2 December, 2002.

Moitra, Bhaswar and Pranab Kumar Das. 'Goundwater Markets in West Bengal, India: Emergence, Evolution and Market Structure', mimeographed. South

Asia Network of Economic Research Institutes V Programme, 2004. Available at http://saneinetwork.net/Files/05_04.pdf, accessed on 24 July, 2013.

Mouffe, Chantal. 'Hegemony and Ideology in Gramsci'. In *Gramsci and Marxist Theory*, edited by Chantal Mouffe. London: Routledge and Kegan Paul, 1979.

Namboodiripad, E. M. S. *National Question in Kerala*. Bombay: People's Publishing House, 1952.

_____. *Reminiscences of an Indian Communist*. New Delhi: National Book Centre, 1987.

Nanda, Ved P. 'The "Good Governance" Concept Revisited'. *Annals of American Academy of Political and Social Science* 603 (January, 2006): 269–83.

National University of Education Planning and Administration (NUEPA) and Department of School Education and Literacy. *Elementary Education in India: Progress towards Universal Elementary Education*. New Delhi: Ministry of Human Resource Development, Government of India, 2011.

Negri, Antonio. 'The Labor of the Multitude and the Fabric of Biopolitics'. Translated by Sara Mayo, Peter Graefe and Mark Coté. *Mediations* 23(2) (Spring, 2008): 9–24.

Overstreet, Gene D. and Marshall Windmiller. *Communism in India*. Berkeley and Los Angeles: University of California Press, 1959.

Patnaik, Prabhat. 'The Left in Decline'. *Economic and Political Weekly* 46(29) (16 July, 2011): 12–16.

Patnaik, Utsa. 'Neo-Populism and Marxism: The Chayanovian view of Agrarian Questions and its Fundamental Fallacy'. *Social Scientist* 9(12) (December, 1981): 26–52.

Pedersen, Jùrgen Dige. 'India's Industrial Dilemmas in West Bengal'. *Asian Survey* 41(4) (July–August, 2001): 646–68.

Peet, Richard and Elaine Hartwick. *Theories of Development: Contentions, Arguments, Alternatives*. New York: The Guilford Press, 2009.

Perelman, Michael. *The Invention of Capitalism: Classical Political Economy and the Secret History of Primitive Accumulation*. Durham and London: Duke University Press, 2000.

Polanyi, Karl. *The Great Transformation: The Political and Economic Origins of Our Time.* Boston: Beacon Press, [1944] 2001.

Pratichi. *The Pratichi Education Report I* (with an Introduction by Amartya Sen), Part I. New Delhi: TLM Books in association with Pratichi Trust, 2002.

_____. *The Pratichi Education Report II: Primary Education in West Bengal, Changes and Challenges* (with an Introduction by Amartya Sen). Shantiniketan: Pratichi Research Team, Pratichi (India) Trust, 2009.

_____. *The Pratichi Report on Mid-Day Meal.* Shantiniketan: Pratichi (India) Trust, Publication Support: Sarva Siksha Mission, Birbhum, February, 2010.

Ramachandran, V. K. 'On Kerala's Development Achievements'. In *Indian Development: Selected Regional Perspectives,* edited by In Jean Dreze and Amartya Sen, 205–356. New Delhi: Oxford University Press, 1997.

Rana, Kumar 'Social Exclusion in and through Elementary Education: The Case of West Bengal'. *Pratichi Occasional Paper 1.* Kolkata: Pratichi (India) Trust in association with UNICEF, February, 2010.

Ray, Rabindra. *Naxalites and their Ideology.* New Delhi: Oxford University Press, 2002.

Ray, Sankar. 'CPI(M), A History of Ideological Chicanery'. *DNA,* Friday, 25 November,2011.Availableat:http://www.dnaindia.com/analysis/1617060/comment-cpim-a-history-of-ideological-chicanery, accessed on 2 July, 2013.

Rosanvallon, Pierre. *Counter-Democracy: Politics in an Age of Distrust.* Translated by Arthur Goldhammer. Third printing. Cambridge: Cambridge University Press, 2012.

Roy, Dayabati and Partha Sarathi Banerjee. 'Decentralised Governance Reforms in Primary Education: Some Reflections from West Bengal'. *Economic and Political Weekly* 47(24) (16 June, 2012): 67–74.

Roy, Dayabati. 'Changing Patterns of Politics in Rural West Bengal', PhD thesis. West Bengal: Burdwan University, 2009.

Rudra, Ashok. 'Loans as Part of Agrarian Relations'. *Economic and Political Weekly* 10(28) (12 July, 1975): 1049–53.

_____. 'One Step Forward, Two Steps Backward'. *Economic and Political Weekly* XVI(25–26) (20–27 June, 1981): A61–A68.

_____. 'Sharecropping Arrangements in West Bengal'. *Economic and Political Weekly* 10(39) (27 September, 1975): A58–A63.

Ruud, Arild Engelsen. 'Land and Power: The Marxist Conquest of Rural Bengal'. *Modern Asian Studies* 28(2) (May, 1994): 357–80.

_____. 'The Indian Hierarchy: Culture, Ideology and Consciousness in Bengali Village Politics'. *Modern Asian Studies* 33(3) (1999): 689–732.

_____. *Poetics of Village Politics: The Making of West Bengal's Rural Communism.* New Delhi: Oxford University Press, 2003.

_____. 'Socio-Cultural Changes in Rural West Bengal', Ph.D. dissertation, London School of Economics and Political Science, 1995.

Saha, Anamitra and M. Swaminathan. 'Agricultural Growth in West Bengal in the 1980s: A Disaggregation by Districts and Crops'. *Economic and Political Weekly* 29(13) (26 March, 1994): A2–A11.

Samaddar, Ranabir. 'Caste and Power in West Bengal'. In *Caste and Class in India,* edited by K. L. Sharma. New Delhi: Rawat Publications, 1994.

_____. *Passive Revolution in West Bengal: 1977–2011.* New Delhi: Sage Publications, 2013.

_____. 'Whatever Has Happened to Caste in West Bengal?'. *Economic and Political Weekly* (7 September, 2013): 77–79.

Sanyal, Kalyan. *Rethinking Capitalist Development: Primitive Accumulation, Governmentality, and Post-colonial Capitalism.* London and New Delhi: Routledge, 2007.

Sarkar, Bikram. 'Benami Transfer: A Move to Frustrate Land Ceiling Laws'. In *Land Reforms in Eastern India,* edited by Manjula Bose, 83–93. Calcutta: Planning Forum, Jadavpur University, 1981.

_____. *Land Reforms in India, Theory and Practice: A Study of Legal Aspects of Land Reforms Measures in West Bengal.* New Delhi: Ashish Publishing House, 1989.

Sarkar, Manabesh and Rana, Kumar. 'Roles and Responsibilities of the Teachers' Unions in the Delivery of Primary Education: A Case of West Bengal'. *Pratichi Occasional Paper No. 3.* Shantiniketan: Pratichi (India) Trust, December, 2010.

Sassoon, Anne Showstack. *Gramsci and Contemporary Politics beyond Pessimism of the Intellect.* London: Routledge, 2000.

Schubert, J. Daniel. 'Suffering/Symbolic Violence', Chapter 11. In *Pierre Bourdieu: Key Concepts,* edited by Michael Grenfell. Durham: Acumen, 2008.

Sen Gupta, Bhabani. *Communism in Indian Politics*. New York: Columbia University Press, 1972.

Sen, Asit. *An Approach to Naxalbari*. Calcutta: Institute of Scientific Thought, 1980.

Sen, Asok. 'The Frontiers of the "Prison Notebooks"'. *Economic and Political Weekly* 23(5) (30 January, 1988): PE31–PE36.

Sen, Mohit and Bhupesh Gupta. *CPM's Politics X–Rayed*. New Delhi: Communist Party of India, 1978.

Sen, Sunil. *Agrarian Struggle in Bengal: 1946-47*. New Delhi: Peoples' Publishing House, 1972.

_____. *Peasant Movement in India: Nineteenth and Twentieth Centuries*. Calcutta: Manisha, 1991.

Sengupta, Sunil. 'West Bengal Rural Scene: A Review'. *Science and People* 1(1989): 13–28.

Singh, Amrik. 'Combining Moral Commitment with Pragmatism: Ashok Mitra Commission on Education'. *Economic and Political Weekly* 28(29/30) (17–24 July, 1993): 1504–10.

Sinha, Aseema. 'Ideas, Interests and Institutions in Policy Change: A Comparison of West Bengal and Gujarat'. In *Comparative Politics across India's States: Case Studies of Democracy in Practice*, edited by Rob Jenkins. Delhi: Oxford University Press, 2004.

_____. *The Regional Roots of Developmental Politics in India: A Divided Leviathan*. New Delhi: Oxford University Press, 2006.

Sinharay, Praskanva. 'A New Politics of Caste'. *Economic and Political Weekly* XLVII(34) (25 August, 2012): 26–27.

_____. 'Re-emergence of Dalits in West Bengal: Matua Mahasangha and a New Politics of Mediation', MPhil dissertation. Calcutta: Centre for Studies in Social Sciences and Jadavpur University, 2013.

Srinivasan, Vivek. 'Understanding Public Services in Tamil Nadu: An Institutional Perspective', Ph.D dissertation, New York: Syracuse University, 2010.

State Council of Educational Research and Training (SCERT). *Implications of Private Tuition in West Bengal: A Report*. Kolkata, September, 2009. Available at: http://righttoeducation.in/sites/default/files/implications_private_tuition_wb.pdf, accessed on 24 September, 2013.

Surjeet, Harkishan Singh. *On CPI(M)-CPI Differences*. New Delhi: National Book Centre, 1985. (This book is quoted from www.revolutionarydemocracy.org/rdv13nl/cpim.htm, accessed on 3 July, 2013).

_____. 'The CPI(M) Programme: Updating in Tune with Changing Times'. *The Marxist* 16(3–4) (July–December, 2000). Available at: http://cpim.org/content/programme-updated-changing-times, accessed on 25 September, 2014.

Taylor-Gooby, P. 'In Defence of Second-best Theory: State, Class and Capital in Social Policy'. *Journal of Social Policy* 26(2) (1997): 171–92.

Thorner, Daniel. *The Agrarian Prospect in India*. New Delhi: Delhi School of Economics, Delhi University Press, 1956.

Veron, Rene, Stuart Corbridge, Glyn Williams and Manoj Srivastava. 'The Everyday State and Political Society in Eastern India: Structuring Access to the Employment Assurance Scheme'. *The Journal of Development Studies* 39(5) (June, 2003): 1–28.

West Bengal Legislative Assembly (WBLA). *Assembly Proceedings: Official Report*, Vol. 64. 44th Session, West Bengal, March–April, 1967

_____. *Assembly Proceedings: Official Report*, Vol. 66(1): 25–31. West Bengal, Calcutta, August 1977.

_____. *Assembly Proceedings*, (manuscripts), file no. 92, 27. West Bengal, Calcutta, March, 1989a.

_____. *Assembly Proceedings*, (manuscripts), file no. 76, 3. West Bengal, Calcutta, April, 1989b.

WBPKS. *The Demands of the Peasants*. The resolution adopted at the 18th Conference, Satgachia, 14–16 October, 1966.

_____. *Report of the 19th Session*. 19th Session, Sonarpur, 1968.

_____. *Report of the 21st Session*. 21st Session, Chinsurah, Hooghly, 4–7 June, 1970.

Webster, Neil. 'Agrarian Relations in Burdwan District, West Bengal: From the Economics of Green Revolution to the Politics of Panchayati Raj'. *Journal of Contemporary Asia* 20(2) (1990): 177–211.

Williams, Glyn. 'Panchayati Raj and the Changing Micro-politics of West Bengal'.

In *Sonar Bangla? Agricultural Growth and Agrarian Change in West Bengal and Bangladesh*, edited by Ben Rogaly, Barbara Harriss-White and Sugata Bose, 229–52. New Delhi: Sage Publications, 1999.

Williams, Gwyn A. 'The Concept of "Egemonia" in the Thought of Antonio Gramsci: Some Notes on Interpretation'. *Journal of the History of Ideas* 21(4) (October–December, 1960): 586–99.

Bengali sources

Bandyopadhyay, Parimal. *Bhumi O Bhumisanskar: Shekal Ekal*. Kolkata: De's Publishing, 2007.

Baske, Boro. '*Purono Alo Nibhechhe, Notun Alo Jwoleni*' ('Old Lights are Out, New Lights Didn't Turn On'), Op-ed essay. *Anandabazar Patrika*, 4 February, 2014.

Chakraborty, A. B *et al. Kalpurush*, 27, 1967.

Chattopadhyay, Boudhayan, *et al.* '*Operation Barga, Ekti Samiksha*' ('Operation Barga: An Analysis)'. *Sahitya o Samaj* 3–4 (Baisakh, 1393B) (1986): 63–123.

Chowdhury, Benoy. '*Swadhinata Uttor Yuger Krishak Samaj-e Poribortoner Swarup*' ('The Changing Facet of the Peasant Society in the Post-independence Era'). *Marxbadi Path* 5(1) (1985): 27–31.

CPI(M). *Bibhinno Front-er Report* (A Report by Various Front Organizations). 14th West Bengal Conference, Calcutta, 27 December 1981 to 3 January 1982.

_____. *Poshchimbonge Jukto Front Bhangar Chokranto Protirodh Korun* (Resist the Conspiracy to Break the United Front in West Bengal). Kolkata: West Bengal State Committee, December, 1969.

_____. *Poshchimbonge Shoshthho Panchayat Nirbachan: Tathya o Shomiksha* (Sixth Panchayat Election in West Bengal: Facts and Overview). Kolkata: West Bengal State Committee, 2004.

_____. *Poshchimbongo Tristar Panchayat Nirbachon* (Three-tier Panchayat Elections in West Bengal) (28 February, 1988): *Janaganer Proti Abedan* (An Appeal to the People). West Bengal: Poschim Bongo Rajyo Committee (West Bengal State Committee), 1988.

Dasgupta, Rangalal. '*Operation Barga: Proshashon Nirbhar Shongoshkarer Sheemaboddhhota*' ('Operation Barga: The Limitations of Administration

Oriented Reforms'). In *Aneek: Pochish Bochhar Probondhho Shankolon*, edited by Dipankar Chakraborty and Ratan Khasnabis. Calcutta: Aneek Prokashona, 1989.

Dasgupta, Sudhanshu. *Proshongo Jonogonotantrik Front, Bam o Gonotantric Front* (On People's Democratic Front, Left and Democratic Front). Calcutta: Nishan Prakashani, 1989.

GoWB. *'Bhoomi Sanskar Ayiner Dwitio Sansodhani* (1981)' [The Second Amendment to the Land Reforms Act (1981)]. Calcutta: Rajaswa Parshat, 1981.

_____. *'Grambasider Dwara Gram Porikolpona* (*Somonwito Jono Udyog Sohobhagi Porikolpona*): *Nirdeshnama'* (Village Planning by the Villagers). Kolkata: Department of Panchayat and Rural Development, 2002.

Gupta, Saibal Kumar. *Kichhu Smriti, Kichhu Kothha* (Reminiscences). Kolkata: M. C. Sarkar and Sons, 1994.

Hembram, Munni. *'Andhakar: Pracheen o Adhunik'* ('Darkness: Ancient and Modern'), Op-ed essay. *Anandabazar Patrika*, 4 February, 2014.

Hembram, Nityananda. *'Labhpur-e Ganadharshaner Ghotona Mormontudo: Tar Mane ki Adivasi Swoshasan Kamyo Noi?'* ('Labhpur Gang-rape Incidence is Heart-rending: Does it Mean that *Adivasi* Self-government is Undesirable?'), Op-ed essay. *Ei Samay*, 4 February, 2014.

Mishra, Surjakanta. *Sreni Drishtibhongite Panchayat* (Panchayat, Looking through the Perspective of Class). Calcutta: National Book Agency, 1998.

Nikhilbongo Prathamik Sikshak Samiti. *Sangram Andolone Nikhilbongo Prathamik Sikshak Samiti (1935-2003)*, Volume I. Kolkata: Netaji Institute for Asian Studies and Progressive Publishers, 2007.

Pal, Madhumoy, ed. *Marichjhnapi: Chhinno Desh – Chhinno Itihash* (Marichjhnapi: Severed Country, Severed History). Kolkata: Gangchil, 2009.

Poshchimbongo Prathamik Sikshak Samiti. *'Poshchimbongo Prathamik Sikshak Samiti-r Itihas'. Prathamik Sikshak* 1 (15 January, 2009).

Rana, Kumar, ed. *Kalamchari: Prathamik Shikshakder Likhito Obhigyota* (Written Testimonies of the Primary School Teachers). Kolkata: Pratichi (India) Trust, 2012.

Rana, Kumar. *Aksharer Kshamata Kshamata-r Akshar* (Power of Words, Words of Power). Kolkata: Camp, 2007.

_____. 'Poshchimbonge Dalit Jagoroner Shomoshya o Shombhabona' ('The Problems and Prospects of Dalit Awakening in West Bengal'). In *Poshchimbonge Dalit o Adivasi*, edited by Santosh Rana and Kumar Rana. Kolkata: Camp, 2009.

Rana, Santosh and Kumar Rana. *Poshchimbonge Dalit o Adibasi* (Dalit and Adivasi in West Bengal). Kolkata: Camp, 2009.

WBPKS. *Krishaker Shomoshya O Shongram* (The Problems and Movements of the Peasants), (by Harekrishna Konar). 14 October, 1966.

_____. 'Krishok Andolon o Gonotantrik Jonomot' ('Peasant Movement and Democratic Public Opinion'), (by Benoy Konar). *Deshhitoishi* (Autumn Number) (1989): 89–93.

_____. *Nuton Poristhitite Krishak Andoloner Kaj* (Agenda for Peasant Movement in the New Situation). 22nd Session, 18–20 November, 1972.

_____. *Report o Prastab* (Report and Proposals). 27th Session, Cooch Behar Town, 19–22 February, 1986.

_____. *Shampadakiya Protibedan* (Secretary's Report). 6th Session of Bolepur Krishak Sabha, Bolepur High School, 2–3 June, 1984.

_____. *Shampadakiya Report o Prastab* (Secretary's Report and Proposals). 25th Session, Bankura, 24–27 February, 1979.

_____. *Shampadakiya Report o Prastab* (Secretary's Report and Proposals). Pandua, Hooghly, 1–4 October, 1982.

_____. *Sonkhipta Report o Grihito Prastababoli* (Brief Report and Adopted Proposals). 28th Session, Udainarainpur, Howrah, 10–12 March, 1989a.

INDEX